Books for the Gifted Child

SERVING
SPECIAL NEEDS
SERIES

Volume *2*

Books *for the* Gifted Child

Paula Hauser
Gail A. Nelson

WITHDRAWN

R. R. BOWKER COMPANY
New York & London, 1988

Published by R. R. Bowker Company
a division of Reed Publishing (USA) Inc.
Copyright © 1988 by Reed Publishing (USA) Inc.
All rights reserved
Printed and bound in the United States of America

Library of Congress Cataloging-in-Publication Data
(Revised for volume 2)

Baskin, Barbara Holland, 1929–
   Books for the gifted child.

   (v. 1: Serving special populations series)
(v. 2: Serving special needs)
   Vol. 2. by Paula Hauser and Gail A. Nelson.
   Includes indexes.
   1. Gifted children—Books and reading.   2. Children's
literature—Bibliography.   I. Harris, Karen H.,
1934–   joint author.   II. Series: Serving special
needs series.
Z1039.G55B37   011'.62   79-27431
ISBN 0-8352-1161-4 (v. 1)
ISBN 0-8352-2467-8 (v. 2)   Rev.

Contents

Preface

Books for the Gifted Child, Volume 2, carries forth on the principles of the 1980 volume by Baskin and Harris. We are indebted to Barbara H. Baskin and Karen H. Harris whose work has provided an exemplary model for our efforts. This annotated bibliography, with 195 entries, focuses on literature that is cognitively demanding principally because of the language complexity of the text and includes works that have merit due to their effective and unique interaction between text and illustrations. Also included are selections that speak to the young reader's imagination and aesthetic sensitivity. Publication dates span 1980 to 1987 and titles are arranged alphabetically by author's last name. There are three out-of-print titles, but they can be found in the public library. A Title Index, Reading Level Index, and Subject Index provide additional ready access.

Like Baskin and Harris's book, *Books for the Gifted Child,* Volume 2, is directed toward librarians, teachers, parents, and others working with gifted children, preschool through grade 6. The growth of school identification and programming practices for gifted children has resulted in a surge of interest in and attention to the intellectual and literary needs of these children. Librarians are among the most responsive proponents of education for the gifted, but their efforts to serve the reading needs of gifted children are often hampered by a lack of appropriate bibliographic materials. *Books for the Gifted Child,* Volume 2, is intended to fill this need, serving as a resource of cognitively challenging books recommended for intellectually gifted youngsters.

The search for appropriate selections had to be carefully conducted since the traditional sources of information, such as lists by professional associations and publishing companies, yielded few titles that met our criteria (see chapter 1). To compensate for the lack of recommendations from these quarters, we turned to librarians for suggestions in order to make this resource as relevant and helpful as possible. Children's literature reviews published in educational journals served as a guide before both public and school libraries' collections were carefully searched for appropriate books. In addition, our professional background and experiences—teaching gifted children—provided us with expertise and awareness of this group and their reading preferences and abilities.

A comprehensive treatment of the nature and characteristics of giftedness was not within the scope of this work. However, chapter 1 discusses unresolved issues defining who are the "gifted" and the importance of guiding intellectually able readers.

We wish to acknowledge Judy Wilson, project director, Microcomputer Information Coordination Center, Kansas State Department of Education, for her expertise in special education technology and express to her our gratitude for giving us this professional challenge. We would also like to recognize the professionalism of Kirsten McBride, copy editor, who generously gave her technical assistance, advice, and encouragement.

Many other professionals provided valuable assistance and made recommendations during the process of selecting titles. We thank the staff of the Johnson County Library System, Kansas, especially Debbie McLeod, children's library specialist, who gave generously of their time. Also we acknowledge the library staff of the Shawnee Mission Public Schools, Kansas, Mary Feisley, Helen Nahrstedt, Judy Tracy, and the professional library resource staff, Rosemary Hallier and Jean Johnson. We appreciate the suggestions of Marilyn Peterson, Linda Meier, and Carol Sandness, librarians, Olathe Public Schools, Kansas. We especially acknowledge June Level, education program specialist of Kansas. We appreciate the opinions provided by Reva Jenkins-Friedman, the University of Kansas. Our special thanks also go to Sandra Hoffman, typist, for her patience.

We are indebted to our families and those closest to us for their patience and understanding throughout this endeavor.

Books *for the* Gifted Child

1
Reading and the Gifted Child

Since the publication of *Books for the Gifted Child* in 1980, the public has continued to maintain an ambivalent attitude toward the gifted; and within the professional community no consensus has been reached on what constitutes giftedness or which children should be labeled "gifted." At the same time, programs for gifted children and youth have increased in an attempt to meet the educational needs of more intellectually able individuals. In spite of these efforts, it has been estimated that as many as half the gifted population are not currently recognized for their potential or given appropriate educational opportunities. These figures include cultural minorities, the handicapped, and others from underserved populations—"those which suffer group neglect in terms of the provision of conditions and opportunities to nurture, stimulate, and guide the full development of the individuals' abilities."[1]

The lack of a clear definition of "giftedness" and the implications for service delivery were intensified in the early 1980s, when federal support for gifted education declined with the abolishment of the Office for the Gifted and Talented in 1981. However, as a result of the growth of parent advocacy groups and the support of other community members and interested legislators, efforts to recognize the importance of gifted children and youth by providing economic support at the federal level have continued. As of this writing, both the House and Senate have passed omnibus education bills, including the Jacob K. Javits Gifted and Talented Children and Youth Act, which calls for appropriations to states and schools and reestablishment of the federal Office for the Gifted and Talented.[2]

In the interim, despite the lack of a federal mandate, many states provide elementary and secondary programs. Some states include the gifted under the regulations of PL 94-142, the Education of All Handicapped Children Act, thereby granting all the rights and procedural safeguards afforded to other exceptionalities, including an individual education plan written by a team of professionals and the child's parents in an attempt to meet each child's unique educational needs.

GIFTEDNESS AS MULTIPLE TALENTS

Typically, educational programs for gifted children are offered within a continuum of services from full-time special classes, seminars, accelerated courses, and pullout programs ranging from a few hours to several days a week to enrichment provided in the regular classroom. Often, program eligibility is based on a multiple-talent conception of giftedness seen as including a *complex* of abilities, talents, and behaviors in contrast to the unitary concept of giftedness as referring to an intelligence quotient. Thus many behaviors other than those related to strict academic achievement are being proposed as elements of giftedness. For example, the ability to think analytically, to acquire and process information, to apply previous knowledge to new situations, conscious adaptation to the environment, and application of practical behaviors are identified as aspects of intelligence by Sternberg in his triarchic theory of intellectual giftedness.[3]

Many other psychologists and educators have identified both intellective and nonintellective factors that purport to define giftedness. The chance factor or luck and environmental influences as well as other nonintellective variables such as achievement motivation, the ability to utilize appropriate meta-learning habits when approaching tasks, combine with superior general intelligence and special aptitudes to facilitate giftedness according to Tannenbaum's psychosocial approach to giftedness.[4]

Although a comprehensive discussion of the definition of creativity or the relationship of creativity to intelligence is beyond the scope of this work, it should be noted that creativity is at the core of many proposed definitions. Several theorists maintain that creativity should be included among the traits considered to comprise giftedness,[5] is synonymous with giftedness,[6] and is "the highest expression of giftedness."[7]

Definitions

In general, the potential for gifted behavior and outstanding performance is being emphasized more than actual or demonstrated accomplishments as a criterion for giftedness. This recognition of potential is evident in the most prevalent definition, stated in the Gifted and Talented Children Act of 1978 (PL 95-561) and used by the U.S. Office of Education, stating that the gifted and talented are:

Children and, whenever applicable, youth who are identified at the pre-school, elementary, or secondary level as possessing demonstrated or potential abilities that give evidence of high performance capability in areas such as intellectual, creative, specific academic or leadership ability or in the performing and visual arts, and who, by reason thereof, require services or activities not ordinarily provided by the school.

Using the U.S. Office of Education definition as a guide, most states have developed their own definitions. Thus there is *no one* definition of giftedness. However, among the several areas of giftedness or talent listed in the U.S. Office of Education definition, probably the most frequently used is general intellectual ability, determined by an individual intelligence test or by performance on an achievement test. Most commonly, school programs for youngsters identified as gifted deal primarily with academic aptitude and demonstrated ability rather than other talent areas.

In addition to the federal definition, another widely accepted educational definition of giftedness—Renzulli's Three-Ring Conception of giftedness—includes many factors other than traditional concepts of intelligence, primarily the interaction of three trait clusters usually depicted as overlapping circles: above average ability, creativity, and task commitment. Traits within each cluster include such intellectual behaviors as high levels of abstract thinking; adapting and shaping novel environmental experiences and rapid information processing; task commitment behaviors such as self-confidence, enthusiasm, perseverance, and creative behaviors, including fluency, flexibility, and originality; willingness to take risks; and receptivity to new and unusual expression of ideas. The interaction of traits within clusters contributes to the manifestation of gifted behaviors. In addition, a multitude of "personality" and "environmental" factors interact with the three clusters to produce gifted behaviors.[8]

Characteristics of Gifted Children

Contributing to the difficulty of identifying gifted children is the absence of one set of characteristics that apply to all children whose potential is outstanding. Instead, gifted children may possess a range of positive traits, such as an extensive vocabulary, fluent expression of ideas, ability to grasp new concepts quickly, sense of humor, wide variety of interests, and the ability to become absorbed in a task. At the same time, many children labeled as "gifted" demonstrate behaviors—often viewed as negative by parents, teachers, and peers—that include a narrow focus of interest in one area, aggressive or dominant behavior in a group setting, impatience with detail and routine tasks, and the tendency to become easily distracted or lose interest in a project. Each child is *unique* and will not exhibit all of these characteristics. Furthermore, children's specific strengths may lie in one or more areas. For example, a highly verbal youngster who learned to read on her own as a preschooler may also be talented in music. Another individual might demonstrate unusual ability in mathematics, yet read at an average level.

Further contributing to the ambivalence regarding the nature of giftedness are the many myths and misconceptions about gifted children that continue to prevail among laypersons as well as many educators. One myth is that gifted children are a homogeneous group. While gifted youngsters may share some characteristics, such as the ability to learn quickly, retain facts and apply knowledge and skills, each child is unique in terms of environment, background of experiences, interests, personality traits, and expression of abilities. "The range of physical, academic, and social variables is almost as great as one would find in a random selection of people."[9]

GIFTED NEED GUIDANCE

Another myth about gifted children is that because they are so intelligent, they will learn on their own. Evidence to the contrary has been found by Whitmore[10] and Rimm.[11] Both of these writers express concern about the underachieving child who is often lacking in motivation, without realistic goals, lacking a positive self-concept, and functioning below anticipated levels. Early recognition and nurturing of young children's giftedness is essential to their continuing intellectual and emotional growth. Support for the environmental influence on giftedness was found by Bloom in his studies of child prodigies and adults whose talents were manifest after nurturance, instruction, and encouragement by significant adults such as instructors, coaches, and parents.[12]

Gifted children need guidance in many aspects of their lives. Of particular relevance in this book is the need for nurturance and direction of their reading to assist them in developing self-directional skills that will enable them to pursue lifelong learning.

Books provide a means by which gifted children can enhance and expand the very behaviors often seen as constituting giftedness, including making choices and exerting control over their learning. In addition, books allow them to expand knowledge, develop new areas of interest and expertise, respond to their emotional needs, and stimulate their imaginations. Books, therefore, offer special features that can accommodate the unique needs of individual children. In the words of Baskin and Harris:

> Books allow a high amount of autonomy for the child in controlling the depth, pacing, direction, ordering, quality, and complexity of intellectual pursuits. Books are available in every content area and every level of difficulty. They allow unrestrained exploration of interests, as much redundancy or pausing for analysis, assimilation, and reflection as desired, and as much leapfrogging or skimming as wished. In short, they are the single indispensable tool for fostering independent learning.[13]

IMPORTANCE OF LITERATURE FOR GIFTED CHILDREN

The important role of literature in the reading process has received renewed emphasis as evidenced by the recent thrust to incorporate literary works as a central part of the elementary reading curriculum. Consistent with this trend, publishers of basal readers are presenting skills lessons around stories from recognized literature of the past and present. As a result, more youngsters of all ability levels are becoming aware of critically acclaimed authors and illustrators and their works. Recognizing the importance of reading, Bill Honig, California state superintendent of public instruction, in 1985 launched the California Reading Initiative, which includes a list of recommended instructional and recreational readings for students in grades K–12 accompanied by a plan for how to integrate literature in the reading curriculum. Overall, a greater prevalence of literature is found in reading programs in schools across the country as a result of Honig's study, which is based on his philosophy that "a love of reading and books is one of the most important gifts that teachers and parents can give our young people."[14]

In addition, one of the recommendations in the Report of the Commission on Reading, "Becoming a Nation of Readers," is for children to spend more time in independent reading, including literature from the different genres.

> With respect to literature, students must be able to understand increasingly complicated plots and characterization. They need to be able to cope with literature in which devices such as flashbacks and flash-forwards are frequent and subtle in realization. They need to be able to appreciate the moral or author's point as well as how the plot is resolved. Particularly in the early grades, made-for-school stories are not as complex as the literature intended for children in the same grades on the shelves of libraries and bookstores. This fact has caused some authorities to wonder whether school reading programs adequately prepare children for genuine literature.[15]

The increase in numbers of school-identified gifted children has resulted in programs for gifted and talented students across the country and hence has created a demand for more quality literature to help meet these youngsters' recognized intellectual needs. For all students, the implications for gifted readers of the increased emphasis on literature in the schools include an opportunity for these youngsters to profit from more exposure to great writing aside from works about their personal interests and beyond texts designed to develop and enhance basic reading skills.

For all readers, but particularly for gifted children, literature should contribute to an understanding of the world around them, propel them into independent investigation beyond the written words, and instill a love and appreciation of quality literature. Gifted children need to read widely and in depth to develop their interests and appreciation of literature.

Charlotte Huck distinguished between helping children develop an interest in reading and gaining an appreciation of literature:

> Interest in reading is developed through the opportunity for *wide reading*, for listening to many stories, through exposure to many books. Appreciation for literature requires knowledge and understanding of fine writing and grows out of the opportunity for reading *in depth*. A child may develop an interest in books

independently, whereas the appreciative reader is the informed reader. Discrimination is developed gradually over a period of time; it requires sensitivity to the idea of the book, and sensitivity to the means of expressing that idea. While enthusiasm and interest in good books may be caught, appreciation and discrimination are almost always taught.[16]

Characteristics of Gifted Readers

Examination of the characteristics of gifted students reveals that they are usually advanced in their reading ability, have long attention spans, express their ideas maturely, question and persist in seeking answers, adapt easily to situations around them, and are able to apply reasoning skills to problems while recognizing relationships and comprehension of meaning. Gifted children's usually advanced level of speech production—evidenced in their word usage, understanding, word selection, and sentence length—facilitates reading ability. Fluent in expression of ideas and with a propensity toward effective problem solving, gifted children are able to conceptualize at high levels even at a young age.

Although these characteristics tend to apply to gifted children in general, the very young gifted child often presents a complex challenge. For example, analysis of the young child's reading comprehension scores may reveal an ability to read on an advanced level but, in reality, the child may not approximate the abstract thinking of older students.

The broad spectrum of intellectual levels in gifted children makes it difficult to designate them to a specific grade or age group for reading selection purposes. For example, some children can read and comprehend at a higher level than their grade placement, but may be socially and emotionally too immature to understand or appreciate literature intended for older children. These children should not be denied the opportunity to satisfy their curiosity by investigating books for older readers, but they should be offered titles that are more appropriate for them.

Many gifted children who are avid readers find refuge in the public library after realizing that their school library is limited in its offerings of mature literary material. Surpassing the juvenile section, these youngsters may seek titles from the young adult or even adult shelves.

> Therefore, whatever the skills demonstrated, and however strong the motivation to learn, gifted children like other children need the guidance and the concerted interest of both teacher and library media specialist as they become involved in the learning process.[17]

Often these children pursue a favorite topic in such depth that they exhaust the material typically available in school libraries. However, qualified adult intervention can guide such readers and teach them to discriminate among available materials. Results of a study on the reading habits of gifted children, with particular reference to selection of library books, revealed:

Some gifted students did select books that could stimulate higher-level thought processes. Interests of the identified gifted were more varied than those in the comparison group and, in some cases, were unique. Even though the gifted students exhibited a comparatively wide range of reading interests and circulated many fine books, they did not consistently self-select works that were intellectually challenging.[18]

READING ATTITUDES AND INTERESTS OF GIFTED CHILDREN

A study on reading attitudes and the gifted reported that "reading is an activity in which gifted students engage and which they perceive as being both easy and enjoyable."[19] However, the results of the study further revealed that these students' perception of reading changes as they mature and progress through school. While young primary gifted students report prolific reading activity, older intermediate, junior high, and senior high students note a downward trend in reading activity. This development may be due to differences in the reading materials typically chosen by younger and older students—the former reading shorter books. However, older students also reported less interest in reading as a favorite leisure activity than younger students.

Like all children, the gifted child is influenced by the fast-paced superficiality of television and other media; and popular novelty-type books and games, puzzles, sports, and other trivia-type fare are attractive to children regardless of their intrinsic value. Books for the very young and the early childhood preschool set abound, many of them in manipulative formats, such as pop-ups. In addition, "choose-your-own-adventure" books, stories on computer discs, and software/paperback combinations compete for children's attention. While these materials have a place in the popular culture and often serve to motivate reluctant readers, for the most part, they are of limited value to the highly able reader who needs challenging language, strong characterizations, and intricate plots.

GUIDING THE GIFTED READER

Independent reading programs based solely on students' interests seldom improve their interests and tastes. Thus, although they may increase the students' knowledge in a particular area, they may neglect subjects unfamiliar to the students. Exposure to a broad range of topics and challenging material will help readers develop and apply advanced reading skills.[20] Even highly able readers require assistance in locating books for independent reading. Characteristically, they quickly learn to understand even complex literary elements; however, it cannot be presumed that they will automatically select intellectually stimulating reading material.

Gifted children need careful guidance in selecting the best literary offerings in their areas of interest to arrive at a balance between those particular interests and challenging books across all genres. Some children's experts contend that since children read primarily for pleasure they should make their own choices. However, considering the abundance of books available, lack of guidance could result in the selection of poor quality literature.[21]

Gifted children differ from the nongifted because of an intellectual capacity that allows them to learn greater quantities at a more rapid pace, their appetite for learning, their breadth and depth of knowledge, and their tendency to engage in creative and productive thinking. Since gifted students master material quickly and display an insatiable appetite for new ideas, much time is needed to locate advanced materials and devise activities to challenge these students. In addition, research has shown that gifted students need more guidance in this area than their nongifted peers and that their interest and involvement improve when they receive such guidance. Students of average reading ability tend to receive more help in selecting material than the gifted, who are left to fend for themselves.[22]

A strong and continuing relationship among the librarian, good literature, and intellectually gifted students must constitute an integral part in helping these students attain maximum reading skills and develop the thinking skills necessary for evaluative behavior.[23]

The responsibility for guidance in selecting appropriately challenging literature for gifted children falls on the significant adults in their lives— parents, teachers, or librarians. Consequently, these individuals must remain cognizant of both the unique characteristics of each gifted child and the finest literary sources. Gifted children and the adults in their lives often turn to the librarian for guidance in locating appropriate books. Traditionally, the librarian has directed the general population of children to books that have received recognition from literary committees and other expert bodies. However, gifted children can benefit from reading books included on lists for the general population when given directed activities designed to evoke higher level responses. Typically, such structured reading lessons are part of the gifted child's instructional reading experience.

The importance of award-winning books is emphasized in schools and libraries as evidenced by lists from which children may select the "best" books of the year. However prescriptive this selection method seems, often it does not meet the gifted child's intellectual reading ability and interests.

> Awards are frequently made on the basis of criteria that are irrelevant to the needs of gifted children. Annual prizes are, by definition, given to the "best" book, according to committee consensus, for that year. Yet some years may be lean in terms of quality entries and others rich in contenders. The results are uneven, leading to the promotion of lesser titles in some years and the neglect of major efforts in others.[24]

Two major award categories underlie the typical lists of acclaimed literature. Winners of the Newbery Award, given for the most distinguished contribution to literature for children, are widely promoted in libraries. Many books that receive this award do not intellectually challenge the gifted reader in language, story, or literary quality, however popular they may be. Annual Caldecott Medals, given for the most distinguished picture book, are awarded for illustrations only. Often these selections do not serve the specific reading needs of gifted children either. However, in both instances, individual titles, due to their intellectual appeal and/or combination of art and text that produced an aesthetic, intellectually stimulating or imaginative treatment, warranted inclusion in this work as appropriate for gifted readers.

Book selections by libraries must be made to meet the reading requirements for the majority of readers. Therefore, gifted readers who do not fall into this population must receive guidance from a knowledgeable adult in selecting appropriate reading material. Gifted programs in the schools and parent advocacy groups in the community have created an awareness of gifted children's characteristics and educational needs leading to a greater recognition among librarians of the unique reading needs of gifted children.

Eager to continue to expand their knowledge in this area, librarians acquaint themselves with the reading interests and skills of gifted children to help them make appropriate suggestions and offer guidance in literary selections. In addition, at many universities the requirements for a library science degree include a course in the education of children with special needs, giftedness included. As a result of these forces, librarians are now more cognizant of gifted children's specific areas of interest as well as what best motivates them to actively engage in reading good literature. In many cases, contacts with parents of these children help broaden the librarian's perception of the child. In addition, rather than being a quiet, checkout and resource haven, public and school libraries now have become places to interact concerning books, and users, including children, are freely encouraged to use reference materials. In essence, the library has evolved into a resource center with well-trained librarians ready to guide and assist children in finding good, appropriate literature.

BOOKS AND THE RESPONSES OF GIFTED READERS

The opportunity for children to respond to books on several levels is an important consideration of book selection. The able reader cognitively calls on his conceptual and experiential background, uses his well-developed language ability, and employs these thinking skills when processing information from books. Thus his reconstruction of new and challenging material allows him to establish a relationship with what he already knows and extend his ideas. Books for highly able readers should encourage readers' responses by fostering language development and enjoyment, providing cognitive challenges on higher levels of thinking, and by stimulating the imagination.

Good literature enhances language development in children by introducing them to the power of the well-chosen word and vivid language patterns while offering qualitative literary experiences. Thus the gifted child's vocabulary becomes enriched from reading complex, provocative, and highly structured literature.

> Language is the single most significant component to be considered in judging books for gifted readers. It should be rich, varied, accurate, precise, complex, and exciting, for language is the premier instrumentality for the reception and expression of thought.[25]

To be challenging to gifted readers, language should be filled with subtleties or suggestions, incorporating fine shades of meaning, multiple meanings, and utilizing wordplays and other humorous inventions.

Specifically, wordplay and riddles can foster fluency in the child's inner and oral expression. Even wordless picture books increase fluency by developing and increasing thought processes that gradually give way to verbal expression. For example, imaginative plays on words, language variances, and riddles provide fun and pleasure while also requiring use of problem-solving and higher-level thinking processes.

Gifted children's fascination with words often entices them to seek further information about etymology and the ways word meanings have changed over the years as in *Murfles and Wink-a-Peeps* by Susan Sperling.

Numerous facets and nuances of language serve to enrich the child's language and total life experience. By exposing children to a rich variety of language models, we give them a sense of the infinite possibilities that exist for experimenting with their own language. That is, as we offer them books, "we provide models, and, through experimentation children increase their ability to use language effectively."[26]

In addition to the language component, another factor in book selection is the level of cognitive challenge. Highly able readers need literature that is intellectually stimulating and demands high-level cognitive functioning—that is, beyond what is purely developmental. Much of school learning is organized around Bloom's *Taxonomy of Educational Objectives: Handbook 1, Cognitive Domain.*[27] Arranged as a pyramid model, the taxonomy begins with knowledge as the basis, followed by comprehension, application, analysis, synthesis, and evaluation. The first three levels—knowledge, comprehension, and application—are usually emphasized in basic skills instruction in the regular classroom. The top three levels require higher levels of thinking. Analysis utilizes skills of comparison and contrast, outlining, and rearrangement of data; synthesis provides for combining elements and creating and devising new structures; and evaluation requires judgments based on previous information or specific criteria. Instruction for gifted children should be based on a reversed pyramid, with more time spent on the higher levels of thinking. Many current reading programs emphasize cognitive level thinking exercises above the knowledge and comprehension levels. Books for highly able readers should offer opportunities for responses on higher levels of thinking.

Many gifted readers exhibit a keen interest in various areas of nonfiction, including scientific topics that stimulate higher level thinking processes and satisfy investigative aspirations. Information books for gifted children should extend their investigative potential, particularly in the case of scientific works, in addition to introducing new and specific information. Thus such works should stimulate curiosity, present or allude to the unknown, incorporate complex ideas, introduce unfamiliar possibilities, and use language characteristic to the topic of exploration.

The gifted child who is interested in science is curious about the workings of the world. She accepts the abstraction of ideas and has a tendency to analyze details, drawing generalizations and perceiving relationships among them. Further, she is usually not content with simple explanations but seeks to discover for herself. Her response to well-chosen books should be to analyze and discriminate from available principles and theories. Evaluative thinking skills are employed to arrive at solutions.

Children need the opportunity to participate in order to become the "scientist" in the field. They need time to use their powers of observation and to experiment. Often conveying a strong sense of excitement, good science books involve their readers and stimulate them through various activities and suggestions to put forth great effort, however patiently, and inquire beyond the known. For example, Sam Epstein and Beryl Epstein's *What's for Lunch? The Eating Habits of Seashore Creatures* takes the youngster beyond basic information in its discussion of the techniques seashore creatures use to escape predators. Its inclusion of unusual animals will encourage children to seek further information about them, all the while contemplating and respecting their skills for survival.

In addition, children may find in science the stimulus to engage in logical thinking. They may find structure and order, a kind of predictability that can offer comfort in what often seems to be an erratic world. But most of all, they may begin to sense the emotional thrill felt by the scientist who is pursuing answers to fundamental questions.[28]

Whether dealing with emotional or cognitive levels, books should evoke active participation and involvement of the reader.

> Gifted children's responses to books within a genre will be unique to each child since reading is a dynamic process brought about, in part, by "the wandering viewpoint." As we read we continually alter our viewpoint. Each unexpected theme that causes us to formulate another meaning, eventually forces us to revise our original meanings and to reassess our own values.[29]

In addition to developing cognitive responses, good literature affords readers an opportunity to extend and develop imaginative responses. Literature develops our imaginative perspective on reality and relates to us in words an unexpressed thought.[30]

In our concern for a child's growth and development, imagination does not always receive sufficient attention. This neglect may partly stem from an inability to define fully the term *imagination*. Pertaining to literature, perhaps we can say that children will be stimulated in different ways and consequently respond in different ways depending on what they bring to the book they are reading. In other words, experience with good literature will enhance their imagination by providing rich nourishment of ideas. Ideally, imaginative literature should permeate children's reading content, thereby providing pleasure while increasing their understanding of literature. The child approaches books on the basis of his imagination, whether developed or not. The quality and complexity of the literature he chooses can substantially enhance that imagination.

Gifted children in need of constant stimulation and challenge may turn to fantasy to satisfy those needs. Fantasy incorporates obscure and dramatic time changes, rich figurative language, contains what appear to be impossible situations, and provokes the reader to leap ahead mentally and visualize conclusions, only to be delighted with a surprise ending.

> By transcending the distracting limitations of what we perceive to be the boundaries of the possible, fantasy can focus our attention on universal concerns. It can, moreover, offer the satisfying resolution—generosity over meanness, love over hate, good over evil—which the dynamic uncertainties of real life deny us.[31]

Good literature must tempt, stretch, and motivate the child's imagination in ways that will affect him emotionally while also evoking a powerful intellectual response that motivates him to pursue and prefer quality literature. In addition, well-chosen and meaningfully employed words, intricate verbal structures, figurative language, and insightful use of metaphor and simile all help the reader develop and express his own imagination.

Gifted children's divergent thinking ability can also be expanded and enhanced by rich, imaginative literature that evokes creative responses and sharpens perceptive ability. Literature concerning the arts, such as *Meet Matisse* by Nelly Munthe, illustrates the product of a keen imagination and divergent thinking in the famous artist's meticulous and creative arrangement of the cut paper figures. Thus each mural and the technique used express Matisse's imaginative and divergent thinking.

In spite of what many pragmatists and contemporary high-tech gurus contend, "literature is not a luxury." Creativity and imagination are essential to the human personality, inseparable from social consciousness and personal awareness.[32] Therefore, we must ensure that all children are encouraged from an early age to develop good reading habits that lay the foundation for lifelong independent reading.

Picture Books

A powerful fusion of art and language, the effective picture book represents a unique genre in children's literature. Traditionally, picture books have served as a vehicle for introducing children to the world around them by describing familiar events and feelings and providing vicarious experiences that often extend the boundaries of the immediate environment, thereby opening new realms of meaning. Consistent with this purpose, picture books serve as an effective introduction to books while also establishing attitudes and values that may lead to a lifelong interest in reading.

> A picture book can be found for almost everyone, for this is a genre that can offer different ways of knowing the meanings and possibilities of life and nature; of stimulating sensitivity, creativity and aesthetic growth; of providing information, emotional involvement, excitement, mystery, and, of course, sheer enjoyment.[33]

Picture books transcend all other literary genres by containing in abbreviated form the elements of any literary work. Picture books are not limited to the very young. Many titles offer stimulating plots, characters, and themes suitable for older sophisticated readers. For example, Richard Kennedy's *Song of the Horse*, in stunning pictures and intriguing narrative, describes the aesthetic relationship of a young girl to her horse. Thus the quality of language expressed in the text uniquely blended with images conveyed by picture book illustrations contributes to the totality of the reader's experience.

Picture books do not always need language to relate a message, however. Thoughtfully rendered, wordless books can express powerful concepts and evoke feelings and contemplation through illustrations only. Aimed at the more sophisticated reader, the exquisite illustrations of John Goodall's *The Story of a Castle*, for example, challenges the reader's ability to experience visually and conceptually the dramatic changes a strategic construction undergoes over the centuries.

In addition to challenging them on a cognitive level, picture books for gifted readers should also extend, stimulate, and develop their imagination and productive thinking. Thus picture books that incorporate fluency, flexibility, and originality in addition to stimulating ideas can encourage youngsters to utilize their own creative thought processes by applying them to solving problems or creating original products in art or literature.[34] An unusual "tell-and-draw" story included in this bibliography is *The Maid and the Mouse and the Odd-Shaped House* by Paul Zelinsky. Line-drawing details elaborate the story as it unfolds, requiring the reader to imagine or project what shape will appear next. *If at First You Do Not See* by Ruth Brown also encourages readers to use their imaginations. On a playful journey through the text, which is written in the margins around each page, readers must use their imaginations to discover disguised objects among more salient shapes such as a strange creature's teeth that turn out to be onions in a sandwich.

By contributing to the child's visual orientation to the world, which to a large extent is the result of most children's extensive exposure to television, graphic aids, such as drawings, photographs, maps, charts, and tables, assume an increasingly important role in the transmittal of information in children's books. In addition, home computers and video recorders have an impact on children's learning. As a result of these powerful electronic forces, the role of visual learning cannot be overlooked. Indeed, many youngsters and adults prefer, and may require, learning through the visual modality or a combination of verbal and visual.

Illustrations may also embody an intellectual component either by complementing the challenging language of a picture book or standing alone without text, as in wordless picture books. Drawings, sketches, watercolors, collages, and other forms of illustrations may be clever, humorous, suggestive, provocative, or ambiguous for the purpose of extending, interpreting, or complementing the text. To be intellectually challenging, illustrations must communicate to the observer messages that stimulate the imagination. This goal can be achieved through such devices as visual paradoxes, as found in Chris Van Allsburg's *The Mysteries of Harris Burdick;* visual allusion, as in Mitsumasa Anno's *Anno's U.S.A.;* or unusual perspectives, as in Louis Phillips's *The Upside Down Riddle Book.*

One of the most widespread type of picture books, alphabet books rely heavily on visual symbols to convey meaning and include such formats as letter-picture-word, object identification, and visual discrimination. Others are designed around a specific topic or place an imaginative emphasis on nursery rhymes.

Alphabet books that utilize unusual, nontraditionally pictured objects as referents for letters of the alphabet along with challenging language are appropriate for young minds. Bert Kitchen, for example, uses a sophisticated, aesthetic approach to illustrating the letters of the alphabet. In his *Animal Alphabet,* readers are required to identify the animal that is pictured along with each letter it represents. Similarly, readers apply observation and discrimination skills as they attempt to find an animal identical to the one given in Demi's *Demi's Find the Animal ABC: An Alphabet-Game Book.* A larger design depicting the same animal in various poses and predicaments adds to the challenge.

Along with alphabet books, concept books are usually among the child's earliest reading experiences. The concept book is an important vehicle for introducing ideas, structuring experiences, and expanding a child's view of the world. Focusing on a single idea, a concept book moves from the general to the specific or from the simple to the complex. By reading concept books, youngsters can learn about numbers, size, shapes, colors, and temporal relationships related to measuring time, the seasons, weather, and so on. Concept books encourage the use of convergent thinking and provide a framework for organizing a young child's experiences and thoughts about the world.

By exploring mathematical or scientific principles, for example, at the young child's maturational level, concept books allow analytical examination of information otherwise not encountered until an older age. Jane Jonas Srivastava's *Spaces, Shapes, and Sizes* is an introduction to the concept of volume. Readers are expected to deduce from text and illustrations that when a potato, for example, is cut into pieces, only its shape is changed, not its volume.

A search among today's picture books reveals those that speak clearly and directly to children, mirror their interests, provoke curiosity, test their thinking processes, and evoke an intellectual response in the reader—the very criteria for recommended reading for gifted youngsters.

Fiction

Much of a child's recreational reading time is devoted to fiction, a broad category that includes realistic fiction, fantasy, and humor. In addition to providing pleasurable reading, fiction affords readers an opportunity to explore other people's problems, beliefs, and responses vicariously. As a result, fiction can enhance the reader's affective and aesthetic development—an important aspect of children's growth—along with cognitive development. Story characters can illuminate viewpoints not previously considered or understood and provide young readers with insights that cannot be acquired through nonfiction.

Although highly able readers are often capable of comprehending adult-level nonfiction in their areas of interest, the same does not hold true of fiction. When selecting fiction, a child's maturational level is an important factor to be considered—there should be a match between a title and the child's psychological or maturity level. Many popular titles—warm stories about caring families and accounts of children and their problems growing up—although valuable because they address the reader's affective needs, seldom possess the literary qualities of more cognitively demanding fiction. Good fiction for young people should possess qualities similar to those of adult novels, such as story characterization and complex plots. The characters should be well-developed, memorable figures whose personalities are revealed in their thoughts, actions, opinions of other characters, as well as the author's narrative. Lukens defines "round character" as:

> The character is so fully developed that we may even be able to predict actions and reactions. Yet, like a real person, the character may surprise us or respond impetuously on occasion. It is as though we know the character so well that the character has become a real person, one we wish we could meet or might enjoy knowing.[35]

Characterization is a critical element in an effective story. Through the actions of dynamic characters, readers are able to experience new viewpoints that may be instructive or lead to a better understanding of others, in addition to helping shape their own beliefs. Theo, in Lloyd Alexander's Westmark Trilogy, struggles with the age-old problem of political injustice. The young girl, Mickle, demonstrates many talents and a strong character as she successfully makes the transition from a wandering street urchin who has lost the memory of her heritage to her rightful position as queen. Another strong character is found in Avi's *Bright Shadow*. Here, Morwenna, who is very mature for her years, is faced with burdening decisions that will affect the outcome of her own life as well as the lives of others.

In addition to rich character development, fictional works for highly able readers should be based on intriguing plots, filled with complexities and occasionally unexpected twists. Stories that require readers to unravel clues, make inferences, decipher meaning, and arrive independently at new conclusions provide cognitive stimulation. For example, in Sylvia Cassedy's *Behind the Attic Wall,* readers are left to ponder the rebellious, insecure, and unloved Maggie and her unusual realtionships with the dolls. After many disappointments, heartaches, and repeated escapes into her imaginary world, Maggie emerges as mature, convincing, and loving—a truly well-developed character.

Obscure, unexpected plots and themes require readers to employ skills of analysis, synthesis, and evaluation to discover relevant meaningful solutions. Plots with intriguing distractions and obstacles encourage high-ability readers to further investigation. Specifically, gifted readers will gain understanding of deep human worth and insights, cultivate values and beliefs, and develop concern for humankind's future based on its past experiences.

Winter of Magic's Return by Pamela Service is a fantasy whose theme reflects contemporary concerns about the aftermath of nuclear war. Here, a lack of belief in science and technology as a means to control our environment is coupled with hope for being able to build a better world by learning from past mistakes.

Beyond character and plot, many authors of intellectually demanding fiction use fantastic settings to unfold imaginary worlds that may or may not contain features of our own surroundings, thereby extending the boundaries of time and place. Often fantasies deal with underlying universal themes of a serious nature such as good versus evil. Magic and inexplicable, impossible circumstances make up the major elements of most fantasy.[36]

Compelling changes, conflict, and adventure are experienced in *The Hounds of Morrigan* by Pat O'Shea, whose characters are dramatized against sweeping backgrounds of imaginary, complex circumstances—real to them and captivating to the reader. In addition, frightening situations are relieved by an element of humor in this story of wonder.

In contrast to fantasy, realism refers to fiction set in today's world with characters and plots that are plausible. Ethel Heins, summarizing trends in children's books, noted a new realism in fiction. In comparison to the "now old-fashioned family story—a much-loved branch of children's literature that celebrated the home as a place of safety and stability, whatever the circumstances,"[37] contemporary children's fiction also deals with the communication difficulties between children and adults as well as problems of alcoholism, child abuse, divorce, drugs, and other social issues.

Again, in the fiction genre, some gifted readers may bring to their reading experience a special sensitivity that allows them to empathize with fictional characters who are resolving conflicts in their lives, such as Oliver and Charlotte in *A Place to Come Back To* by Nancy Bond.

Always enriching the imagination, fiction may deal with real-life experiences, as in *Gaffer Samson's Luck* by Jill Walsh, or fantasy in the beguiling whimsy, *The Mysterious Toyshop* by Cyril Beaumont. In either case, children observe and participate in the main characters' motivations and their discovery of self and the world around them, thereby gaining valuable vicarious experiences.

Humorous fiction, a special fiction subcategory, appeals to many children. Highly able readers, in particular, can recognize subtle humor and the various devices used to convey humorous thoughts. Puns, exaggerations of characters, actions, absurd circumstances, and incongruities may require interpretation and an extensive vocabulary in order to be understood.

In Maggie Davis's *The Best Way to Ripton,* absurd humor delights the intellect in a nonsensical tale about an old man's feelings of patience, perplexity, frustration, anger, and finally, satisfaction. In *The Whipping Boy* by Sid Fleischman, the reader is allowed to share vicariously the humorous experiences of Jemmy, the prince's whipping boy who eventually becomes the steadfast friend of the prince who used Jemmy to take his punishment.

Nonfiction

Natural curiosity, the ability to remember details and discern relationships in and among them, and an undaunted desire to find out how things work are among the personality traits that stimulate gifted children to seek out specific information from nonfictional works. Nonfiction books for children include a broad range of titles from the arts to the sciences. Although many works are read for pure pleasure, others are selected to satisfy the reader's need for specific information. The trend of the past ten years has been "to publish informational books that are not in a series, that are about an interesting topic, and that have an attractive format."[38]

Many recent nonfiction titles for young people contain visually appealing drawings and photographs that go beyond merely illustrating the text and carry a major responsibility for communicating its message. For example, specialized photographic processes reveal microscopic views as well as features of distant solar objects in *Hidden Worlds: Pictures of the Invisible* by Seymour Simon. Similarly, Patricia Lauber uses dramatic photographs to describe graphically Mount St. Helens in *Volcano: The Eruption and Healing of Mount St. Helens.*

One of the most promising contributions of current children's literature is the growing number of books in the nonfiction genre on single topics that reflect the specific interest of children. For example, *Flash, Crash, Rumble, and Roll* by Franklyn Branley introduces readers to the nature of thunderstorms at a level commensurate with young children's reading and thinking ability. Many current nonfiction books also address personal or societal problems such as endangered animals. For gifted children many of these informational books encourage further exploration and investigation, thereby challenging them to independent and creative pursuits. Many of the titles in this bibliography exemplify these trends in current nonfiction for children. For example, *Saving the Peregrine Falcon* by Caroline Arnold explicitly illustrates the stages in the life of this endangered bird by carefully explaining the methods used to protect their eggs.

> The new approach to juvenile nonfiction, which applies to all age groups, from preschool picture books to titles aimed at young adults, is characterized by four key features: a close focus on one significant aspect of a topic that will serve to reveal other aspects; a concise, tightly written text that will catch and hold the interest of young readers; a built-in emphasis on illustrations, whether they are photographs or drawings or a combination of the two; careful attention to the overall design of the book to make sure it is visually inviting.[39]

Gifted children need books from this genre that are not too simplified and, particularly in science, works that speak to them and require them to engage in actual investigations.

Fascinating books are available on a multitude of topics in the pure sciences: mathematics, astronomy, physics, chemistry, earth science, life science, and ecology, to mention a few. In many, authors and illustrators have combined their expertise to explain topics and concepts once reserved for older readers. For instance, young readers are shown how to use the scientific method in *How to Think Like a Scientist* by Stephen Kramer. Planetary topics are explored in depth in Patricia Lauber's comprehensive narrative *Journey to the Planets,* which invites the reader on a voyage into the universe. In other works, such as Peggy Thomson's *Auks, Rocks and the Odd Dinosaur: Inside Stories from the Smithsonian's Museum of Natural History,* otherwise broad, general treatments yield a behind-the-scenes adventure into the fantastic scientific collections of the museum.

Informational books exclusively conveying factual material were not included in this bibliography due to their failure to meet the criteria previously discussed. Obviously, selections from a nonfiction genre must include facts as a basis for high levels of thinking. But more important considerations for gifted readers include whether a book was likely to stimulate the reader to engage in further investigation or contemplation about the topic; whether the work elicited higher-level thinking responses such as analysis, synthesis, and evaluation; and if the young reader was either placed in the role of a professional in the discipline or introduced by example to the particular language, methods of study, and problem-solving techniques unique to the given discipline.

After being exposed to several accepted theories, readers are left to decide for themselves why the dinosaurs disappeared in *Dinosaurs, Asteroids, and Superstars: Why the Dinosaurs Disappeared* by Franklyn Branley. Readers apply scientific techniques—observation and discrimination—as they scan the drawings and search for camouflaged creatures in *How to Hide a Butterfly: And Other Insects.* One of several books by Ruth Heller, this title shows various creatures in their natural surroundings carefully camouflaged from predators. A similar "professional" approach is used in *Digging to the Past: Excavations in Ancient Lands* by W. John Hackwell, where readers get an on-the-scenes look at procedures, tools, and attitudes of archaeologists uncovering remnants of ancient civilization in the Middle East.

In contrast to the field of science, few recently published books about mathematics are of exceptional value for highly able young readers. Therefore, to obtain advanced information on mathematical topics, young readers usually need to consult adult sources. However, some books express higher concepts on a more understandable level for youngsters. Among these is Mitsumasa Anno's *Anno's Mysterious Multiplying Jar,* which introduces factorials through pictures supplemented by minimal text. Similarly, *How Much Is a Million?* by David Schwartz attempts to make concrete the abstract concept of a million by comparisons presented through humorous drawings.

As in fiction, humor is found in the nonfiction genre, especially in puzzles, riddles, and games. Combined with the unique characteristics of these subgenres, humor enhances their potential for stimulating cognitive growth. Specifically, riddles may expand vocabulary and encourage exploration of multiple meanings of words. *Riddles & Rhymes & Rigmaroles* by John Cunliffe humorously explores a variety of poems, riddles, and rhyming stories. In Monika Beisner's *Book of Riddles,* readers obtain meaning from both text and illustrations as they search for answers.

Books that focus on language features—wordplays of unusual combinations of words, humorous, exaggerated descriptions, absurdities, paradoxes, and puns—can serve to develop the divergent thinking skills of fluency, flexibility, and originality. For example, in Marilyn Burns's *The Hink Pink Book or What Do You Call a Magician's Extra Bunny?,* readers are encouraged to consider using humor and rhyme to define familiar objects and everyday incidents. *Too Hot to Hoot* by Marvin Terban invites readers to search for palindromes, words that are spelled the same way forward or backward.

Within the nonfiction genre, few titles in the visual or performing arts were found to be of major merit to gifted readers. Specifically, chronicles of the history of a particular school of painting or an era were not included because they fail to convey the individual artists' techniques and use of materials that communicate cognitive and affective messages. An exception to this is *Faces* by Giles Waterfield, an in-depth study of portraits that evokes both aesthetic and cognitive responses in readers as they analyze and compare various methods of portraying the human face.

Poetry

Good poetry is in itself incomplete, leaving much for the reader to ponder, question, consider, and investigate—whether imaginatively, creatively, or emotionally. By its form and deliberate use of rhyme, meter, figures of speech, and other poetic elements, poetry differs from other genres. "A poem is not a casual construction. It has design or form, a plan in the mind of its creator."[40]

Children should recognize poetry as another form of communicating life's experiences, not as a separate entity. To be meaningful to children, poems should be within their experiential background or level of understanding. Like other literary genres, poetry should speak to, not at or about, the child. As a means of sharpening our awareness of feelings and events, poetry contains an affective component in addition to content, thereby giving readers an opportunity to respond at both levels.

In terms of selection criteria, Sutherland proposes that the following questions be asked when selecting poetry for children:

> First, *does it sing*—with good rhythm, true, unforced rhymes, and a happy compatibility of sound and subject—whether it is nonsense verse or narrative or lyric poetry? Second, *is the diction distinguished*—with words that are rich in sensory and connotative meanings, words that are unhackneyed, precise, and memorable? Third, *does the subject matter of the poem invest the strange or the everyday experiences of life with new importance and richer meaning*?[41]

Poems that deal with mature themes such as love, death, and philosophic issues beyond the experiential level of children are inappropriate reading selections. Consequently, they have been omitted from this bibliography. Although for a different reason, poems with predictable end rhymes or forced rhythms have also been left out. Although often appealing when read aloud, such poetry offers little cognitive or emotional value.

Poetry that utilizes concise, figurative language places intellectual demands on readers by requiring them to separate layers of meanings and piecing together a new interpretation before they reach full understanding. *A Swinger of Birches* introduces the thought-provoking poetry of Robert Frost to readers of all ages. For example, Frost's beautifully illustrated "The Road Not Taken" allows the reader to identify with the difficulty of having to make choices. Two roads or directions cannot be traveled at once, and when we embark on a certain course without turning back, we may be influencing the rest of our life.

Poetry can stimulate children's imaginations by introducing a new perspective of an ordinary experience. For example, Marcia Brown's translation of Blaise Cendrars's "La Féticheuse," or "Shadow," is a tone poem that evokes imaginative, mysterious, inexplicable shadows enhanced by the artist's colorful collages. Inevitable in any discussion of the characteristics and value of good poetry is its emotional impact on the reader. Thus, in addition to stimulating children's imagination, poetry may require them to respond at both an emotional and aesthetic level. Many gifted children have developed a high sensitivity to the feelings of others and the aesthetic value of nature— topics frequently chosen by poets. Through emotionally and intellectually stimulating verse and illustration, Ted Hughes's *Under the North Star* portrays the desperation of animals trying to survive. This collection of poems was chosen for inclusion here because of its powerful aesthetic impact, as well as its demanding language.

Poetry is available in anthologies, the collected works of a single poet, or as books of poems focusing on a specific topic. To be most useful, anthologies should be arranged thematically rather than chronologically. This format allows readers more easily to make comparisons and analyze various poetic forms of expression. X. J. Kennedy and Dorothy M. Kennedy's anthology *Knock at a Star* is especially valuable for introducing children to poetry. Clear, understandable comments directed toward young readers set the tone and motivate readers to respond to the poetry that follows.

Folklore

Folklore, or traditional literature, includes myths, legends, folktales, and fables. Originating as stories transmitted orally by anonymous storytellers, folklore expresses the values, beliefs, and customs of specific cultures. As such, it serves as a vehicle for transmitting cultural heritage and has merit for all readers. Knowledge of folklore also contributes to better understanding of literature in general, since many books contain allusions to legendary and mythical characters and events. Folktales, fairy tales, and fables are appealing and stimulate the imagination, but generally offer little cognitive challenge to gifted children. Characters are frequently prototypes, themes are explicit, plots are predictable, and good usually triumphs over evil.

Baskin and Harris characterize fables as having little to offer the highly able reader, describing them as short and simple, didactic forms of literature that require little intellectual effort to make analogies from the characters encountered to real-life situations. Morals are usually clearly defined and specific, without ambiguity in their message.[42]

However, some worthy examples are included in this bibliography. Exceptions to the standard formula for fairy tales and folktales are stories dealing with abstract ideas and those written in complex, poetic language. An excellently executed fairy tale, *East of the Sun and West of the Moon* by Mercer Mayer is such an example. Lavishly illustrated, this version of the Norwegian tale chronicles a young girl's quest and dedication to correcting a mistake.

In addition, mythology contributes to the gifted reader's rich literary experience. A myth is a simple and primitive effort of the imagination to identify the human with the nonhuman world. Some of the earliest forms of literature stem from myth, the storyteller's explanation for nature's cycles and changes in weather. Replete with tales of gods, goddesses, and heroes, mythology is filled with adventure, dangerous missions, overcoming obstacles, and sacrifices and losses that somehow all turn out well at the end of the tale.

Over the centuries, mythology has started to merge with literature and has become a structured principle of storytelling. Simplified versions of many well-known myths and fairy tales are available. More complete, challenging editions utilizing complex metaphorical and analogous language structures are recommended for intermediate and older children. For example, the adaptation of *The Adventures of Hercules* by I. M. Richardson adheres closely to the original myth while offering children fine literature that encourages them to investigate more in-depth works of Greek mythology.

A simpler form of myth, pourquoi tales, or "why" stories, explain phenomena. For example, in *Daughter of Earth: A Roman Myth,* Gerald McDermott retells the myth of how the seasons began, making an otherwise difficult tale accessible to readers in the intermediate grades. Paul Goble's retelling, *The Great Race of the Birds and Animals,* is another example of a tale from Cheyenne and Sioux mythology that describes people's dominion over animals.

Similar to myths, legends are based on actual historical figures with little emphasis on the supernatural. For example, King Arthur actually existed, but the well-known legend about him is not historically true.[43] Many excellent adaptations of translated legends are available for young children. Included in this bibliography is Margaret Hodges's retelling of *Saint George and the Dragon* taken from Spenser's *Fairie Queene.* Trina Schart Hyman's detailed, colorful illustrations combine with the rich, vibrant language to create a poetic narrative of this well-known legend. Another legend adapted for young children is *Brothers: A Hebrew Legend* by Florence Freedman. In this story two brothers have developed a lifelong friendship that culminates at the top of a hill that later becomes the site of Jerusalem.

Biography

As pointed out previously,[44] biography is one of the most difficult genres from which to select titles for gifted children because good biographies are rare. Biography has the potential for providing insight into notable individuals' lives as well as allowing readers to explore different historical periods and places. At their best, biographies must be accurate and present an authentic view of the protagonist and his or her role in history. Because the subjects of biographies often serve as models for young readers, they should be worthy of study—individuals who have made significant contributions to society through science, the visual or performing arts, politics, or religion. Equally important, biographies should present a balanced view—both positive and negative qualities or experiences. Finally, effective biographies should provide more than the isolated life story of an individual by also depicting the person's impact on his or her social, cultural, and historic period.

> Beyond this, it is crucial that readers be able to experience vicariously the circumstances and events that made the subjects of the books exceptional, the costs and rewards to them, and how they viewed themselves and were viewed both by their contemporaries and subsequent generations.[45]

Two biographies included in this bibliography meet these criteria by presenting an honest, well-balanced treatment of their subjects. In *Queen Eleanor, Independent Spirit of the Medieval World: A Biography of Eleanor of Aquitaine* by Polly Schoyer Brooks, we meet Eleanor, a powerful ruler, queen of both England and France, who paved the way for better treatment of women. *The Chemist Who Lost His Head: The Story of Antoine Laurent Lavoisier* by Vivian Grey truthfully portrays both the scientist's successes and failures, including not only his scientific contributions but his political activities in late eighteenth-century France. The biography illustrates a scientist's endurance and perseverance amidst multiple obstacles.

In addition to providing worthy role models and elucidating specific facets of interesting careers and lives, well-written biographies of significant persons offer another potential benefit to gifted children. By reading biographies, gifted children may meet characters with personality traits much like their own, thereby being able to identify with unique needs which often are not understood by friends and peers. For example, Robert Burleigh's *A Man Named Thoreau* illustrates the solitary life and isolated feelings of Henry David Thoreau, his need for unstructured "thinking time," and his unique observations of humans' purpose in the world. Gifted children are often interested in the ideas and values literature has to offer. For example, they respond to the complexities and events that shape the main character's life in biographies by contemplating the worth and purpose of struggles encountered and evaluating the methods used to surmount them. For example, the reader is encouraged to examine and decide whether Thoreau was truly a great philosopher based on the descriptions of important periods in his life.

In each of these biographies the authors have attempted to portray authentically the person as a human being. Thus, in addition to describing events surrounding the protagonist, the authors have focused on how struggles were met and weathered, thereby emphasizing the universality and commonality of problem solving.

NOTES

1. Joanne Whitmore, "Conceptualizing the Issue of Underserved Populations of Gifted Students," *Journal for the Education of the Gifted* 10 (1987): 141–153.
2. *Gifted Children Monthly* 8 (November 1987): 4.
3. Robert J. Sternberg, "A Triarchic Theory of Intellectual Giftedness," in *Conceptions of Giftedness,* ed. Robert J. Sternberg and Janet E. Davidson. Cambridge: Cambridge University Press, 1986, pp. 223–243.
4. A. J. Tannenbaum, "Giftedness: A Psychosocial Approach," in *Conceptions of Giftedness,* ed. Robert J. Sternberg and Janet E. Davidson. Cambridge: Cambridge University Press, 1986, pp. 21–51.
5. Joseph S. Renzulli, "The Three-Ring Conception of Giftedness: A Developmental Model for Creative Productivity," in *Conceptions of Giftedness,* ed. Robert J. Sternberg and Janet E. Davidson. Cambridge: Cambridge University Press, 1986, pp. 53–91.
6. Tannenbaum, *"Conceptions of Giftedness,"* p. 49.
7. Barbara Clark, *Growing Up Gifted,* 2nd ed. Columbus, Ohio: Merrill, 1983, p. 30.
8. Renzulli, "The Three-Ring Conception of Giftedness," p. 83.
9. Joyce Juntune, "Myth: The Gifted Constitute a Single, Homogeneous Group!" *Gifted Child Quarterly* 26 (Winter 1982): 9–10.
10. Joanne Rand Whitmore, *Giftedness, Conflict, and Underachievement,* Boston: Allyn & Bacon, 1980.
11. Sylvia B. Rimm, *Underachievement Syndrome: Causes and Cures.* Watertown, Wisc.: Apple, 1986.
12. Benjamin S. Bloom, ed., *Developing Talent in Young People.* New York: Ballantine, 1985.
13. Barbara H. Baskin and Karen H. Harris, *Books for the Gifted Child.* New York: R. R. Bowker, 1980, p. 39.
14. Bernice Cullinan, "Books in the Classroom," *Horn Book* 62 (November/December 1986): 766–768.
15. "Becoming a Nation of Readers: The Report of the Commission on Reading." Washington, D.C.: National Institute of Education, 1985, p. 67.
16. Charlotte S. Huck, "Strategies for Improving Interest and Appreciation in Literature," in *Reaching Children and Young People through Literature,* ed. Helen W. Painter. Newark, Del.: International Reading Association, 1971, pp. 37–45.
17. Philip D. Baker and David R. Bender, "School Library Media Programs and the Gifted and Talented," *School Library Journal* 27 (February 1981): 21–25.
18. Betty Carter, "Leisure Reading Habits of Gifted Students in a Suburban Junior High School," *Top of the News* 38 (Summer 1982): 312–317.
19. Margaret A. Anderson, Nona A. Tollefson, and Edwyna C. Gilbert, "Gifted-

ness and Reading: A Cross-Sectional View of Differences in Reading Attitudes and Behaviors," *Gifted Child Quarterly* 29 (Fall 1985): 186–189.

20. Barbara W. Moller, "An Instructional Model for Gifted Advanced Readers," *Journal of Reading* 27 (January 1984): 324–327.
21. Bernice E. Cullinan, *Literature for Children: Its Discipline and Content.* Dubuque, Iowa: Brown, 1971, p. 2.
22. Charles E. Martin, "Why Some Gifted Children Do Not Like to Read," *Roeper Review* 7 (November 1984): 72–75.
23. Phyliss B. Leonard, *Choose, Use, Enjoy, Share: Library Media Skills for the Gifted Child.* Littleton, Colo.: Libraries Unlimited, 1985.
24. Baskin and Harris, *Books for the Gifted Child,* pp. 44–45.
25. Ibid., p. 46.
26. Dorothy Strickland, "Promoting Language and Concept Development," in *Literature and Young Children.* Urbana, Ill: National Council of Teachers of English, 1977, pp. 38–58.
27. Benjamin S. Bloom, ed., *Taxonomy of Educational Objectives: Handbook 1, Cognitive Domain.* New York: David McKay, 1956.
28. Jo Carr, ed., "Clarity in Science Writing," in *Beyond Fact: Nonfiction for Children and Young People.* Chicago: ALA, 1982, pp. 43–53.
29. Susan Steinfirst, "Reader-Response Criticism," *School Library Journal* 33 (October 1986): 114–115.
30. Glenna Davis Sloan, *The Child as Critic: Teaching Literature in the Elementary School.* New York: Teachers College Press, 1975, p. 7.
31. Michael Cart, "A Light in the Darkness: Humor Returns to Children's Fantasy," *School Library Journal* 33 (April 1987): 48–49.
32. Lloyd Alexander, "Literature, Creativity, and Imagination," paper presented at the Association for Childhood Education International Meeting, New York, October 1970, in *Childhood Education,* ed. Monroe D. Cohen. Wheaton, Md.: Association for Childhood Education, 1973.
33. Patricia J. Cianciolo, *Picture Books for Children,* 2nd ed. Chicago: ALA, 1981, p. 28.
34. Nancy Polette, *Picture Books for Gifted Programs.* Metuchen, N.J.: Scarecrow, 1981, p. 61.
35. Rebecca J. Lukens, *A Critical Handbook of Children's Literature,* 3rd ed. Glenview, Ill.: Scott Foresman, 1986, pp. 46–47.
36. Ruth Nadelman Lynn, *Fantasy for Children: An Annotated Checklist and Reference Guide,* 2nd ed. New York: R. R. Bowker, 1983, p. 1.
37. Ethel Heins, "A Decade of Children's Books: A Reviewer's Response," *Catholic Library World* 58 (September/October 1986): 75–80.
38. M. Jean Greenlaw, "Books in the Classroom," *Horn Book* 62 (September/October 1986): 634–636.
39. James Cross Giblin, "A Publisher's Perspective," *Horn Book* 63 (January/February 1987): 104–107.

40. Helen W. Painter, *Poetry and Children.* Newark, Del.: International Reading Association, 1970, p. 72.
41. Zena Sutherland, Dianne Monson, and May Hill Arbuthnot, *Children and Books,* 6th ed. Glenview, Ill.: Scott Foresman, 1981, p. 257.
42. Baskin and Harris, *Books for the Gifted Child,* p. 54.
43. Lukens, *A Critical Handbook of Children's Literature,* p. 24.
44. Baskin and Harris, *Books for the Gifted Child,* p. 61.
45. Ibid., p. 62.

2
A Selected Guide to Intellectually Challenging Books

This chapter consists of annotations of juvenile books whose specific qualities make them appropriate for gifted children ranging from the prereading stage—including beginning, intermediate, and advanced readers—to grade 6. The annotations are arranged alphabetically by author's surname. In addition, the reader will find a helpful index section at the back of this work, listing books by title, subject, and level. Each annotation is composed of a summary of the book's contents and a discussion of the features that deem the work appropriate for gifted children. When included, quotations are selected to communicate an author's particular style.

The philosophy on which title selections were based is that books for highly able readers should demonstrate (1) appropriate form and content wherein the language is sufficiently complex to call on gifted readers' abilities to deal with abstractions, ambiguities, and other reasoning tasks and (2) an interface of text and illustrations. In addition to their tangible features, books were selected that afford readers an opportunity to respond *cognitively* while containing features that also allow them to respond *emotionally* and *imaginatively.*

Many factors influence a child's book selection. The child's age, maturity level, interests, preferences, background of experience, and other factors combine to determine whether a specific title is appropriate for a particular child at a given time. Every book described here is not appropriate for every intellectually gifted child. As noted, the population of identified gifted children demonstrates a wide range of reading levels and conceptual understanding.

Most books included in this work can be read independently; however, some titles are best read to a child or shared by a child and adult. The annotation will reflect our recommendation in this regard.

Assigning a level designation to a title is difficult for many reasons. For example, grade designations are inappropriate because children span several years within a grade level. Also, many youngsters need books on a variety of reading levels, depending on their specific academic abilities. A child who demonstrates high ability in mathematics would probably need advanced books in that field, but introductory- or intermediate-level books in science. We have used the three broad reading level designations of the first volume that include not only features of books but also the skills and background of information that children bring to the reading experience. The reading level designations are beginning, intermediate, and advanced.

READING LEVEL DESIGNATIONS

Beginning level Beginning-level books are for the youngest readers or those new to the subject area. With some exceptions, this category includes picture books, alphabet and counting books, materials directed at preschoolers, and books intended to be read aloud. Not all require the ability to read: Some are textless, and some are intended to be shared by adults and children. Although some genres are usually thought of as encompassing only easy titles, the examples included here are more sophisticated and challenging, surpassing similar offerings in their demands of young readers. In addition to the expected literary fare, topics covered range from art to zoology.

Intermediate level Except for textless works, all intermediate-level titles require reading proficiency. If nonfiction, they presume some prior acquaintance with the topic or a willingness to plunge directly into a substantive consideration of problems central to the discipline. If fiction, they may make considerable demands in terms of both structure and content, often encompassing ambiguities and paradoxes. In either event, books on this level generally display a demanding vocabulary and a treatment of their topic that is deep as well as broad.

Advanced level Advanced-level works are directed toward extremely bright children who may even be functioning on an adult level intellectually. They presume a high stage of literary sophistication, an advanced vocabulary, considerable background knowledge, absoprtion in the topic, and a willingness to confront exceptionally demanding material. Enjoyment is predicated on deriving satisfaction from mastering high-level intellectual challenges.

Adkins, Jan. *Letterbox: The Art and History of Letters.* Illus. by author. New York: Walker, 1981, 48 pp. (Intermediate)

Beginning with the earliest forms of communication, *Letterbox* chronicles the history of writing from simple, crude drawings and symbols, known as pictographs, to modern type. Pictographs mostly related facts (e.g., sun represents day) rather than feelings and emotions since the latter cannot easily be pictured in a concrete fashion. However, the combination of symbols represented complex ideas or things as well as feelings that cannot be seen, such as love and work. For example, a picture of a mother and child conveyed the more complex feeling of "love." Adkins refers to Chinese calligraphy as an example of symbolic writing that is considered an art. The cuneiform tablets of Mesopotamia are briefly introduced before the reader is presented with a more extensive explanation of Egyptian writing. Ideograms, phonograms, hieroglyphics, hierotics, and demotic forms of symbol writing samples remained in use thousands of years after the Egyptian civilization declined.

Adkins contrasts ancient Egyptians and their interest in the natural world with the Phoenicians, who were mainly interested in trade and immediate profit. Consequently, Phoenician writing reflected this fast-paced life-style, the symbols being quick, brief, and angular, whereas Egyptian writing was more decorative and graceful. Eventually, the Greeks changed Phoenician writing, developing the Greek alphabet that is still used today. From the Greeks are derived the names of our letters: "A" meaning alpha and "B" meaning beta, and so forth.

Later, the Romans adjusted the Greek alphabet to their own style, retaining 13 of the 21 Greek characters and developing the rest of their alphabet using many Greek similarities. The inscription on the base of the Trojan Column in Rome represents the style and dignity of Roman culture. Beautiful as writing for mainly decorative purposes was, the emergence of laws, record keeping, important documents, and more widespread communication necessitated a standard form of writing that could be quickly written and generally understood.

After a brief history of the decline of the Roman Empire, the Carlovingian miniscule, the familiar rounded form of handwriting, was introduced. This was the style in which laws and literature of Greece and Rome were re-copied and preserved. As art and architecture underwent change, so too did Carlovingian. The rounded letters became more vertical and pointed in keeping with the Gothic style of architecture that was flourishing.

The effect of cultural change on writing was dramatic. For example, during the Renaissance, a focus on writing, reading, and more effective means of printing books emphasized the importance of communicating new ideas. To illustrate this point, Adkins explores Gutenberg's enthusiastic development of the printing press in an effort to facilitate the flow of the written word. Over the years the printing press was modified and different type styles developed—each reflecting the historical changes within a culture and expressing its ideas, values, and beliefs. As a result of the strong influence of writing during the Renaissance period, the Italian type of handwriting we know as italic developed.

Adkins offers famous quotations to illustrate various kinds of type for comparison. In addition, decorative type such as that used in advertising is examined. For example, a double-page spread shows words that convey to the reader the concept of the words, such as "window" written with large open letters and "thud" printed in heavy, black block letters.

Emphasis is also placed on how writing styles are influenced by the instrument used, whether it be a red pen or a stub pen or a stylus used on wax tablets or lead sheets. The reader is invited to try writing unicals, and half unicals, using different strokes called ascenders and descenders.

In another section of the book the invention of the typewriter is detailed along with its effect on writing pertaining to business and industry in contrast to the personal, warm, artful handwriting produced directly by the human hand.

Adkins's artful narrative style enlivens the origins of a subject most of us take for granted. He repeatedly involves the reader with suggestions that they try their hand at different forms of writing using the appropriate writing instruments. For example, he includes a double-page spread of illustrations of tools and pen points and shows the reader how to use them effectively, always emphasizing writing as an art. Illustrations are in black-and-white pencil on cream-colored paper that lets the symbols and letters stand out and complements the text. The printing is clear and readable, and the evolution of the alphabet and various forms of writing is effectively covered. The particular value of the book is that it invites readers to examine the relationships between the art and utility of written communication.

Ahlberg, Janet, and Allan Ahlberg. *The Baby's Catalogue.* Illus. by authors. New York: Little, Brown, 1982, 32 pp. (Beginning)

Beginning and ending with illustrations of babies, this book employs a developmentally appropriate viewpoint that highlights the activities of parents and siblings throughout a young child's typical day. Soft shades and tints of color are used to illustrate the variety of everyday situations and objects in a young child's environment. Arranged in rectangular shapes like photographs in an album, drawings show babies crying, sleeping, nursing, peering from a crib, and enthralled with a toy. Babies at various developmental stages from the very young to those being toilet-trained and with different colored hair, eyes, and skin—even twins—are depicted. Large, dark brown-toned type contrasts with the white background and colorful illustrations to label the categories in the catalog, such as "Moms and Dads," "Mornings," and "High Chairs and Breakfasts." Both moms and dads assume a variety of roles—providing child care, preparing meals, doing laundry, and going off to work.

Catalog-fashion, specific labels for individual toys, items found in a grocery story and in gardens, as well as common pets, appear next to the drawing of each object. Other illustrations are unlabeled, giving youngsters an opportunity to develop oral language expression as they interpret the actions themselves. Included in the shopping list are "Baby Things"—with illustrations of a pacifier, baby powder, booties, diaper pins, and ice cream. The shopping list also contains six different sizes of cans, with various types of openers, including a sardine can with its key opener and an oil can with a pointed nozzle. Placed in the row of baby carriages for young readers to discover are two smaller carriages—a toy carriage and a stroller. Many scenes are appropriately labeled with action words. Games are described as "Bouncing," "Piggyback," "Catching," "Climbing," and "Peekaboo." The page about books shows babies independently looking at books and listening to adults read to them. A careful look reveals twins sitting on their mother's lap reading *The Baby's Catalogue*. Baby's head stuck between the bars of a fence, and baby playing with makeup from mother's handbag, feeding cake to the family dog, and dropping keys down a sidewalk grate are but a few of the accidents depicted. One especially familiar event is the illustration of an older sister lifting baby from her lap as the reader sees a dark stain on her dress.

The Baby's Catalogue provides preschoolers with more than a mere listing of objects. The witty and detailed illustrations give young readers an opportunity to practice discrimination skills by identifying color, size, shape, and function. Feelings and moods are represented in the faces of babies and in the concerned, happy, and sometimes irritated expressions of their parents.

Alexander, Lloyd. *Westmark*. New York: Dutton, 1981. 184 pp. (Advanced)

Westmark is the first of a trilogy. In the kingdom of Westmark, Theo, a printer's apprentice, is uprooted when his master's print shop is overtaken by soldiers pretending to conduct a Royal inspection for King Augustine. After striking a soldier while trying to protect his master and the printing press, Theo becomes a wanted man and consequently flees. On the road, he meets with Las Bombas, a clever charlatan who wanders the country, altering his occupational schemes and disguising both himself and his dwarf assistant, Muskrat, to fit the occasion. Theo decides to join the trio after Las Bombas devises a quick scheme to disguise Theo from approaching soldiers, thereby saving his life.

Soon the group comes to include Mickle, a fragile, ragged waif who was in the crowd during one of Las Bombas's medicine shows. It is during this show that she displayed her unusual gift for ventriloquism and mimickry; and recognizing her as a profitable opportunity Las Bombas convinces her to join his troupe. As their friendship develops, Theo teaches Mickle to read and write; she, in turn, teaches him sign language.

Eventually, Theo's conscience makes it impossible for him to continue to take people's money fraudulently. He sets out on his own and opens up a shop, using the name DeRoth, as a public letter writer in Freyborg. He is aided in this undertaking by a man who led a small band of rebels who are opposed not only to the harsh treatment of people ordered by Cabbarus, King Augustine's chief minister, but also to the idea of a monarchy.

King Augustine, in ill health and grieving over the death of his daughter, Princess Augusta, six years earlier, wants to find a person who can contact his daughter's spirit. While the court physician, Dr. Torrens, tries to restore the King's health, Cabbarus continues to supply occultists and spiritualists, who cause Augustine's health to grow worse. Hungry for more power, Cabbarus tries to persuade the King to adopt him as an heir to the throne. As part of his selfish pursuits, Cabbarus convinces the King to banish Torrens. Pretending to leave the country, Torrens is attacked by one of Cabbarus's spies. The doctor survives, however, and is found floating along the river by two scavenger children, Sparrow and Weasel. Along with a journalist, Keller, the two care for him.

Hearing that Mickle and Las Bombas are in trouble with the law because of their deceptive ways, Theo comes to their rescue in Nierkeeping, along with Florian, a rebellious son of a nobleman, who is planning an attack on the city's arsenal. Theo and Mickle are reunited, if only for a short while, and Florian's men succeed in breaking into the arsenal. After learning about Las Bombas and the amazing girl who supposedly contacts the spirit world, Cabbarus, still bent on his plan to get rid of the King, arranges to capture the group and bring them to the castle. Here he arranges a show in which Mickle pretends to be Princess Augusta and urges her father to abdicate the throne and name Cabbarus his successor. During the performance, Mickle, seemingly in a trance, dramatizes her near death from drowning as Princess Augusta at the hands of Cabbarus. Recognizing her voice, King Augustine pronounces Cabbarus a murderer. Cabbarus flees and nearly falls to his death from a belfry, but is saved by Theo.

Theo and Mickle part again and she resumes her role of princess. At Dr. Torrens's (now back at the castle) suggestion, Theo travels throughout Westmark to learn more about the citizens' concerns and how to remedy injustices.

The story is a fast-moving balance between the tragedy of Mickle's life and her sense of humor and talent for mimickry. Most able readers will independently seek the other books in the trilogy. In *The Kestrel*, Theo travels throughout Westmark, detailing instances of political and economic injustices and continues his inner struggle to justify his actions. The characters are fully realized in the concluding part of the trilogy, *The Beggar Queen.* Arranging for an election and abdicating her position as queen, Mickle, along with Theo, leaves Westmark. The trilogy explores the struggle between ethics, loyalty, and individual responsibility. Colorful characters enliven the suspenseful, tightly woven plots. Of particular challenge to gifted readers are the wit and multiple meanings employed in the books.

Aliki. *How a Book Is Made.* Illus. by author. New York: Crowell, 1986, 32 pp. (Beginning)

Orchestrated in an entertaining fashion, this publication is highly informative as it systematically illustrates the method of making a book from story idea to the completed volume.

Aliki uses cartoonlike illustrations of cats to explain the step-by-step bookmaking process. Thus, we first meet a little cat asking who made the storybook he is reading. A chorus of cats, composed of all the participants in the process, answer that they all contributed, and the pages that follow proceed to demonstrate how it is done.

First, a little cat comes up with an idea for a story, completes her manuscript, and sends it to the editor of the Goodbooks Publishing Company. This stage is depicted in a sequence of cartoon frames over two pages with text inserted between frames and comments in conversation balloons. The satisfied editor issues a contract to the author, who will illustrate her own book. From there, the reader learns of each step along the way: the artwork, design, editing, typesetting, and proofreading of the book and the technical aspects of cost estimates, production schedule, mechanicals, color separation, printing procedures, binding, sales, and reviews. Finally, we see the book delivered to libraries and stores where it will reach children who want to read it.

Gifted children and their teachers will welcome this remarkable book. After reading this entertaining treatment of the subject, children will have respect and admiration for the many people involved, and many will be inspired to try writing a book themselves. Unique in its approach to this topic for younger children, *How a Book Is Made* will be a valuable resource for older children also. The presentation is succinct, accurate, clear, and entertaining without minimizing the complexity of the task. The book has a picture-book format, without need of an index to the elements of the well-documented bookmaking process.

Aliki. *A Medieval Feast.* Illus. by author. New York: Crowell, 1983, unp. (Intermediate)

"The king is coming to visit" begins this unique book about the elaborate preparations carried out to celebrate this noble visitor. Plans are announced that the King and company are stopping over at Camdenton Manor. The King's party includes the Queen, knights, squires, and everyone else making up his court—a retinue of 100.

The Lord of the manor immediately became very busy to ensure a satisfactory feast. First, he called on his serfs and instructed them to start preparing for this phenomenal event. They began refinishing the Royal Suite, weaving new fabric for it, embroidering the King's emblem on linens, painting it on his chair, and so forth. Next, they tidied every room in the house, prepared quarters for the horsemen and their horses, and most important, began to gather the food for the feast. This group of dependable loyal subjects hunted all kinds of animals and birds, caught various varieties of fish, gathered fresh fruits and vegetables, and collected honey from bees. They ground flour for breads, made butter and cheese, and brewed wine.

After these long-range plans, the actual food preparation began, and the huge, vaulted, great kitchen in the manor bustled with activity. Many cooks and scullion boys assisted in the monumental task: They roasted pigs, deer, and wild boars and prepared salted meats for highly seasoned stews. In medieval times, foods were consumed that are unheard of today, such as swan, heron, peacock, and blackbirds. Each dish was prepared to appeal to the eye as much, or more than, the palate.

Everybody had a job to do. The King was coming and the impression counted. When all was ready, the great hall was opened and the tables set. Customary ceremony and ritual preceded the serving of food; for example, everybody washed his or her hands in scented water, which was first tasted by the Ewerer, or water pourer, before it was poured over the King's hands. Silverware was not provided, only napkins; wine glasses were shared. Then the serving of the fancy and ostentatious dishes began, including such extravaganzas as a castle molded from pastry and stuffed with foods and delicacies. The feast lasted until dark and resumed the next day.

Aliki's account is magnificently detailed, demanding readers' skills of observation and synthesis. It is a visual feast of a multitude of preparatory activities that culminate in a grand party indeed fit for a king. Children may be surprised and amused at some of the foods consumed in medieval time, not always sharing their taste and choice.

Jewel-colored illustrations are reminiscent of tapestries. A caption or explanation at the bottom of each complements the text. At the bottom of several pages, we see the travelers journeying through the forests en route to Camdenton Manor. The borders of each page are decorative and informative, showing labeled pictures of many of the foods. Much of the vocabulary is unfamiliar, but is explained in part by illustrations or text. There is no glossary, which would have been beneficial to readers. The author has presented an unusual topic with clarity, detail, and pomp that will interest young readers and perhaps stimulate further research.

Anno, Masaichiro, and Mitsumasa Anno. *Anno's Mysterious Multiplying Jar.* Illus. by Mitsumasa Anno. New York: Philomel, 1983, unp. (Intermediate)

In this book Masaichiro Anno and Mitsumasa Anno describe the concept of mathematical factorials in two presentations—first, in colorful, detailed drawings of real objects and then by using tiny red dots and factorial notation in an abstract manner. Factorial numbers express numerical relationships. For example, 3! = 3 × 2! = 1 × 2 × 3 which is the product of the number 3 multiplied by the next smaller number and so on down to 1.

Starting with a painting of a beautiful blue jar on the book's cover, the Annos give readers a visual treat. For example, there is an elegant apothecary jar of oriental blues and white, and clear, rippling blue water flows across the ensuing pages on which an antique ship is introduced. The next two pages show a solitary island that contains two countries, each featuring three mountains. Using the technique of a scene-within-a-scene the story continues to build toward an understanding of factorials, such as 4 walled kingdoms, 5 villages, 6 houses, 7 rooms, 8 cupboards, 9 boxes, and 10 jars. At the conclusion of the pictorial section, the Annos ask readers how many jars were in all the boxes and then reveal the factorial symbol for 10 that means 3,628,800.

In the second presentation, the Annos retell the story numerically, using tiny red dots to signify the countries, mountains, and so on. The text used in the first story appears again at the bottom of each page with the appropriate number of very small red dots in the center and the factorial notation at the top. The last double-page spread is so filled with small red dots representing 8! that the rest of the story (concluding with the 10 jars in each of 9 boxes) is told solely in text without the use of dots.

In an afterword the Annos carefully explain factorials, giving examples of the phenomenal possibilities of huge numbers and emphasizing the order and beauty of our world. Adults might find the book a useful tool in teaching youngsters the meaning of large numbers, and very capable young readers can understand the concept of factorials when they know how to multiply, since the visual presentation is cumulative and clearly drawn. The concept remains abstract, however, and should present a challenge to young readers.

Anno, Mitsumasa. *Anno's Counting House.* Illus. by author. New York: Philomel, 1982, unp. (Beginning)

In this wordless picture book designed to help children learn to understand numbers, the reader gradually witnesses ten children—five boys and five girls—and their belongings move from one house to another. Differentiated by color and architectural style, interior and exterior views of each house appear on alternating pages. While the exteriors are shown in color, the interiors are sketched in black and white, providing a contrast to the colorfully clothed children in the rooms.

The story begins by showing the interior of a house and its ten occupants. The next page depicts the exterior of the second house, to which the children move, one at a time, throughout the pages of the book until all ten of them have vacated their original home. House exteriors feature cutout windows that reveal either children or furnishings inside. While going about the task of packing and unpacking, each child is shown in different rooms in each house, thereby adding interest and challenging the reader to account for every child and his or her location.

Anno begins by suggesting to the reader how to use the book. In concluding notes to parents and other adults, he explains the importance of children gaining mathematical understanding and appreciation (as opposed to rote learning) through concrete experiences acquired as they observe and interact with the environment: Visual-memory skills and discrimination of details come into play as young readers scan the interiors of the two houses, count the children, and observe the differences between the two floor plans in this gamelike book.

The book offers more than one way to enjoy and learn and/or reinforce the counting process. Anno suggests that the reader can interact with the pages by placing two contrasting sets of counters on the boys and girls in the first house to determine that the number of remaining counters represents the number of children who have moved into the second house at a given time. The book can also be read backward; that is, the children appear to move from the second house to the first. By reversing the order, repeated counting practice is encouraged. Highly able youngsters will delight in solving the visual mystery of locating the children as they move from house to house. The book also offers the potential for noting similarities and differences and creating stories to accompany the illustrations.

Anno, Mitsumasa. *Anno's U.S.A.* Illus. by author. New York: Philomel (originally published by Fukuinkan Shoten, Tokyo, 1983, under the title *Tobi No Ehon IV*), 1983, unp. (Intermediate)

The unusual city skyline on the front cover with King Kong waving frantically from atop a building, city streets with no automobiles, and two buildings—one with red and white stripes, the other with white stars on a blue background representing the American flag—tell readers that this will be no ordinary pictorial of the United States.

Anno, the lone traveler in this wordless picture book, journeys across America starting at the West Coast, going across the land backward in time, or departing from the East Coast as one of Columbus's ships looms on the horizon. Appearing as a man on horseback, cloaked in blue garments (as he does in some of his other books), Anno merely passes through each scene, observing but not reacting to the characters and actions portrayed in murallike paintings that cover the entire double-page spreads. Placed throughout are characters from literature and the popular media, historical landmarks, and scenes from famous paintings. For example, the traveler encounters Plains and Pueblo Indians, early settlers in covered wagons, cattle ranchers, cotton plantation workers, musicians and artists, riverboats, the Alamo, the Liberty Bell, Independence Hall, the Governor's Palace in Williamsburg, and Preservation Hall in New Orleans. One of the many memorable scenes in the book is a New York parade featuring Paul Bunyan and his blue ox, Babe, Maurice Sendak's characters from *Where the Wild Things Are,* a statue of the lone traveler on horseback, a big apple, various zoo animals, and the lions of the New York Public Library. In the distance, early Dutch traders and American Indians are seen, presumably bargaining for the purchase of Manhattan.

Anno cleverly adds humor to serious events from the nation's history. Among the incongruities illustrated are Little Orphan Annie with Sandy greeting Daddy Warbucks near the Capitol with the well-known statue of the Marine Memorial in the distance, the subject of a James McNeill Whistler painting in the same scene as Sesame Street characters, and figures representing *American Gothic* a few feet away from a red-costumed Santa Claus conversing with a local shopkeeper about a sled for sale.

Anno's watercolor and ink drawings are amazingly detailed without any one set of figures assuming more importance than another. Understanding the book requires a wide background of knowledge and finely honed observational skills and visual perception—skills that make demands on most young readers, including the intellectually gifted. The book invites rereading to locate previously missed allusions and encourages beginning readers to ask questions of their more experienced reading companions.

Arnold, Caroline. *Saving the Peregrine Falcon.* Photog. by Richard R. Hewett. Minneapolis, Minn.: Carolrhoda, 1985, 48 pp. (Intermediate)

This highly informative book explains, in clear and carefully chosen terms, the scientific process employed to save one of the most majestic birds in the country, the peregrine falcon. A brief description of the peregrine falcon's nesting places is followed by information about some of its major characteristics and the causes of this fantastic bird's endangerment.

To compensate for the harmful effects of DDT that the falcons consume during their winter stay in Central and South America, scientists rescue the fragile eggs for safekeeping until they hatch. The book illustrates how skilled mountain climbers retrieve the eggs, leaving plaster ones in their place, and take them to the Santa Cruz Predatory Bird Research Group Laboratory. At the laboratory the eggs remain in an incubator under careful scrutiny until they hatch. When the chicks are three days to one week old, they are placed in a nest of an imprinted mother peregrine until they are ready to return to the wilderness at three weeks of age.

Colorful and exquisite photographs illustrate all the facets of this challenging, and sometimes dangerous, effort to save the falcon from extinction, including a chronicle of each stage of the chick's development. The exceptionally arranged pictures do not need captions with the coordinating text. A glossary is included to define the vocabulary introduced in heavy type throughout the book.

The thoughtful reader will appreciate the thorough research and the patience expended in the effort to save the peregrine falcon. The book is easy to read and understand in its presentation of the unusual circumstances that surround the preservation of a most noble creature.

Arnosky, Jim. *Secrets of a Wildlife Watcher.* Illus. by author. New York: Lothrop, 1983, 66 pp. (Intermediate)

Sharing his personal experiences of observing wild animals and birds in their natural habitats, Jim Arnosky invites readers to begin what could become a lifelong interest in learning about wildlife. Readers are given a lesson in how to detect specific details of various animals' colors and markings, feeding habits, nesting behaviors, grooming, posturing, and warning signals. Animals observed include those found in woodlands and near open fields and marshes.

Specifically, in a discussion of animal ranges, Arnosky informs readers where to look for hawks and owls and what surface signs, such as gnawed bark, mounds of soil, and tracks, indicate the presence of wildlife. The reader also learns how to remain quiet and unseen through techniques such as crouching low to the ground and using a blind. (Steps for constructing a simple blind are also detailed.) Clues on how to identify whether a bird, turtle, frog, or deer is male or female or juvenile are found in their colors, markings, and sizes.

One of the humorous anecdotes in this informational and sensitive book is about a descented skunk Arnosky kept as a pet. This unusual pet never lost his wild nature as he disrupted Arnosky's household with his antics.

More than facts about wildlife are presented in an interesting manner that entices readers to go outdoors and begin applying their observational skills. Readers are shown techniques for making their own discoveries. Arnosky's personable writing style reads almost like a diary. Every page contains labeled drawings that surround the text and give his account the informality of a sketchbook.

The value of the book for intellectually able readers is that it serves as a guide for developing one's senses—skills that may be applied in other areas of scientific pursuit. An implied theme throughout the book is a respect for all forms of life.

Avi. *Bright Shadow.* New York: Bradbury, 1985, 167 pp.
(Intermediate)

This is an intensely intriguing story that draws in the reader immediately by requiring active participation. What choices would the reader make if placed in a similar situation? The time and place are not specified as this fantasy unfurls and sets the reader upon an enthralling adventure.

A dying wizard must pass on five unused wishes that remain with him, and anxiously approaches the palace of the king to find a successor. Because of his prolonged illness, the wizard is unaware that King Ruthvin is cruel and demanding and is much hated by the people. King Ruthvin, mistaking the wizard for a beggar, lashes out at him in disgust. As the wizard lies dying, Morwenna, an assistant to the chambermaid, happens upon him and tries to help. Able to pass the five wishes on to the confused girl, the wizard asks for her forgiveness before dying and turning to dust.

The burdened people of the land have long hoped that someone would rescue them from their terrible plight, and they believed that the time was near for this to happen. The king's army chief, Sibald, relays this story to the king, who vaguely remembers an old man trying to tell him something. Obsessed with trying to find the wizard, Ruthvin prepares to execute people randomly to demonstrate his authority and power over his people.

Meanwhile, Morwenna is trying to sort out her thoughts about the wizard's five wishes. She finds it difficult to believe that she owns them, but continues to hear echoes of an irrepressible voice in her ears, cautioning, encouraging, and sometimes threatening her. She becomes distracted and preoccupied in conversation with Swen, her longtime friend who takes her home from the palace each day. Swen, slightly older than the 13-year-old Morwenna, is lacking in maturity. He happily lives for the moment, finding pleasure in the simplest things of life, and content to be a mule-cart driver.

Each time Morwenna is tempted to tell Swen of the incident with the wizard, a voice prevents her from doing so. Suffering from low self-esteem and self-centeredness, Swen thinks she isn't interested in him, and begins to brood and yearn for a way to win Morwenna's admiration. When the oppressive king arrests Swen as the wizard, he believes the attention will proclaim him important.

Experiencing strange visions and dreams, Morwenna pulls more and more into herself. Longing for help and understanding, she is unable to seek any, for the voice reminds her of silence concerning the wishes. This only increases the burden she carries.

When the king prepares to hang Swen publicly, Morwenna uses one of the wishes to save him. Swen, wishing for his life at the same time, thinks he has saved himself and that he is truly the wizard. Morwenna and Swen ride deep into the forest to escape where they encounter Gareth, an old man, and his small band of people who are hiding from the king. Disguised as a beggar, the king enters the village but is recognized by Morwenna. She is torn between a desire to escape and let Swen take care of himself and a certain loyalty she feels toward her friend. When the king kills Swen, she uses another wish to bring him back to life. Gareth finally discovers that Morwenna is the true wizard and begins making plans for how she can save his people from the ruthless king. He allows Swen to continue believing that he possesses magical power and lets him lead the people to the city to overthrow the kingdom.

Morwenna is becoming increasingly torn in her inability to tell Swen the truth. Closely guarded by Gareth's men, she cannot leave the village. Swen, criticizing her for not believing in him, rejects her and joins the throng of people who instill in him a feeling of importance. Meanwhile, King Ruthvin believes he has finally killed the wizard and prepares to enforce his power by destroying anyone who questions it.

On the march to the city, Morwenna's conscience once again persuades her to save Swen from death by the king's men. The exasperated Gareth tries to convince her to destroy Ruthvin, thinking she has many wishes to use. But she knows that when all five wishes are gone, she will be gone too. At the palace she must once again use another wish to turn the army's arrows to dust, and she is left with only one wish. When Swen is dying from the king's dagger, Morwenna is faced with the choice of whether to save him or not, knowing that she will die when she dispenses the last wish. She decides to live and let the last wish remain with her.

The story ends with the question of what the reader would do if placed in Morwenna's predicament. One wonders whether Morwenna ever uses the last wish by choice. The protagonist struggles with whether or not to sacrifice herself. This overall theme of a classical dilemma is an illustration of risk taking with which gifted children will identify.

Avi has written a sensitive, yet complicated story of a girl's conflicting desires. The strong character manifested in Morwenna compels the reader to resist putting the book down. Depicted as a young girl, but mature in her thinking, the character of Morwenna will allow gifted children to identify with her. This tightly woven tale is truly haunting and mysterious. It is fast-paced and ends in a unique way.

Balian, Lorna. *Humbug Potion: An A B Cipher*. Illus. by author. Nashville, Tenn.: Abingdon, 1984, unp. (Beginning)

Discovering an old recipe for a Magic Beauty Potion written partly in code, a homely witch who wishes to become beautiful brews the required ingredients in her cauldron. A colorful illustration on each page shows the witch and the miscellaneous animals—black cat, mice, and a crow—usually associated with witches. In addition to her traditional black dress and pointed hat, Balian's red-haired witch wears a shawl and colorful petticoats, which soften her appearance to make her nonthreatening, almost grandmotherly.

The reader soon becomes involved in decoding the recipe whose ingredients are printed in a simple code that substitutes numerals for alphabet letters. One alphabet letter appears at the top of each page. Upper- and lowercase letters are printed side by side (Aa, Bb, etc.), and the cardinal number corresponding to each letter (A is 1, B is 2, etc.) is printed directly below the given letter. One line of text using code for one or two words appears at the bottom of each page. An alphabet/numeral decoding chart is located in both the front and the back of the book for easy reference. The word to be decoded on a given page begins with the letter featured on the page. For example, for the letter "Cc," the text reads "and a 3-21-16 of 3-15-4 liver oil" (and a cup of cod liver oil).

The observant beginning reader will detect a second story line in the facial expressions and antics of the witch's black cat, nestled at her feet with one eye peering at its mistress and displaying curiosity, playfulness, and skepticism. Tiny mice can be seen scampering about, and a black crow assists the witch in her endeavors by bringing an odd assortment of objects to be added to the brew. Ignoring the directions to stir with a smile, the witch is unsuccessful in her attempt to become beautiful.

More complex than most alphabet books, *Humbug Potion* is most appropriate for beginning readers who already have a basic knowledge of letter names, sound/symbol relationships, and alphabet letter sequence. The illustrations reveal words to be decoded. For instance, the witch is shown pinching her nostrils closed as she drops an egg into the cauldron. Despite the obvious pictorial clues, young readers with limited spelling skills will be challenged to decode the words. Convergent thinking is used to decode the words; however, the possibilities exist for divergent thinking if young readers imagine the results of combining items depicted or try to predict which ingredient the witch will select next. Beginning readers who have developed competence by decoding the words might want to read the book to a younger child. The illustrations offer so much detail and originality that the book can be read repeatedly with enjoyment.

Bang, Molly. *The Grey Lady and the Strawberry Snatcher.* Illus. by author. New York: Four Winds, 1980, unp. (Beginning)

Stunningly illustrated, this whimsical, wordless picture book offers an entertaining story about an old lady, called the "grey lady" (she is portrayed as solid gray except for her hands and face), and a spirited character known as the "strawberry snatcher."

The smiling grey lady is observed buying a box of plump, red strawberries and carrying them home. In the meantime, a strangely clothed character is lurking nearby. His bright blue body dressed in a glaring green and red cape and a purple pointed hat, this creature surreptitiously follows the grey lady, who is unaware of his presence. Suddenly, the "thing" reaches for the bag of berries, and not until then does the grey lady realize that someone is behind her, as the reader can see by the expression on her face. When the creature tries to grab her bag, she runs, narrowly missing a woman on a skateboard carrying a snake in a basket. All three of them appear to collide with an oncoming bus.

The next scene shows the grey lady still carrying the strawberries and the "snatcher" now riding the skateboard. The pursuit is continued through a murky swamp where tree branches look like arms reaching out grotesquely. The lady is somewhat camouflaged behind a huge gray tree as the strawberry snatcher stealthily prowls the forest looking for her. She barely escapes by climbing the tree and swinging away on a vine.

Now more obsessed than ever, the "thing" ferociously flies after her with teeth bared, but is mystified as the lady becomes totally obscure in a dense gray fog. Just when the snatcher seems defeated, it happens on a large berry patch and abandons the pursuit to gobble up his delicious discovery. The grey lady arrives safely home with the luscious red strawberries and all is well again.

Bang's brilliantly illustrated wordless story captivates the imagination. Only the bright, neon colors of the snatcher and the smug, smiling face of the lady are visible. An element of delight tinged with anticipation creates a somewhat humorous situation, while leaving the reader to ponder the question: Will the strawberry snatcher catch the grey lady? Readers are continually reminded that it is the strawberries the creature is after, not the lady. Youngsters must employ skills of observation and visual discrimination to discern the lady's whereabouts, as she is not always readily visible. Here the traditional theme of the villain and the innocent has a new, refreshing twist that will encourage children's creative contemplation.

Baylor, Byrd. *A God on Every Mountain Top: Stories of Southwest Indian Sacred Mountains.* Illus. by Carol Brown. New York: Scribner, 1981. unp. (Intermediate)

Poetically presented, this unusual work brings the myths of Southwest Indians' mountains to life. These traditional stories describe the beliefs of Apache, Navajo, Pueblo, Zuni, and several other tribes concerning their sacred or holy mountain. Divided into sections—Beginnings, Changes, Protection, Power, Magic, Mystery and Dreams, and The Beings in the

Mountains—each story-verse emphasizes some aspect of a particular tribe's perception and beliefs about a mountain.

Each verse expresses honor and respect for the tribe depicted and sensitively conveys that tribe's wishes and dreams. "The Way to Make Perfect Mountains" describes the construction of a mountain representing the directions by means of color. For example, the Mountain of the East is made from shell and sand with pigeon eggs placed at the top, explaining the Navajo color for East as white. South is called blue, as it is made from turquoise; yellow-red sand and abalone make yellow for West; and North consists of black sand and jet. In this manner, the "perfect mountain" is formed. In another tale, "The Flood," the people try to make their mountain "grow" above the rising water but are finally turned to stone above the waterline. Hence, they become known as People-Rocks.

Each story is told imaginatively but with adherence to the underlying original Indian myth. Baylor uses an appealing format with lots of white space complementing the stark black-and-white illustrations by Brown. Each drawing cleverly evokes humor but not ridicule. Children will delight in these engaging retellings, and interested youngsters may independently pursue original sources of Indian mythology as a result. The book includes a brief introduction, notes, and bibliography.

Baylor, Byrd. *I'm in Charge of Celebrations.* Illus. by Peter Parnall. New York: Scribner, 1986, unp. (Intermediate)

Writing in her journal, Byrd Baylor records those observations of desert life she considers worth remembering the rest of her life—experiences such as being attracted to the sight of whirlwinds or dust devils; a triple rainbow shared with a jackrabbit standing on his hind legs and a greenish cloud shaped like a parrot. Later, she makes each event an annual celebration. For instance, she celebrates Coyote Day by leaving food for a coyote she had met on a trail; she also celebrates her own New Year by beating a drum and admiring the blooming cactus and the animal life in her favorite places.

Each special event described in Baylor's lyrical prose is accentuated by Parnall's exquisite illustrations. His bright splashes of earth colors—orange, red, gold, and green—enhance the reader's feeling of the wide, open spaces of the Southwest. The exaggerated size of animal tracks suggests their importance.

Both the text and illustrations speak to readers of diverse ages. Readers with a sensitivity to the world of nature will appreciate the author's message and may begin marking their own celebrations. Gifted children, often very individualistic, can identify with the author's need not to conform but to choose her own ways to celebrate special events, seasons, and experiences.

Beaumont, Cyril W. *The Mysterious Toyshop.* Illus. by Wyndham
Payne. New York: Holt, Rinehart & Winston, 1985, 32 pp.
(Intermediate)

Enchantment and wonder await the fortunate reader between the covers of
this fascinating book. Truly a work of art, *The Mysterious Toyshop* starts out
as quite an ordinary story, but with extraordinary use of language found in
English classics. The book was originally published in 1924 and is now part
of the Metropolitan Museum of Art collection. The facsimile, beautifully
written and illustrated on fine paper, will become a favorite treasure for all
who read it or hear it read aloud.

The story begins in the late 1800s in old Londontown just before the
holiday season, when an interesting toyshop suddenly appears in an old
building on a side street without anybody ever having heard construction
noises or seen any other telltale signs of a new business. It just appeared one
day. Soon the shop was open, its windows filled with delights that charmed
even the most reluctant shopper: old-fashioned toys of every imaginable
kind, games, soldiers, wooden horses, castles, tops, boats, dolls, books—all
attractively arranged. The joy of such a display brought smiles to everyone's
faces, and children reluctantly tore themselves away, filled with dreams of
what they hoped to buy first. People came and went, some making purchases, others just looking, but always returning—magnetically drawn to the
magic of this newfound shop.

Above two floors of delightful toys, a third constituted the owner's quarters and storage for some valuable dolls and toys. Occasionally, a customer
was allowed to the top floor, but could not purchase any of the toys there;
for the owner, a rather wizened old man with white hair, who rarely left his
room, preferring to perfect the dolls and toys in solitude, did not often part
with these precious items. Downstairs, two almost identical clerks handled
the business quite well, using few rather predictable responses and animated jerky movements. Customers preferred the limited conversation, hyp-
notized as they were by all the mystery surrounding them.

News of the unusual shop traveled throughout London, and soon possession of a toy from it became the most important topic of conversation. Then,
one day, a very important man entered the shop after having seen a certain
doll in a friend's home. Determined to own an identical one, he asked to see
the proprietor, but was refused admittance to the top floor by one of the
shop assistants. After several refusals, the customer finally gained access to
the old man only to be informed that toys from the top floor were not for
sale to him. Angered, the obnoxious visitor argued with the owner, gradually wearying him. Observing this weakening of will, the visitor pressed on
until he literally undid the old man. The customer then rushes from the shop
in alarm. Frightened at this disturbance, customers returned home to discover that toys bought from the shop would no longer operate. The next

day, when customers came to return the broken toys, they discovered that the shop was no longer there. The doors were locked, the windows empty, and its contents had disappeared mysteriously.

Beaumont's wonderful story will delight young and old at holiday time or any time. The sparkling magic captured on these pages and the rich language so vividly describing each detail will not soon be forgotten. While particularly appealing to the curiosity of the gifted child, the underlying intrigue that is entwined throughout the story challenges the reader's creative and divergent thinking processes. In contrast to many traditional tales that move toward a happy ending, this story concludes open-ended. The book's structure, unusual arrangement, and sequence of events will entice gifted children first to wonder, inquire, and contemplate upon them. Finally, the children will accept the enchantment unquestioningly without eliminating the original element of imagination the story evokes. Enhanced with quaint, four-color illustrations, the story will leave children pondering the spirit of goodwill so effectively portrayed.

Beisner, Monika. *Book of Riddles.* Illus. by author. New York: Farrar, 1983, unp. (Beginning)

A beautiful series of puzzlements is in store for the reader of this tastefully designed volume. Verses written on cream-colored pages are riddle-type puzzles that rarely end with a question as do ordinary riddles. Rather, each is written in a rhyming fashion with seven to nine verses on a page. Bright, colorful illustrations on the facing page consist of little creatures and objects that hold the answer to each puzzle.

The search for the solutions to the puzzles is delightful, and many answers are amusingly hidden—for example, a cow on a cliff and birds in a bush along with several objects that are obviously out of place. In another painting, a majestic peacock perches on a table and another is atop a bush. Children of any age will enjoy this book, particularly those with inquisitive minds.

The author's use of vivid, rich, jewel-tone colors lends a quaint splendor to the paintings. The beauty of the book, combined with 101 challenging word puzzles, makes this volume a wonderful addition to a collection. Each riddle or puzzle is numbered and the corresponding solution is listed at the end of the book. Most puzzles are new, different, and challenging for very young readers. The fun lies in finding the solutions in the pictures.

Bell, Neill. *The Book of Where or How to Be Naturally Geographic.* Illus. by Richard Wilson. Boston: Little, Brown, 1982, 119 pp. (Intermediate)

In an entertaining, somewhat humorous style, this book, another in the Brown Paper School book series, introduces the reader to concepts of geography ranging from awareness of one's immediate surroundings to more complex information such as the continental drift theory.

Bell involves youngsters by requiring them to find their way around their neighborhood, understand the meaning of street names, and realize why there may be gaps in numbered streets. For example, activities on direction and instructions for making a compass can be applied to making a simple map that helps the reader gain an understanding of cartography. Also, children are shown how to read a street map through a dialogue between two taxi drivers who are trying to interpret a street map.

Moving beyond their immediate neighborhood, readers are introduced to activities related to location and borders of counties and states before progressing to an explanation of physical maps. The physical terrain of the United States is discussed as it appears from an airplane. Readers are asked to identify various geographic features such as rivers and mountains and their locations through questions, scrambled words, and puzzles.

Going wider and wider geographically, readers are introduced to a world globe by means of a grapefruit that helps convey an understanding of hemispheres, latitude, and longitude. Subsequently, they are asked to pinpoint exact locations according to latitude and longitude on the globe. Similarly, the international date line and time zones are clearly explained, again accompanied by questions to be answered.

The book concludes with a discussion of glaciers, icebergs, active volcanoes, and oceans, before branching out to explore the vast continents of Asia and Australia. After a final ocean-floor investigation of mountains and basins, readers are returned to their homes with a better understanding of the world around them.

Bell brings an amazing amount of material on geography to a level of understanding appropriate for intermediate-level readers. By means of Wilson's clever drawings and diagrams, the text holds the readers' attention throughout. Much of the information is explored using riddles and problem-solving situations with solutions provided in smaller print on the same page. Although the contents listing is detailed, topics are not in alphabetical order, and there is no index.

Able readers are challenged to use skills of analysis to determine their whereabouts and skills of synthesis to understand the larger world in which they live. Also, they continually employ evaluative thinking as they try to realize just where they are. Bell's friendly style converts a sometimes dry subject to a lively and interesting one. Some readers will want to explore many of the specific topics in greater depth after reading this book.

Berger, Melvin. *Star Gazing, Comet Tracking, and Sky Mapping.* Illus. by William Negron. New York: Putnam, 1985, 80 pp. (Intermediate)

Without the use of a telescope, a careful observer can learn about the many marvelous objects in the night sky and perhaps even make a few scientific discoveries. In the first of the three chapters listed in the title, Berger tells the reader how to locate 30 constellations that are visible from almost any part of the United States. Accompanying star charts show the constellations at their culminating or brightest point at 9:00 P.M. on the sixteenth day of the month from a latitude of 40° north. Differences in star colors and magnitudes are explained in simple terms and indicated by the varying sizes of black dot symbols placed on top of gray drawings of each animal or human figure for which the constellation is named. For instance, black dot symbols connected by straight lines are positioned over a drawing of the upper body of a bull to indicate Taurus (black dots represent the stars that comprise the constellation). A brief summary of Greek legends and myths is also included to explain each constellation name.

In the chapter on comets, Berger presents a concise explanation of these fascinating sky travelers, using vocabulary such as "nucleus," "coma," and "subatomic particles." To assist readers in understanding elliptical orbits and parabolas, he suggests simple demonstrations using string. Interested amateur astronomers will also find directions for how to search for yet undiscovered comets, how to check for accuracy, and how to report comet sightings.

The chapter on sky mapping is filled with directions for how to make instruments using inexpensive, common materials and methods for how to estimate time, distance, and number of stars observed. Instructions are given on how to construct a star plotter—a piece of plexiglass used to mark positions of stars with a grease pencil. Star locations can later be transferred using tracing paper and pencil so the star plotter can be reused. Directions are also given on how to make a simple astrolabe to help locate constellations and map the sky. A few suggestions are also mentioned on the use of photography to map the night sky. Finally, Berger shows how, by using one's hands, the reader can make rough estimates of time and distance. A pencil held in the hand can serve as a crude sun dial. Arms extended with hands and fingers pointed toward the horizon can be used to determine an estimate of degrees and thus locations of objects in the sky. Taking numerous sightings of stars viewed from a cardboard tube and multiplying by a formula number will yield an estimate of the number of stars that can be seen.

Star Gazing, Comet Tracking, and Sky Mapping provides young aspiring astronomers with many opportunities to practice skills and engage in activities similar to those of trained scientists. Readers are asked to apply the skills of the astronomer, including estimating, observing, and constructing and using measuring instruments and recording data. The text conveys the explicit message that amateur observers can make contributions to the field of astronomy. Gifted youngsters with a beginning interest in astronomy can spend many rewarding hours reading this book.

Blocksma, Mary. *Amazing Mouths and Menus.* Illus. by Lee J. Ames. Englewood Cliffs, N.J.: Prentice-Hall, 1986, 48 pp. (Intermediate)

Against a backdrop of dinner menus for each day of the week, 35 mouths, including the human mouth, are investigated. An introduction of the basic mouths of mammals, reptiles, fish, and birds is followed by an informative discussion of the structure of the mouth, including teeth and tongue, and the preferred diet of each creature.

The book's format is appealing, with the menu for each day appearing at the beginning of each section followed by a description of the featured animal's unique habits. Children will employ skills of analysis as they are continually required to make comparisons between mouths and corresponding menus.

Each section is well illustrated with black-and-white diagrams and pictures. Some illustrations, such as a vampire bat hovering over what appears to be a saucer of blood, may be a bit unsettling for very young children but sure to entertain older ones. Using scientific terms such as "carnivores," "insectivores," and "herbivores," Blocksma offers a wealth of information ordinarily found only in more advanced science books. The text explicitly describes the habits of predators, such as a rattlesnake swallowing a small animal.

This unusual book deals with a topic of interest to curious and able readers and one that will most likely encourage further investigation.

Blumberg, Rhoda. *Commodore Perry in the Land of the Shogun.* New York: Lothrop, 1985, 144 pp. (Advanced)

Intriguing headings—"The Coming of the Barbarians," "Aliens Arrive"—signal the effect of the American ships' arrival in the fishing harbor at Edo Bay near the Japanese capital in 1853. Commodore Matthew Perry led this U.S. Navy expedition to propose a treaty between the United States and Japan, a land heretofore closed to outsiders, or "barbarians." The proposal allowed certain ports to be opened, provisions of coal and other goods for American whaling ships, and better treatment of sailors shipwrecked off Japan's rough coastal waters. At the time Perry arrived, many merchants and scholars were eager to end the isolation and open up Japan to foreign trade.

Arriving during the Tokugawa period, or "The Great Peace," Perry encountered a Japan that was not involved in war, in which the arts and education thrived, and where government was highly organized but very restrictive. Not understood by Perry, Japan was a medieval feudal society, tightly regulated and lacking freedom. Wielding more power than the emperor, shoguns established codes of conduct and laws regulating the behavior of the lords, or daimyos—landowners who ruled territories from their castles—and samurai who were in charge of the farmers, artisans, and merchants. The emperor, revered as a god but isolated in the Imperial Palace where he studied the classics, had contact with the outside world only through the shogun.

Met at first by unfriendly soldiers and cannons on shore and told to leave, the American expedition was gradually accepted. Official members of both cultures participated in gift exchanges, enjoyed food and drink together at dinner parties and dances, and adapted to each others' strange customs—the Japanese tolerated the Americans' loud talking and crude table manners, and the Americans demonstrated their politeness by following the Japanese practice of taking away dinner leftovers in their pockets.

Both sides engaged in military pageantry and display, including music played by naval bands and the Japanese construction of a temporary structure to house the first meeting in which Perry presented President Fillmore's letter to Japanese officials. Nine days after their arrival, Perry and his men left, adding the accomplishment of a peaceful meeting to the other achievements of Perry's distinguished military career.

Perry planned to deliver President Fillmore's letter of requests to the emperor, sail to Hong Kong, and return in the spring. However, suspecting a long delay due to the news of the shogun's death shortly after the Americans had left and concerned that the Russians or French might negotiate their own treaties in the meantime, Perry returned to Japan on February 13, 1854. After several weeks of talks, the Japanese agreed to reconstructing the Treaty House, and on March 31, 1854, the treaty was signed. Including a provision for a U.S. consul, the treaty opened the way to future trade agreements between Japan and the United States.

This account of an important event in the history of both East and West uses authentic details and anecdotes about Japanese and American participants' perceptions of each other and their initial fears, superstitions, and misunderstandings. There are a few references to self-sacrifice or suicide customary in Japanese feudal society. Some descriptions are taken from Perry's diary and other official documents. The vivid reconstruction of social interchanges and communication efforts between representatives of the two cultures enlivens the account and results in a "you are there" involvement on the part of the reader. The large, attractively designed book is a superb blend of text and illustrations. The illustrations include drawings based on those made by artists on the Perry expedition, art from Japanese handbills sold in the streets in place of newspapers, and contemporary Japanese art.

The well-documented nature of this work is also evident in an extensive amount of appended material that includes both the Japanese and American leaders' letters to each other, a list of gifts presented to the heads of state of both nations, the text of the Treaty of Kanagawa, notes organized by chapter, an index, and a bibliography. The extensive research provides a worthy example for upper-intermediate-grade readers interested in an exciting chapter of world history and serves as a model on how to conduct historical research. Understanding the process of political negotiation and the concepts involved in Japanese feudal society places cognitive demands on readers, rendering the book most appropriate for sophisticated readers.

Bodecker, N. M. *Carrot Holes and Frisbee Trees.* Illus. by Nina Winters. New York: Atheneum, 1983, 40 pp. (Intermediate)

Prepare for a preposterous tale of phenomenal proportions in Bodecker's bright and witty story of an industrious little couple who grows the biggest vegetables in the land without really trying.

At first, William and Pippin Plumtree were proud of their prize produce, especially the carrots, but when the carrots grew as large as third graders, they puzzled over what to do since they had grown enough to fill a school. Their problem was compounded by the huge holes left to fill after pulling up the carrots. These holes were sometimes accidentally "filled" by an unsuspecting visitor dropping by, or in.

To manage their bumper crop, the Plumtrees sold carrots, gave some away, and cooked and canned as much as possible. Pippin served all manner of carrot dishes—side dishes, seasonings, drinks, and desserts—and looked forward to next year's garden, hoping it might be less bountiful. In the spring, William arrived at what he thought was a solution for the mammoth carrot holes. He ingeniously planned to use them as postholes by planing the seed and removing the carrot when the hole reached the desired diameter. This idea captured the attention of people needing holes, and business bloomed. But the Plumtrees soon became overwrought from running all over the country measuring the size of carrot holes.

As an alternative, their next venture consisted of selling posthole-grower kits by mail. For this project the Plumtrees only needed to keep a plentiful supply of carrot seeds, which they accomplished by allowing a couple of carrots to grow as large as trees, thereby producing seeds the size of Frisbees. Soon the Plumtrees were again much more involved than they wished to be. They longed for their former simple, quiet life. Finally, when they had accumulated more than enough money, they decided to give it all away, but then William Plumtree became ill. While he was in the hospital, a huge carrot began to grow on their lawn. William returned home and that winter, he and his wife "listened" to the carrot grow as it creaked and cracked the frozen ground.

In the spring and summer they enjoyed the shade of the towering carrot tree that dwarfed their little house, until one evening they felt the rumbling of what seemed to be a small earthquake and immediately called for a crane. The crane and accompanying workers arrived and set to work heaving and hoing until finally the unwieldy carrot gave way and emerged the size of a factory chimney. The monstrosity was taken to a sawmill, and the weary Plumtrees decided to take a walk.

On returning to their little house, they received a congratulatory call from the sawmill informing them of the great strides the couple had made for the lumber industry by providing them with enough wood to last a long time.

The prosperous Plumtrees had hoped to give their "luck" away, but again their efforts had been unsuccessful. Reminding themselves of their rationale—do what you know how to do best—they continued to grow giant carrots to supply the world.

This small book contains exaggerated language that will appeal to older children. The illustrations are grayish-white drawings that depict a warm, peace-loving couple, cozy with their little house and garden.

Gifted children with a keen sense of humor will delight in this ridiculous and absurd story. Yet they will also be caught up in the seriousness of the Plumtrees' dilemma and hope for a comfortable outcome for the pleasant couple, who are portrayed as kind, generous, and enterprising young people. This book is an invitation to imagination-plus, eliciting a chuckle from the reader throughout. This blatantly exaggerated tall tale lends a humorous balance to gifted children's reading. The language is straightforward, written in a refreshing folksy style.

Bond, Nancy. *A Place to Come Back To.* New York: Atheneum, 1984, 187 pp. (Advanced)

Charlotte and Oliver, longtime close friends, are part of a loyal teenage group that includes Kath and Andy, a brother and sister. The foursome spend leisure hours ice skating and tobogganing in a New England setting. Although Charlotte is usually paired with Andy and Kath with Oliver, Oliver and Charlotte emerge as the central characters in the story, each experiencing many emotional changes as they grow up and their relationship matures.

Oliver, quiet and withdrawn much of the time, lives with his great-uncle, Commodore Shattuck, as a result of his parents' divorce. His mother has remarried and is too involved in her Washington career to show much concern for her son. Similarly, his father, living in California, virtually ignores Oliver. It is only his uncle, his dog, Amos, and his friends that give Oliver a sense of worth.

Charlotte's family, on the other hand, is loving, kind, and sincerely interested in their daughter's well-being and happiness. Their caring extends to Oliver and the Commodore, who is admired and respected throughout the community. At 82 years of age, the Commodore has become an endearing friend to Charlotte and her friends. When he suddenly dies of natural causes, feelings of shock and regret are felt by all who knew him. Oliver, however, withholds all emotion until the end when he allows Charlotte to share his feelings. Knowing his life will change drastically now that his uncle has died, Oliver decides not to report the death for a couple of days to give himself some time to think. Only Charlotte is informed of the secret and she is appalled, frightened, and resentful that Oliver would do such a thing. Though her friend convinces her of his reasons to keep the death secret for a while, Charlotte finally persuades Oliver to tell her family and let them assume the necessary responsibilities.

Oliver comes to stay with Charlotte's family until all funeral arrangements are made, and his mother and stepfather take him to London to live with them for a year. Oliver knows he is unwanted in his new family, but as a minor he has no choice. He knows, too, he will have to give up Amos, whom he truly loves.

Charlotte's changing feelings toward Oliver are complicated by his un-emotional, complex behavior and his refusal to talk. His almost rude, indiffer-ent manner of protecting his feelings confuses Charlotte, making her both irritated and sympathetic. Eventually, Oliver requests that Charlotte wait for him until he returns from London since he has inherited his uncle's house and property. Charlotte feels pressured and committed beyond her maturity to pacify Oliver. In addition, she recognizes that her feelings for him are deeper than those of friendship.

Bond's characters are well delineated, strong, and memorable. Both Char-lotte and Oliver display the full range of emotions as they each experience deep pain for different reasons. This sensitively written story appeals to ma-ture middle graders. Detailed flashbacks acquaint the reader with background information. A rich, personal story that demands the reader's attention throughout, its theme is unique and its plot thought-provoking, focusing on the young people's dilemmas and how they handle them. Able readers are left to ponder the future of Charlotte and Oliver using problem-solving skills to tie together the loose ends in a sensitive but ambiguous ending.

Boyd, Candy Dawson. *Charlie Pippin.* New York: Macmillan, 1987, 182 pp. (Intermediate)

Enterprising young Charlie is a sixth-grade, black girl who sets out to be-come an accomplished businesswoman. Consequently, she takes advantage of every opportunity to supply her classmates with needed materials such as pencils. It is during one of these projects that she finds herself in violation of the school code that states that each student must be a "responsible learner." When her parents are notified of her activities, Charlie is upset, for she really cannot see anything wrong with her activities.

Charlie, which is short for Chartreuse, obtains extra school supplies from her grandfather's store to fill her orders. She shares a special relationship with each grandparent since they do not live together but still care for each other. Her spunky grandmother, known as Mama Bliss, involves Charlie in her own business ventures consisting of making items for local craft fairs.

Charlie's older sister, Sienna, who is caught up in a teenage world of boys, does not prove to be a helpful confidante in times of trouble and even selfishly takes advantage of Charlie. Charlie is hurt by the feeling that Sienna is closer to their father. Her mother acts as a buffer in family arguments, demonstrating an understanding of Charlie's independent ways, yet willing to enforce the consequences of broken rules.

Charlie's favorite family member is her Uncle Ben. Mr. Pippin, Charlie's father, and Ben do not always get along and usually end up in heated arguments over the issues of the war in which they both served.

Charlie's relationship with her father is very trying, for he does not communicate with her other than to establish restrictions. His failure to answer her questions about the Vietnam War frustrates her even more. A social studies project at school has peaked Charlie's interest in this topic and Charlie is determined to learn how the war changed her father. She thoroughly researches the war and interviews others for their opinions. Her class co-workers are Chris, a sixth-grade intellectual, and Katie Rose, a good friend who takes turns staying with each of her divorced parents.

After delving into the war, Charlie discovers the issues surrounding the causes and cures to be confusing, but she is able to grasp some of the issues and develops her own strong opinion to eliminate war completely. Charlie's father seems embarrassed, hostile, distant, and angry that his daughter is involved in the project. Nevertheless, Charlie continues her search for answers about the war and finally wins the school oratory contest. She prepares her speech for the district contest but loses her train of thought when her father shows up unexpectedly. Her mistakes cost her first place, but she does win third. Disappointed and unhappy, Charlie blames her father for her losing the contest.

Soon Charlie is involved in another money-making project at school and begins to make plans for items to sell in her class. During this preparation, Charlie receives an invitation from her Uncle Ben to go to Washington, D.C., to visit her Aunt Jessie. This is her opportunity to see the war memorial, but her father forbids the trip because she is in trouble for her recent business project in school. Charlie becomes obsessed with the trip and makes secret plans to go anyway. Her plan is successful until she arrives in Washington where she learns that her aunt must call her father to let him know she has arrived safely. At this point, Charlie panics and tells the truth to Uncle Ben and Aunt Jessie. She then calls her parents and tells them where she is, knowing she must deal with harsh consequences when she returns. But while in Washington, she gets to visit the memorial and obtain rubbings of the names of the two close friends her father lost in the war.

When they finally talk about the war, Mr. Pippin eventually realizes the meaning it has for Charlie. He is impressed with her persistence and her reasons for going to Washington, and is very proud that she would bring the names home to him. He shows deep emotions concerning the war and how it changed him. The event establishes a bond of understanding and communication between the two.

Charlie is characterized as a determined, strong-willed girl who won't be ignored. Although she disobeys her father, her rationale for doing so is meaningful. Boyd writes in a way that does not condone Charlie's behavior but justifies it according to her character's unselfish motivations. The theme may be unfamiliar to many children, but the issues are presented from more than one viewpoint, thereby acquainting readers with important historical information.

Gifted readers may identify with the strong, singular interest Charlie has for a topic and may find her business projects informative. Charlie keeps moving ahead in her thinking and actions, regardless of disappointments and mistakes. The book will appeal mostly to middle-grade readers, but older children may find the details of the Vietnam War interesting.

Boyer, Edward. *River and Canal.* Illus. by author. New York: Holiday, 1986, 48 pp. (Advanced)

As a major means of transportation and trade before the railroad in the early nineteenth century, canals overcame obstacles created by impossible rapids and linked the coast with inland towns. Trade between settlements along the coast where rapids prevented further travel could be handled by small boats. However, transportation to cities springing up inland was difficult and expensive. Canals provided a solution to this problem by allowing heavy transportation and cargo to move easily between coast and inland cities.

Based on historical facts, *River and Canal* is a unique fictional account of the building of early canals in eastern North America. The author has created a story of a canal company composed of Horne, an inventor and engineer, and Warren, a surveyor who wanted to build a canal connecting the western settlements. The partners obtained money for the construction by selling shares. Permission to build was granted through legislative action giving them an exclusive charter.

During the task of surveying the land connecting the coast to the Ohio River Valley, Horne and Warren discovered coal in one of the mountains and formed a coal company to mine and market it. After establishing a community at the base of the mountain, they built a railroad to transport coal from the mountain to the mines.

Ironically, 30 years after the building of the canal, railroads marked the end of the canal company's monopoly on transportation by being more practical—they could be built less expensively and more quickly than canals. In addition, winter weather limited the operation of canals, whereas railroads could operate year-round. Thus, within ten years' time the railroad took over and after 100 years of service the canal was terminated.

Boyer explicitly illustrates with diagrams each step in the canal-building process. Accompanying technical and precise explanations provide readers with a comprehensive inside view of this intricate construction. New vocabulary, such as "cofferdam," "locks," and "miter gates," is introduced and explained before it is encountered in the book. For example, "Locks are watery stairs that enable boats to move from one level to another.... The lock's doors are called miter gates because they meet at an angle."

Boyer's enthusiasm and knowledge, plus his extensive research of canals, provide readers with specific details about this intriguing topic that extend far beyond general information. The imaginary owners of the Pocosink Navigation Company personalize factual information and present a close look at problems surfacing throughout their complicated endeavor. The author's shared experiences about the subject will peak readers' interest in locating the remains of old canal, helped by a list of sites in the back of the book. A glossary and an index are included. Illustrations are detailed, and labeled pencil drawings are profuse. Interior aspects of machines, equipment, and tools involved in canal building help clarify construction. An aerial view illustration of the Pocosink Navigation Canal Path resembles an engineer's blueprint.

This well-written book is intended for gifted children, intermediate and older.

Branley, Franklyn M. *Dinosaurs, Asteroids, and Superstars: Why the Dinosaurs Disappeared.* Illus. by Jean Zallinger. New York: Crowell, 1982, 84 pp. (Advanced)

In spite of much speculation, no one knows why dinosaurs have disappeared. Branley's book tackles each theory behind the huge beasts' extinction in a straightforward and logical manner, without attempting to explain any unknown causes.

The story begins with the puzzle of the dinosaurs, including their first appearance on earth, which can be scientifically determined by rock content. An explanation of rock dating and geological time is clearly presented followed by an analysis of each era in the history of the earth to determine particular dinosaurs' existence and the time during which they flourished.

The author then delves into their mysterious disappearance explaining that every living creature and plant, whether extinct or not, affected each theory. Least prominent life continued to survive while more prominent plants and animals died out, causing great gaps in geological knowledge that are still unexplained.

One of the theories—that dinosaurs, as a group, died of old age—has never been scientifically accepted, turtles have survived, although they are known to be as old as triceratops from the Cretaceous Period. Another theory advanced is that poisonous plants containing alkaloids may have been consumed in large quantities by plant-eating dinosaurs, thus causing their death. However, meat-eaters, flying dinosaurs, and dinosaurs living in the seas disappeared at the same time, making this hypothesis questionable. If disease and illness ended the dinosaurs' existence, why weren't all creatures on earth also affected, eliminating 80 percent of all life?

According to Branley, paleontologists maintain that the destruction of dinosaur eggs and baby dinosaurs by predators—still another theory—does not account for the disappearance of all dinosaurs on earth. The discovery of thin-shelled eggs indicates problems in the dinosaurs' diet, possibly causing them to die out. Yet this theory is not satisfactory either, as it does not account for why the rest of life did not vanish.

Perhaps the big dinosaurs died as a result of extreme climate changes, while the small reptiles burrowed into the earth and survived. Abrupt temperature changes may extinguish all life that cannot make the necessary adaptation. However, this explanation still leaves the unanswered question of what caused the proposed climate change, if indeed it happened. Such a change would necessarily have to be quick, encompassing the entire planet. This conclusion leads the author to explore events that could have brought about a sudden drop in temperature severe enough to destroy most life.

Branley proceeds to the continental drift theory, according to which the discovery of dinosaur remains in various places in the world has led scientists to conclude that one giant landmass broke apart and formed the individual continents. This theory explains why rock formations on one continent have been matched with those on another, and fossils have been found on landmasses that are now separate. Further evidence for this theory is found in tectonic plates that are still moving today.

The author continues to challenge the reader's curiosity about this phenomenal occurrence by exploring superstars and a possible encounter with an asteroid, but neither of these is totally accepted by all scientists.

Volcanic eruption, another theory behind the extinction of dinosaurs, even if widespread, would not kill all dinosaurs directly. However, the atmospheric changes caused by such eruptions could have had an effect on all life. Branley recounts the effects of major eruptions on temperatures around the world.

According to some scientists, a ring of ash circling earth caused severe weather patterns. Under these conditions large dinosaurs would not have survived, but smaller animals could.

While presenting all these many possibilities for the extinction of dinosaurs, in thorough and easy-to-read detail, Branley leaves the reader with the unanswered question. Readers eagerly begin each chapter hoping to arrive at reasons for the disappearance of dinosaurs. The book is an excellent investigation of an intriguing subject. The mystery remains and motivates young paleontologists to pursue its solution.

Pen-and-ink illustrations of these engaging creatures add emphasis to this clearly chronicled account.

Branley, Franklyn M. *Flash, Crash, Rumble, and Roll.* Illus. by Barbara Emberley and Ed Emberley. New York: Crowell, 1985, 31 pp. (Beginning)

Thunderstorms often appear mysterious and threatening to youngsters who do not understand their origin. Branley clearly and accurately explains the unknown using concrete, vivid language complemented by colorful, attractive illustrations by the Emberleys.

From the very outset of the book, a quiet, still, hot day sets the stage for a storm. Gathering clouds change from fluffy white to gray to almost black. This change is explained by diagrams showing the directionality of air movement from earth to clouds and the building of thunderheads against a bright blue sky. Water vapor and how it condenses is also clearly explained so young children can understand the process. For example, a diagram shows what could happen to an airplane if it flew into this rushing air.

Lightning is introduced as the result of electricity in the clouds, followed by thunder. To illustrate, the author uses the example of the sound produced when a balloon is popped. As a fun, but useful rule of thumb, children learn to determine the distance of a thunderstorm by counting the seconds between lightning and thunder after examining the chart illustrating this phenomenon. In addition to the simple-to-read-and-follow explanations of scientific and meteorological events, Branley addresses the dangers of lightning and offers thorough, specific safety precautions in bright pink.

He alleviates the fear some children have of violent weather conditions. In keeping with this reassurance, the book concludes with a clear, blue sky and a beautiful rainbow to remind children that storms do end and all becomes calm again.

The enlightening and reassuring information presented in this book simplifies a complex topic for children without obscuring the facts or minimizing possible danger. Simple, cartoonlike illustrations are direct, expertly labeled, and brightly colored. Synthesization of elements and factors required to produce a full-blown thunderstorm elicit a higher-level thinking skill in even young children. This is a worthwhile book for the young beginning reader to investigate.

Brooks, Polly Schoyer. *Queen Eleanor, Independent Spirit of the Medieval World: A Biography of Eleanor of Aquitaine.* New York: Lippincott, 1983, 183 pp. (Advanced)

Queen Eleanor (1122–1204), who ruled first as queen of France and later queen of England, is the worthy subject of this fascinating biography, which also describes feudal society, tournaments, the hardships of the Crusades, and courtly love and manners. In spite of the feudal pyramid of classes—peasants, barons, counts, dukes—all under the king, Eleanor's father, Duke

William X of Aquitaine, was more powerful than the king of France, Louis VI. Eleanor was remarkable for her beauty, intelligence, political diplomacy, and leadership, in addition to such qualities as generosity, contributions to music and poetry, and courtly manners.

After marrying Prince Louis at age 15 and shortly thereafter becoming queen of France, Eleanor moved to Paris where she learned to question prevailing traditions as she listened to scholars and students using techniques of debate and reasoning. Mother of two girls, Eleanor became dissatisfied with her timid husband, who seemed more devoted to the church than to enhancing his power, and eventually arranged for an annulment of their marriage. Eight weeks later, she married Henry, duke of Normandy, a younger, bold, and temperamental warrior knight more suited to her ambitions for land and power. Due to her new husband's claim to the English throne, at 32 Eleanor also became queen of England.

While Henry established a trial by jury system and provided a foundation for English common law, Eleanor encouraged troubadours and wandering minstrels, thereby becoming instrumental in the development of romantic literature. Influenced by Eleanor, court poets retold old Celtic stories in verse, adding romantic tales of knights battling not only to increase their holdings but to prove their love and loyalty to women.

Marring the relative tranquility of Henry and Eleanor's marriage, Thomas Beckett, once a close friend and adviser to Henry, grew closer to the church and became Henry's enemy. Eventually, Beckett was beheaded by Henry's enthusiastic knights, who believed this act demonstrated their loyalty to the king.

Adding to their difficulties was Henry's affair with the young and beautiful Fair Rosamond, which caused Eleanor's return to Aquitaine. Trying to make it an independent duchy, Eleanor prepared her favorite son, Richard, rather than Henry, to be recognized as her heir to Aquitaine. Over the years, several of Eleanor's ten children—five girls and five boys—married members of the ruling class in various countries. Assisted by her first child, Marie, who came to live with her, Eleanor trained Aquitaine's youth in courtly manners by applying her knowledge of legal matters to "courtly love." For example, Eleanor, Marie, and their ladies served as jurors in mock trials in which young men presented their problems or questions about love. Through these and similar efforts Eleanor paved the way for better treatment of women as well as the concept of "gentleman."

Angry with their father for not giving them more land to rule, and encouraged by their mother, Eleanor and Henry's three older sons aligned themselves with King Louis. Henry finally captured Eleanor and held her prisoner for 15 years. After Henry's death, Richard, known as the Lion-Hearted, became king, and Eleanor, freed from her long imprisonment, improved social and political conditions in England through prison reform and a uniform system of coins, weights, and measures.

Later, Eleanor, who was also skilled and respected in diplomacy and other political matters, secured the release of Richard, who was held prisoner by the Germans after the Third Crusade. Eleanor's other accomplishments included traveling throughout Aquitaine granting charters to townspeople to govern local affairs and gaining support for her youngest and less popular son, John, to become king of England.

Black-and-white illustrations of medieval manuscript paintings, nineteenth-century engravings, and other museum pieces add authenticity to the text. Included are a chronological listing of major events, a bibliography, and a detailed index. Written in a fast-moving, readable style, the book is suited to sophisticated young readers who have the intellectual ability to integrate and interpret the social, personal, and political events described.

As a strong, positive force and a woman with the courage of her convictions who was "ahead of her time," Eleanor serves as a model for advanced readers.

Brown, Ruth. *If at First You Do Not See.* Illus. by author. New York: Holt, Rinehart & Winston, 1982, unp. (Beginning)

If at First You Do Not See—then turn the book around until you do see something unusual, something strange, and finally, something familiar. This very different approach to a children's picture book awards the reader with a special surprise whenever the book is turned upside down. Illustrations, verging on the bizarre, are magnified and colorful. Some children will find them frightening, but others, especially the gifted, will accept the challenge they present to the imagination.

The story begins with a giant mother butterfly ordering her little caterpillars to eat their leaves, but one defiant creature decides to seek more tempting morsels and crawls away. After this introduction, the story is written around the margins of the pages and as the book is turned upside down the text describes the picture that appears. For example, an illustration of the caterpillar eating from a basket full of vegetables becomes a very strange man in a woven hat who warns him away.

Similarly, a clump of grass he tries to eat becomes a giant's nose, and two tasty-looking ice cream cones reveal a pair of clowns. A mushroom is merely the space between two huge scary men, and a wrapped bouquet of flowers becomes a wicked witch in her pointed hat. As the reader follows the caterpillar across the pages, they find two well-endowed hamburgers, a couple of fierce-looking creatures whose teeth are really the onions and the sauce in the sandwiches.

By now, the little caterpillar is hungry, tired, and frustrated and decides to take a nap. Unknowingly, he chooses a scarecrow's hat as a resting place where he soon falls fast asleep. The friendly scarecrow puts the caterpillar in his pocket for safekeeping. Later, when the little worm awakens at the end of his metamorphosis and falls to the ground, his scary adventures start right away. The first thing he sees are two incredible faces that turn out to be leeks growing in a field. Next he encounters a huge creature whose symmetrical wings resemble two menacing eyes. The caterpillar finally realizes the creature is another butterfly. He himself has also become a butterfly, and the two fly away together.

The text of the story is brief, but the rich vocabulary provides an element of discovery as the book is turned around. Illustrations require higher-level skills of analysis and synthesis to discern objects and creatures. The approach is sophisticated for a young child's picture book but will be appreciated by the precocious and the curious, especially if the first reading is shared with an adult.

Burleigh, Robert. *A Man Named Thoreau.* Illus. by Lloyd Bloom. New York: Atheneum, 1985, 31 pp. (Intermediate)

Henry David Thoreau, the son of a well-known family, grew up in the 1800s in Concord, Massachusetts. The inhabitants of the little village perceived him as a strange child for taking solitary walks every day, any season. Becoming a Harvard graduate did not satisfy the people, who expected something more useful from him than just walking. However, Thoreau was determined to live his life as he pleased, not to please others. During his walks, Thoreau was thinking and observing nature, and at the end of each day he carefully recorded his thoughts. He spent many hours by Walden Pond, observing and listening to the sounds of nature. Later, he built a small, simple house near the pond where on some days he swam and gardened and on others, he simply sat. Eventually, he was to write how much he grew in thought during those quiet times alone.

Throughout, Thoreau was obsessed with nature and all its inhabitants. He studied every living thing he came upon and how and where it lived, expressing appreciation for the most minute creature. Feeling that most people were discontent and materialistic by nature, Thoreau tried to demonstrate how simply people could live. He believed the things a person owned ruled the person instead of the person governing his or her surroundings. Thoreau's interpretation of value was the quality of a person's life. With simplicity as his motto, Thoreau belittled his college education, asserting that it did not really teach him the real meaning of life.

After writing of his experiences at Walden, Thoreau moved on to learn about life in other places. He believed that when too much routine sets in, it's time to change.

Thoreau's mysteriousness intrigued others. Solitude was very important to him, but he did have many friends and activities. He was personally acquainted with well-known writers and philosophers such as Emerson and Hawthorne. Regardless of his occasional sociability and sense of humor toward himself, he was sometimes difficult to get along with and was much criticized. He, too, became critical of other life-styles and the government.

For example, he opposed certain taxes and subsequently served a jail sentence. He also disagreed with the war between the United States and Mexico and opposed slavery.

In his early forties, Thoreau became ill and returned to Walden to die. After his death, his simple approach to life and writing became famous and was studied by great men and women.

Accompanying the text are soft, dreamy charcoal portrayals of Thoreau's Walden Pond and the countryside he loved. Burleigh's story of this well-known philosopher focuses on the man and his ideas. Gifted readers can identify with the informal and unstructured time Thoreau spent just thinking and can appreciate his contribution of thoughts to humankind. The book includes a list of important dates in Thoreau's life and a brief bibliography.

Burningham, John. *Where's Julius?* Illus. by author. New York: Crown, 1986, unp. (Beginning)

Aided by an active imagination, young Julius Troutbeck conjures up adventures that involve him too much for him to join his parents for family meals. Consistent with that theme, the story consists of a series of episodes in which either Mr. or Mrs. Troutbeck announces the breakfast, lunch, or dinner menu asking, "Where's Julius?" with their son subsequently explaining why he cannot join them for the meal: He is busy digging a hole to the other side of the world, climbing to the top of an Egyptian pyramid on the back of a camel, throwing snowballs at wolves while riding across Russia in a sleigh, or watching the sun rise in Tibet. Julius uses common household objects to create his world of fantasy, his cluttered playroom supplying his props—chairs, a broomstick holding up a blanket to serve as a tent or a mountaintop. His parents accept his imaginary flights and sometimes are shown in the scenes of his adventures wherever Julius's wanderings take him—Mr. Troutbeck mountain climbing, tray in hand, and Mrs. Troutbeck balances a tray as she steps on rocks in a South American river.

The value of *Where's Julius?* to gifted children is that the story lets youngsters know that imaginary games and adventures are acceptable, and, in this case, understood by parents as a part of childhood play. Burningham's unique drawings juxtapose the reality of daily meals with the excitement of faraway places, the food tray representing a link to reality. The large typeface is appealing to preschoolers. The story would be an enjoyable read-aloud for both parents and child.

Burns, Marilyn. *The Hink Pink Book or What Do You Call a Magician's Extra Bunny?* Illus. by Martha Weston. Boston: Little, Brown, 1981, 48 pp. (Intermediate)

This book of hink pinks—one-syllable, two rhyming words—is full of different versions of this type of wordplay. Hink pinks are the answers to riddles stated in their usual format: A dog who steals hamburger from a plate is called a *beef thief.* In addition, Burns includes hinky pinky riddles—two-syllable rhyming words—When you have fixed a wobbly leg on a dining room chair you have a *stable table*—and hinkety pinkety ones, three-syllable words that rhyme.

The riddles are categorized into 29 cleverly organized subject areas, from fish to mishmash—money, animals, sports, numbers, music, and monsters, just to name a few. Each page is illustrated with pen-and-ink cartoonlike drawings (similar to those in other books by Burns). A most intriguing aspect of the book is the location and arrangement of solutions to the puzzles. Answers are written upside down, backward, and sometimes both ways. Many are not found on the same page as the riddle but on the adjacent page. Consequently, it's a puzzle just to locate the solution. This extra effort may be frustrating and perplexing to many children. However, children who enjoy language play will find it fun to scan the pages, searching for solutions.

This collection of humorous and imaginative riddles, answered with Burns's choice of hink pinks, is fun to read and challenges children who enjoy word puzzles and language games.

Burns, Marilyn. *Math for Smarty Pants.* Illus. by Martha Weston. Boston: Little, Brown, 1982, 128 pp. (Intermediate)

Challenging math and reasoning problems make up the seven provocative chapters of this book, another in the Brown Paper School book series, offering everything from shapes to stats for fun and exploration. Burns tells readers that being smart in math means being able to demonstrate different skills: calculating quickly, visualizing shapes, playing strategy games, and solving logic problems. For a special appeal to reluctant math students, Burns emphasizes that math can make sense and that practice is the key to success. Instruction is made fun by humorous sample problems presented in minimal text supported by abundant use of comic strips, stories illustrated with fantasy and realistic characters, rhymes, and tricks.

Without sounding overly didactic, Burns suggests approaches to problem solving: organizing information in tables and charts, simplifying the problem, searching for patterns, and working backward. Readers are asked to make predictions, and answers are not always provided. One activity involving spatial relationships asks readers to fold a piece of paper in half twice, cut a small shape on the fold, and draw what the paper will look like when unfolded. An opportunity to make predictions consists of predicting whether adults' and children's food preferences are the same or different. To find out, readers are encouraged to conduct a survey.

Some of the card and memory tricks are variations of familiar ones. However, they offer underachieving readers an opportunity to develop a sense of competence by enabling them to master a few tricks. For example, "Math for Two" includes calendar games, tic-tac-toe variations, the guessing game Bagels, card games, and a calculator activity.

"Logical Puzzles" presents probably the greatest cognitive challenge. Here children must manipulate several facts as they solve deductive logic problems using a chart, make many combinations using pizza ingredients, and apply reasoning skills when confronted with several types of paradoxes.

Numeration, geometry, logical reasoning, paradoxes, statistics, permutations, large numbers, factorials, and probability are briefly introduced and clarified by both realistic and fanciful—and definitely humorous—vignettes and problems. Armed with pencil, paper, and a calculator, eager readers can engage in such hands-on activities as constructing a large wobbly cube and drawing common geometric shapes from memory.

Burns's language is conversational and sprinkled with humor as in her use of illustrations, slang, and multiple word meanings. For example, "Math Talk" elucidates the peculiar meanings of words such as "perfect," "positive," and "negative" when used in a mathematical sense. To illustrate the lack of reliability of a small sample in statistics, all children at a party, except one, are depicted making faces and reacting negatively to one girl's favorite food—cold creamed turnips. In addition, locating and interpreting the answers is often a challenge in itself. Printed upside down and backward for easy reading when held up to a mirror, answers to individual problems are camouflaged among text and graphics throughout the book.

Specific topics are not as easily located as they would be if an index had been included. However, the table of contents is detailed.

This fun-filled book will stimulate and tease math lovers while also motivating children who otherwise think they don't like or don't understand math. Concepts are presented with a keen sense of humor that gifted students usually find appealing. Burns encourages readers to interact with ambiguity and abstractions and to explore various possibilities before arriving at a solution. For many, *Math for Smarty Pants* will whet the appetite for further exploration in mathematics.

Calvert, Patricia. *The Hour of the Wolf.* New York: Scribner, 1983, 147 pp. (Advanced)

Jake has two years of high school left when he attempts suicide using his grandfather's old gun. His father, a well-known, ambitious lawyer, decides to send his son from suburban Minnesota to Alaska to finish school and relieve the stigma felt by his socially oriented family. Unable to meet his demanding father's expectations of what he should be in life, Jake leaves for Alaska with mixed feelings—those of being a failure and fear of rejection.

In his new school Jake makes a good friend, Danny, who is a dog handler. Danny's dream is to run the famous Iditarod dog race from Anchorage to

Nome. When Danny finds himself unable to live up to his family's expectations, he attempts suicide and succeeds. Jake is distraught and astounded that Danny shared feelings similar to his own. As a memorial to Danny, Jake decides to train for and enter the great dog race. Although he knows very little about dogs, Jake is able to pick up enough tips and information to help him get started. Besides, he discovers that he has learned more than he thought from Danny. Eventually, Jake tells his father about his plans to enter the race, and his father willingly provides the necessary money for the entry fee and costly supplies and equipment.

In his search for dogs, Jake ends up in Danny's village where he meets Kamina, Danny's sister, who seems to hold a grudge against the world and particularly against Jake whom she considers an "outsider." Reluctantly, Kamina gives Blue Jeans, a huge, bluish hound, to Jake and "B.J.," as Jake names him, unexpectedly becomes the best lead dog.

Kamina decides to enter the race too, using the fine birch sled that Danny had been preparing. Kamina has a serious accident on the trail but is saved by Jake, who has become a close friend. Kamina wants Jake to finish the race with Danny's sled. Through harsh weather, fighting cold and nearly impossible passageways, Jake completes the race, winning the red lantern award for coming in last.

Jake's isolation in the white arctic country provides him with plenty of time to think. He realizes that his self-esteem has improved tremendously since he entered the race. He is no longer a confused, self-conscious teenager. Rather, his perseverance to finish the race instills in him a sense of pride. Later, in a meeting with his father, Jake feels at peace with himself and realizes that he no longer requires the approval of others.

In Jake, Calvert has created a character that will wrench readers' hearts. The turmoil and uncertainty that culminate in such dark despair that he wants to end his life is vividly portrayed. Furthermore, his conclusion that he must be an outcast when his father wants to send him to Alaska is almost too tragic to bear. But the courage Jake exhibits by competing in one of the most difficult competitive races reveals an inner strength that many young people have without always realizing it. Similarly, the demands exerted on this teenager by his well-meaning, prominent family, along with their lack of sincere selflessness required to know and understand their son, are concerns experienced by many older children.

Calvert allows the reader to see Jake's shortcomings and failures without criticism. In his loneliness, Jake grows from feeling hopeless to becoming a person of value and meaning. This book's portrayal of Jake's feelings of isolation, rejection, and aloneness will appeal to gifted children who sometimes experience the same range of emotions. Overcoming a tendency to separate from society and moving from despair to success, Jake demonstrates a perseverance to proceed undauntingly toward a goal he has set to honor his friend. Many sensitive, gifted children will identify with this story about dedication to a cause.

The details of the Iditarod race are explicit and visually presented, thanks to the author's excellent use of language.

Carrick, Carol. *What Happened to Patrick's Dinosaurs?* Illus. by Donald Carrick. New York: Clarion, 1986, unp. (Beginning)

Patrick, a little boy out raking leaves with his older brother, Hank, casually brings up the question of dinosaurs. Wondering whatever happened to them and why they became extinct, the two boys discuss this topic as they continue to rake the leaves. When Hank informs Patrick that the world may have become too hot for the huge beasts, or that perhaps they were destroyed by an asteroid, Patrick denounces these suggestions, claiming to have his own theory. He proposes that dinosaurs and people were once on friendly terms, and that dinosaurs built houses, made cars, airplanes, and roads, and even entertained people with tricks and performances.

When finished raking, the boys put the leaves in bags and toss them into the back of a truck. Finally, the boys are seen lying on the stuffed bags in the truck dreamily discussing the idea that dinosaurs, tired of working all the time, built a fantastic spaceship, boarded it, and left the earth forever. The boys' delightful discussion is conducted against a wash of blue sky and fluffy clumps of clouds that resemble various species of dinosaurs.

A magnificent illustration shows the dinosaurs lumbering up a huge stairway to the spaceship as clouds of blue smoke float out from its base. A final scene portrays cave men in their natural surroundings digging up a car key left over from the highly industrialized dinosaurs. The last page shows a spaceship as it soars away from earth into a black sky filled with constellations of dinosaur shapes.

Inquisitive, challenging questions that capture the reader's interest are combined with luscious detailed watercolor illustrations that will delight any reader. For example, a dinosaur is seen carrying lumber on its back to help build several houses high in the branches of a broad, ancient tree. Dinosaurs are also depicted as operating a "wind-up" station for cars where they must fit a giant key to the customer's car to make it go. Several sizes and species of dinosaurs are seen rolling tires, sitting on an air pump, and preparing to wash windshields. Two unusual airplanes, also made by dinosaurs, fly high above an active volcano. The neck of a great dinosaur becomes a bridge for cars during a road-building operation. Other dinosaurs are shown guiding a steamroller, painting center lines on the new highway, operating a toll booth, and acting as a flagman to slow traffic.

A wonderful study in imagination, this book excels in the creative composition of both text and illustration. The story encourages creative and imaginative thinking and is therefore appealing to gifted younsters. Older children with some knowledge of dinosaur theories will enjoy the humor presented. Very young children may need reassurance that this is truly a story of make-believe.

Carrick, Donald. *Morgan and the Artist.* Illus. by author. New York: Clarion, 1985, 32 pp. (Beginning)

This is a lovely picture-book story about Frederic Toll, an artist, who wants desperately to become a good landscape painter. Disillusioned with his results so far, Frederic one day happens to paint a tiny, enchanting character into his work and includes this little woodcutter figure in other landscapes.

Frederic decides to name the little character Morgan, and paints a path that allows him to come out of the painting. Entering with a mischievous little grin as if he knows something the artist doesn't, Morgan claims to be the artist's spirit. Frederic paints a place for Morgan to stay and everything else he needs, including food to eat.

Because only Frederic can see Morgan, their visits to the art museums, for example, make the guards nervous, as Frederic reacts to Morgan jumping in and out of the paintings. Morgan further directs the artist to go to see the landscapes he wishes to paint. Accidentally, Morgan falls into the water can and is vigorously dashed around in the oily water each time the artist dips his brush. Finally, he grabs the brush and surprises Frederic with his sudden appearance. But Frederic still is not satisfied with his work and destroys a painting, thereby also nearly drowning Morgan again.

When they return home, Morgan informs Frederic that he finally has found his own way to paint. His paintings begin to sell and collectors' demands grow. Frederic begins to reproduce his own work, making Morgan so unhappy that he attempts to destroy his paintings. In his anger, Frederic paints over the little guy. As Frederic continues to make copies of his work, collectors look elsewhere. The artist sinks into despair and realizes how much he misses Morgan.

One day, he accidentally scrapes away some old paint and discovers Morgan underneath. Morgan explains that he is unnecessary in a studio of reproductions, but he is persuaded to stay by Frederic promising to paint him a delicious meal. Frederic soon begins to paint from his heart again after learning from Morgan that an artist must believe in himself. The ending is slightly unpredictable as Morgan remains as a visible observer of the artist's work.

The artist's conscience is charmingly portrayed by the enchanting little Morgan who flits from page to page. Illustrations are soft pastels depicting the cluttered, but creative, environment of an artist's studio.

The story has various subtitles that allow the reader to identify the different stages of emotional struggle an artist may experience. Gifted children will find the book imaginative, yet realistic, amusing, and unique. Carrick, who usually illustrates, has produced a beautiful book—perhaps written of his own experiences as an artist.

Cassedy, Sylvia. *Behind the Attic Wall.* New York: Crowell, 1983, 315 pp. (Advanced)

Rich in imagination, Cassedy's first novel explores the memorable experiences of Maggie, an unruly and willful girl who longs for the love and care others try to give her but self-protectively responds with contempt.

Maggie has been dismissed from numerous schools for her disorderly and obnoxious behavior. She is truly an outcast by her own design, forever fearful of letting anyone get close to her emotionally. Her very appearance matches her behavior, exemplifying an unkempt, rebellious attitude toward herself. As an almost last resort, Maggie is sent to stay with two old great-aunts who formerly operated a girls' school. She is brought here by her Uncle Morris, a teasing and perplexing individual who appears to be a challenge for her because he doesn't react to her questionable reputation. Reluctantly, the two great-aunts decide to rehabilitate Maggie to their own liking. Maggie is scrutinized and criticized by her two aunts.

In her new dwelling, a huge, old stone house filled with countless rooms, Maggie soon begins to hear voices. Amusing conversation and reprimanding comments beckon her to search the rooms for the source. When she discovers that the dolls in the attic actually speak and carry on conversations with her, Maggie feels at home—she finally has found somebody who accepts her and welcomes her. As a result, she becomes a regular visitor to the attic room for afternoon tea, and the dolls become her friends. For the first time in her life, Maggie learns what loving and caring are about. Eventually, she takes out her frustration and anger on her new friends by throwing them across the room. Frightened, the dolls wonder if Maggie is really someone they want in their secret world and they cease to communicate with her. Whenever the dolls can no longer move and talk, Maggie suffers immeasurable despair and longs for the return of her friends. It is Uncle Morris who finally restores the dolls' lifelike character, and becomes one himself. This unexpected ending leaves the reader with much to ponder and inspires independent conclusions.

In Maggie, Cassedy presents a well-developed character who comes full circle. The reader realizes the growth and new-found security in this wayward individual. We identify with her and want her to find love and be able to return it. The story moves at a brisk pace, constantly making the reader anticipate the next event. The well-thought-out and exciting style will challenge and intrigue the gifted.

Cassedy, Sylvia. *M.E. and Morton.* New York: Crowell, 1987, 288 pp. (Advanced)

Eleven-year-old Mary Ella (M.E.), desperate to have a friend of her very own, withdraws into an imaginary world. Told from her viewpoint, this sensitive story presents a very detailed description of every thought M.E. has.

Fantasizing about being popular and admired at the private school she attends, M.E. appears shy, reserved, self-conscious, and very miserable in her hunger for friends. Her only brother, 14-year-old Morton, has learning problems and has been retained in his grade at his special school. Ashamed of Morton, M.E. tries to hide her brother's very existence and willfully says things that hurt him when he embarrasses her in front of other children by asking questions all the time. Through her thoughts and cruel behavior, one gets the feeling that M.E. literally loathes Morton. Indeed, she blames Morton for her own lack of friends.

When Polly, an unusual girl, appears in the neighborhood, M.E. imagines what it would be like to have her as a close friend. Soon Polly comes to play with M.E. who she puzzles with her almost enchanting actions. She tries new things with M.E.'s treasured paint bottles, the very ones M.E. pretends are little ladies with beautifully colored dresses. She flits from one thing to another with a fresh and delightful spontaneity that further inhibits M.E. and keeps M.E. off balance. Not only is her behavior odd to M.E., but Polly even looks different—her clothes are too large and unmatching, her fingernails are dirty, and her hair is stringy. However, regardless of the peculiar picture the reader may have of her, one doesn't pity this charming little imp.

When Polly discovers Morton, whose existence M.E. tries to conceal, she immediately transfers her attention to him, preferring to play with his train set. Morton is mesmerized. Usually, no one comes to play with him, and Polly does not seem to mind, or even notice, that he is different. M.E. watches in awe as Polly and Morton set up the railroad track and make the cars do all sorts of inventive things. Morton is delighted, while M.E. is astonished and perplexed at Polly's fickleness and the comfortable manner in which she becomes Morton's playmate instead of hers.

M.E.'s parents' relationship with their two children is realistically portrayed. For example, the father expresses frustration and displays a rather short temper whenever Morton does something awkward. His patience appears limited from years of toleration of his son's clumsiness. The mother escapes into her own world, muttering despairing comments to herself whenever she leaves the room.

In trying to win over Polly, M.E. begins to imitate Morton's behavior, dress, and even pretends to be slow. Her parents decide to send their son away to a special farm where he can learn and associate with peers having the same kinds of problems. Most of all, they find it necessary to separate him from M.E., since he obviously has a negative influence on her.

When Morton lies in the hospital in a coma after a serious fall, M.E. realizes how important he is to her. Again, Polly assumes a pivotal role when she comes to visit Morton and brings his favorite train car—the one he was trying to retrieve from the roof terrace when he fell. For the first time, Morton opens his eyes as she places the car in his hands.

This is an engrossing, thoughtfully written story peopled with very real and memorable characters. Cassedy reveals the change and maturity M.E. undergoes as she begins to understand what true friendship is all about. Gifted children's capacity to empathize and sympathize with others will be intensely provoked as the author offers one compelling incident after another that requires the reader's perseverance to see this complex story to a satisfying end.

Cendrars, Blaise. *Shadow.* Trans. and illus. by Marcia Brown. New York: Scribner, 1982, unp. (Beginning)

Using a combination of tissue paper, acrylics, printing, and painting, Caldecott winner Marcia Brown has translated in bold illustrations and text the French poet Blaise Cendrars's "La Féticheuse," from conversations with African storytellers and shamans. The tone poem calls forth the inexplicable shadow with all its mystery and surrounding superstition.

Brown uses collages of deep blues, gray, and sunset colors of red and orange, combined with jet black silhouettes, to establish an eerie quality, setting the mood. The graceful trees of the forest become lively, fearful creatures when night falls, and the dancers are depicted in such rhythmic motion that one can almost hear the soft sounds of their feet against the earth. The sharp, black images of the warriors appear three dimensional as they march across the colorful pages, spears pointed. Shadow is described as having no voice or hunger but simply being there and everywhere.

The bold, intriguing illustrations will appeal to a wide audience, but young children will treasure this unusual picture book for its stunning design and verse. This dramatic portrayal of shadows is a perfect marriage of text and illustration, allowing the reader's imagination to play at will.

Chambers, Aidan. *The Present Takers.* New York: Harper & Row, 1983, 128 pp. (Intermediate)

Eleven-year-old Lucy Hall becomes the victim of a bullying trio led by Melanie Prosser in this engrossing story of school children in Britain. Ridiculed, humiliated, hurt, and physically attacked by the gang, Lucy internalizes her fear and resentment because Melanie has always been able to get away with her cruel behavior even when teachers are aware of it. Lucy knows it would not be different this time, and realizes that to tell would only make things worse for her.

Melanie and her sidekicks, Sally-Ann and Vicky, repeatedly seek out some unsuspecting student and surprise her by tormenting her verbally and physically. Melanie's purpose is to force her victims to bring her "prezzies," or presents, to appease her. Having hassled big Clare Tonks into submission, Melanie tires of badgering her and moves on to Lucy. Lucy is determined not to allow Melanie to reduce her to tears and begs to be left alone; however, she loses the battle when the three girls confiscate Lucy's bookbag, taking with them her treasured and secret notes written to her by Angus Burns. When Melanie threatens to post the notes throughout the school, Lucy finally breaks, trying to protect Angus from embarrassment, and allows the group to make a fool of her in front of all the other children. Angus, determined to stop Melanie from harming Lucy further, eventually proves to Lucy that he is a true friend—willing to risk getting into trouble at home or school, for her sake.

Finally, it is Angus who learns of Melanie's plan to implicate Lucy in a shoplifting scheme. He tries to save Lucy, but the incident has already been brought to her parents' attention by the store owners. When Melanie's mother refuses to listen to Mrs. Hall's information concerning her daughter's activities, and her father physically punishes her, Lucy as well as Angus and his parents realize there is nothing more they can do. The children must work out their own problems as best they can. Therein lies the crux of the story.

The opportunity to expose Melanie's insensitive and cruel behavior toward others arises when their teacher plans an end-of-the-year wall newspaper. Angus, Lucy, and Clare collaborate with the other students to write about their feelings and attitudes toward those students who have been bullying others. They decide not to reveal names, but their descriptions are so accurate that everyone knows it is Melanie they write about. Justice is finally done. Melanie reacts violently and is removed from school.

This well-written story, with its occasional Briticisms, captures readers' attention and keeps it until the last page is turned. Lucy's frustrations and emotional agony are sensitively and realistically described, and her relationship with her parents is authentically portrayed. Children who have been treated unfairly by their peers may identify with Lucy's experiences.

Through his strong, convincing characters who undergo genuine transformations, Chambers appeals to the reader's sense of empathy, justice, and courage—emotions typically evoked and echoed in the gifted.

Cobb, Vicki. *How to Really Fool Yourself: Illusions for All Your Senses.* Illus. by Leslie Morrill. New York: Lippincott, 1981, 142 pp. (Intermediate)

Intriguing and mysterious to most of us, optical illusions are particularly challenging to intellectually gifted children. Cobb's book offers insights into many familiar perceptions, in addition to introducing new ones for exploration. The book consists of eight chapters dealing with reality, strange feelings, sounds and tastes, shapes and signs, mirages, and misconceptions that have prevailed throughout the ages. The focus is on physical properties, sensations, and knowledge gained from past experiences.

Children are encouraged to assume a participatory role from the very beginning, as the author invites them to experience some simple illusions about the book they are holding. Thus, she examines the term "reality" and presents previously held concepts of the term before launching into a general description of the book's contents, carefully explaining what is meant by "perception."

After referring to historically held theories and concepts about our physical feelings, Cobb encourages her readers to try Aristotle's illusion and other easily conducted experiments to prick their perceptions. Investigations of the senses of taste, smell, and sound are equally intriguing. Some are familiar, such as "listening to a shell"; others are less well known, including "verbal alternation" and the taste tests.

The visual illusions presented in the book continually compel readers to test their imagination. Examples are clearly and accurately illustrated, as the Poggendorf illusions of lines and the Ames window, for instance.

The section on color illusion might have been better illustrated with colorful pictures rather than black and white, but the scientific explanation is lucid and readers are required to try the tests using actual colors. To illustrate motion and movement illusions, Cobb examines the optical ability of our eyes using simple experiments. One of the most unusual is that of a waterfall illusion demonstrating that by shifting the gaze, one can visualize water falling up. Similarly, snow can be made to appear as if rising from the ground.

Another illusion, the "phi phenomenon," may be unfamiliar to many children. The author explains how it is observed using light sources and presents a brief description of animation that will appeal to children who are intrigued with this technical illusion. Mirage and "seeing spots" require the reader to focus on themselves introspectively concentrating on images that are always present in our eyes but of which we are usually unaware.

In other sections of this informative and fun work, the author scientifically disproves previous misconceptions and incorrect notions, such as the earth is flat, the earth is the center of the universe, objects come to rest in their natural places, and heavy objects come to rest in their natural places, and heavy objects fall faster than lighter ones.

Cobb's book is filled from cover to cover with exciting and fun experiments eager readers will want to try. Many adults, including teachers, will find this a useful sourcebook. For example, the illustrations can be presented to small groups of youngsters to examine and discuss. The book offers a welcome treatment of an elusive area of science that is particularly thought-provoking for intellectual minds. An engaging added little feature in the book is the picture of an eye in the upper right-hand corner of each page, in various positions of movement. Whenever the pages are flipped quickly, the reader is delighted with eye winking and blinking—truly an eyeful of entertainment.

Cobb, Vicki. *The Trip of a Drip.* Illus. by Elliot Kreloff. Boston: Little, Brown, 1986, 50 pp. (Intermediate)

What better title could prepare the reader for the complete cycle of the water we use? Cobb has written a sparkling clear, easy-to-read-and-understand account of water and its use in our lives. The little book is divided into five chapters with an added section on suggested experiments readers may try.

The first chapter begins with an illustration of the everyday practice of turning on the water faucet, with thought-provoking questions accompanying the diagram. The next paragraphs present scientific facts about our bodies' need for water and how inefficient the world would be without clear, running water. Cobb ends the chapter with several stimulating questions about the water we take for granted.

A thorough explanation accompanied by diagrams of water resources for country living introduces the second chapter. Cobb makes scientific descriptions of cesspools, septic tanks, artesian wells, and the water table easily understood. Dowsing is also explained in detail and contrasted with facts about how to locate water sources.

Chapter 3 speculates on the amount of water needed by each person. Storage systems, treatment plants, and water purification procedures required for human use are carefully detailed. Simple experiments sprinkled throughout the book entice the reader to test water samples for various reasons. This section will particularly challenge gifted readers.

The problem of polluted water in our environment is substantiated with information in chapter 4, including the devastating results of factory waste in our streams. The reader will find a new appreciation for our strict water purification standards after reading this book.

Finally, the travels of a drop of water end in chapter 5 with black-and-white diagrams and a series of what-if questions. The story is highly informative and enjoyable. Cobb details and simplifies a complicated process by employing technical language in a masterful style that young readers can clearly understand. In addition, the author engages the reader's active participation throughout the book.

Cole, Joanna. *Cars and How They Go.* Illus. by Gail Gibbons. New York: Crowell, 1983, unp. (Intermediate)

The task of using correct terminology and at the same time make a complex topic understandable to young people is accomplished in this picture book through a combination of text and simple illustrations. For example, the relationship of the gears, pistons and cylinders, crankshaft, drive shaft, wheels, and axles is explained in answer to the question of how the car moves. The cooling, lubrication, steering, and braking systems are also examined, and dashboard instruments and a few safety features are depicted. Different types of engines are discussed along with the possibility that additional power sources may be available in the future.

The simple text is accompanied by illustrations and diagrams. Brilliant colors and uncluttered, neatly labeled illustrations explain the car's systems and part locations from side-front and top-view perspectives. Diagrams are clear and well proportioned so the reader can recognize objects on the car from the shapes of the drawings. For inquisitive youngsters, capable of analyzing parts and functions, who want to examine how an automobile works, this book provides a valuable introduction to what's underneath the hood.

Conly, Jane Leslie. *Racso and the Rats of NIMH.* Illus. by Leonard Lubin. New York: Harper & Row, 1986, 280 pp. (Intermediate)

This sequel to *Mrs. Frisby and the Rats of NIMH* chronicles the adventures of Racso, Timothy, a field mouse, and other intelligent rats who outwit humans as they prevent a dam from flooding their valley and destroying its wildlife. The adventure begins as Timothy, Mrs. Frisby's son, who is a third-year student at the school headed by the superintelligent Rats of NIMH, is preparing to leave for school.

Along the way, Timothy saves Racso from drowning. This brazen rat, off to seek his fortune and learn how to read and write, is the son of the rebellious, cynical Jenner. The conservative, serious Timothy and the cocky, city rat, with a penchant for chocolate and flipping his tail, soon become friends and continue their travels together. One night, Timothy is injured by the talon of an owl as he throws himself in front of Racso to protect him from being killed. Racso devises a sling of sticks and a harness to carry Timothy, thereby enabling the unlikely duo to continue their journey. Soon they are met by Justin, Brutus, Isabella, and Brendan, rats from Thorn Valley sent to search for Timothy when he did not show up at school on time.

Back at school in Thorn Valley, the group is welcomed by Nicodemus, founder of the rat community, and the other rats. Eager to learn to read and write and impatient for success as a result, Racso lies about his family background, for fear he would be denied an education if the truth about his rebellious father were known. Nicodemus uncovers the truth but at Racso's request, keeps it a secret. Concerned about the welfare of his family, Jenner discouraged the youngsters from learning to read and write. So Racso had left home.

Alarmed by the rising river, the rats send out scouting parties to try to find the cause and learn ways to avoid the impending danger. In the process, Beatrice slips into a trailer where she reads the plans for constructing a computer-operated dam to flood the valley.

Mrs. Frisby, who comes to check on her injured son, reports conversations she has overheard at the Fitzgibbons' barn regarding the farmers' anger about being asked to sell their land for campgrounds and motels after the dam is built.

While the rats are proposing actions for how to prevent the dam from becoming a reality, Racso, daydreaming about a past encounter with a computer, has a sudden burst of insight—they could program the computer to destroy the dam. His idea is accepted, and through cooperation and teamwork, the rats begin learning about computers and programming.

Racso is among those selected to implement the sabotage plan. In spite of frantic efforts, time runs out and, believing they have failed, the rats prepare to leave when a power failure suddenly occurs. Knowing of the impending flood and that Racso, who is unable to swim, is nearby, Jenner has caused the power failure by chewing through a wire, thereby bringing about his own death. By now, Racso is accepted at Thorn Valley and even Isabella, who at first scorned Racso, begins to show an interest in him by preparing a batch of candy for him.

Racso's mischievous, selfish acts, such as picking all the peppermint leaves to make candy, are balanced by his kindness and heroic deeds, such as letting Isabella take credit for saving Christopher's life and his willingness to risk his life as part of the sabotage team. The book's underlying themes include misuse of the land, overcoming one's fears, and the value of group concerns, cooperation, and sharing as opposed to seeking the spotlight or being a hero. However, at the conclusion, Nicodemus acknowledges that there may be some value to daydreaming and Jenner is recognized as a hero. The ingenuity of the rats and the blend of humorous episodes and serious concerns for safety combine in a fast-moving plot that should appeal to gifted readers.

Connolly, James E., collector. *Why the Possum's Tail Is Bare: And Other North American Indian Nature Tales.* Illus. by Andrea Adams. Owings Mills, Md.: Stemmer, 1985, 64 pp. (Intermediate)

Fourteen nature tales and myths from eight Native American tribes are arranged in this book according to their origin among eastern and western tribes. As part of this organizational pattern, the geographic location, social and economic structure, and status of each tribe (Iroquois, Cherokee, Ojibway [Chippewa], Micmac, Sioux, Blackfoot, Cree, and Chinook) are briefly described in the introduction.

The tales not only teach morals but also reflect the Indians' respect for living creatures. The collection includes pourquoi tales such as "How the Rabbit Lost Its Tail." In this version of the turtle and rabbit race, the turtle uses his intellect to outwit the rabbit and win the race. Many tales employ trickery, such as the title story in which a barber cricket fools the vain possum by clipping the hairs off his tail.

Factual information about the animals' physical characteristics, their food, survival defenses, and relationship to humans precedes each tale. Black-and-white line drawings are realistic and true to the animals depicted, yet convey humor and a sense of the emotions underlying each story.

This collection of tales would make an effective read-aloud. Although the format allows readers to relate the factual information to the fictional tale, conclusions are not always obvious. As a result, readers are challenged to arrive at their own predictions for the ending—a feature particularly appropriate for gifted students.

Costabel, Eva Deutsch. *The Pennsylvania Dutch: Craftsmen and Farmers.* Illus. by author. New York: Atheneum, 1986, 48 pp. (Beginning)

This unique and informative book introduces young children to an important immigrant culture, the Pennsylvania Dutch, through a tapestry of the arts, crafts, and customs of these German settlers in America.

In her introduction, Costabel acquaints readers with the etymology of the word "Dutch" and briefly chronicles the history of the Dutch, emphasizing their characteristics, such as perseverance and self-sacrifice. Without sentimentality, the author characterizes these thriving people as loving in their relationship with families, communities, and churches and as dedicated and enterprising in their work, whether skilled or unskilled.

Each topic in this picture book is presented in one to two pages covering its history, construction, and the material and technique used by the respective craft workers. Simple, beautiful illustrations in bright, cheerful colors show families at work in the garden, kitchen, or the barnyard. Other drawings decoratively illustrate the arts and crafts of these highly industrious people, including weaving, quilting, fractur (a kind of calligraphy), scissor cutting, folk art, decorated tinware, pottery, glass, and woodenware. Tombstone art, clockmaking, and blacksmithing are also described. More surprisingly, the Pennsylvania Dutch are also credited with the introduction of the Kentucky rifle and the Conestoga wagon.

In keeping with the mood and overall topic of the book, its charming cover depicts a man and woman in costumes of the late 1600s, while endpapers are scissors-cut silhouettes of folk art. Titles of each topic are written in Old English letters. In addition to a table of contents and index, a bibliography and a brief listing of museums owning collections of folk art stimulate further reading and exploration.

This handsome book is appropriate for young children who are mature enough to comprehend the role of specific cultures in our overall heritage. The language and vocabulary are unique to each topic without being very technical, yet shared reading with an adult would facilitate understanding.

Cummings, E. E. *Hist Whist: And Other Poems for Children.* Illus. by David Calsada. New York: Liveright, 1983, unp. (Intermediate)

E. E. Cummings looks at the world through the eyes of a child in his selection of 20 poems. The collection, originally printed privately in 1962, appears here with detailed line drawings by Calsada. The luxurious, delicately sensitive depiction accompanying each poem captures its spirit.

Animals, children, and less tangible topics as dreams and happiness make up the content of this literary work. Imagistic and rhythmic without being sentimental, Cummings's poems delight older readers by recalling days of a carefree life when a kite flying high in the sky was a special visual treat.

Some of the selections are utterly nonsensical, as in "0 the Sun Comes Up-Up-Up in the Opening." Others are mysterious, as in "Hist Whist." In another poem, "Who (is? are) Who," a father and his child are watching snowflakes fall gently. The accompanying picture sensitively illustrates the close relationship between the two spectators. One poem uses slang words more appropriate for mature minds.

The poems strongly appeal to the senses with very little use of repetition and rhyme. The selections stretch the reader's imagination to the fullest and allows him or her to identify with the subject. Each poem and its childlike words evoke myriad responses in children who come to respect the poet's ability to see the world through their eyes. Gifted children will understand and appreciate these magnificently illustrated poems. They are meant for enjoyment and sharing. Children, young and old, will enjoy these moments of wistful dreaming.

Cunliffe, John. *Riddles & Rhymes & Rigmaroles.* Illus. by Alexy Pendle. New York: Deutsch (dist. by Elsevier-Dutton), 1982, 80 pp. (Intermediate)

Rigmaroles—confusing or nonsensical talk—are part of this collection of witty riddles and rhymes. The author provides answers and descriptions to issues raised in the numbered rigmaroles, riddles, and rhymes making up the volume.

Riddle entries are clever and will challenge the gifted reader. The rhyme section of the book, in turn, begins with a verse about "Kippers" and ends with a question the reader has to answer using the clue and description in the solution section. Solutions include garbled nursery rhymes, verses about animals and fish, puns, and various other literary forms without repetition of style.

Some of the rigmaroles consist of short paragraph stories that are literally endless. For example, one of them tells about a boy who tidily makes his bed, lies in it, thereby causing it to become unmade, gets out, makes the bed again, lies in it, and so on. Other stories end abruptly, such as one about a hunter who thinks he is dreaming of a tiger until the tiger consumes him. In the story of the "whatsit," the narrative continues for what seems like forever until its hilarious end. Yet another story has no beginning, but does have an ending.

Gifted children, who usually have a keen sense of humor, will delight in "Mrs. Gittipin's Recipe," written with periods and commas in the wrong places. Two drawing-stories, reminiscent of long ago, are also included in this section—one about a pig, the other about an astronaut.

Cunliffe's book is refreshing and different from more traditional riddle collections in that it utilizes an assortment of subjects and amusements. The purpose is to entertain and that is well accomplished. Intricate black-and-white drawings lend a nice balance to the text. The language is stimulating and illustrative, encouraging such creative thinking skills as divergence, fluency, and extrapolation.

Cutchins, Judy, and Ginny Johnston. *Are Those Animals Real? How Museums Prepare Wildlife Exhibits.* New York: Morrow, 1984, 96 pp. (Intermediate)

Showing the step-by-step process of preparing animals for a museum exhibit, this book answers questions many youngsters and adults alike have about how an animal can look real but yet not be alive.

Not all animals in dioramas were once alive—some are foam, wood, or papier-mâché models. Cutchins and Johnston explain many preservation techniques by using examples of a wide variety of species. One chapter details the taxidermy work done on Godzilla, a favorite zoo gorilla, and Jumbo, the circus elephant. Tanning the skins, making an artifical body, painting the face, and adding glass eyes are related in a simple, straightforward manner. Avoiding unnecessary detail, the authors state that although an animal's actual fur, nose, ears, claws, and whiskers may be used in mounting, "On the inside, though, nothing is the same."

To provide another example of taxidermy, Cutchins and Johnston describe the preparation of whistling swans. New swan eyes were selected from an array of glass eyes and the actual beaks were painted with black paint. Peregrine falcon chicks, long-preserved in a jar of alcohol on the shelves of an old museum storage room, were restored and placed with a mother falcon in a nest display. Before being placed in the display, the chicks' feathers were dried and fluffed with a hair dryer. To solve the problems inherent in a snake display, the authors relate how the museum artists chose to construct a rubber model of a timber rattler. The step-by-step process using a plaster mold is detailed in text and photographs.

The special problems related to designing large and small exhibits are also presented and a solution offered in the example of a large great white shark fiberglass replica and the chemical preservation of a small luna moth. The processes of freeze-drying and protection in a clear plastic mold are illustrated in the display of a tarantula. The authors also describe how after observing a praying mantis outside the museum, an artist decided to sketch the insect and prepare an oversized plastic and foam replica for display outside the museum's front door. Adhering to the belief that no museum would be complete without dinosaurs, the book also illustrates how fossil bones are assembled and the dinosaur's body is prepared. Finally, plastic leaves and water and foam rocks are among a few "secrets" revealed about the contents of dioramas, which are the setting for many museum exhibits.

Throughout the book, focus is on the skills of museum artists: careful observation and matching of authentic colors and decision making related to the most appropriate methodology of preparation. Large black-and-white photographs on nearly every page depict the individual stages of preparation, showing tools used, artists at work, and the before and after animals. Terminology is kept simple without talking down to readers. Many words are defined in the context of the text; there is also a glossary of definitions of such words as "diorama," and "herpetologist."

Although of interest to a wide audience, the book offers highly able, curious readers a rare opportunity to get a behind-the-scenes look at how one group of professionals, museum artists, conduct their work. Implicit in their activities are patience and planning skills. The book reveals how problems are identified and solved, enticing young gifted readers to wonder more about the preparation of museum displays.

Dann, Max. *The All-Amazing Ha Ha Book.* New York: Oxford University Press, 1985, 82 pp. (Intermediate)

This unusual book contains 18 different, amusing stories, jokes, activities, and poems that will appeal to gifted children who have a sense of humor and imagination by clever combinations of slapstick and satire that are not beyond their understanding.

For example, there is a short story about a boy who can't stop jumping from the time he is born. Everyone marvels at this odd spectacle, but the real fun begins when he enters school. Teachers cannot get him to stop, so eventually the whole school joins in the jumping, loving every leap of it! A matching-food quiz, sandwiched in between the stories, deals with a familiar list of dishes, such as lamb chops, to be matched with a drawing. In this case—a sheep with an ax.

Another hilarious experience awaits the reader in a story-in-rhyme about a little boy who hates school so much he decides to eat everything in sight, including the furniture, play equipment, books, friends, teachers, and everything else he can find. However, interesting things start to happen to him; he discovers that he cannot read, spell, write, or add. He becomes ill and must see a doctor who informs him that he must undergo surgery to release all the people and things he has eaten. It's an outlandish tale written in couplet-style rhyme that gifted children will enjoy for its clever use of language.

Elsewhere in the book we come across a new version of the story about the frog who would become a king, and a tale about a hungry "bunyip." A poem introduces sausages that talk; another, three aunts who experience some entertaining episodes. In a short story about a chicken, "Mrs. Cluck," we learn of the chaos she created when she enters a classroom. Another episode involves a little boy who is influenced by a tale his Grandpa tells him about a snail that carries his house on his back and overeats trying to keep his own house.

Problems for everybody follow when Hugh and Aunt Gerty take a huge umbrella to the beach and everything goes wrong when everyone else's privacy is invaded. In another little story, Mousefink gets into trouble with the Icing Gobbler over a cake, and both are reprimanded for the mess they make.

In an illustrated poem, a crow explains how he lost his beautiful singing voice to be left with just a "caw."

The book ends with a story about a proud and haughty magician who makes Murphy the rabbit vanish but cannot bring her back because she didn't like the way her master left her out of the glitter and fame of the magic show. Murphy chooses to return at unexpected moments and finally makes the magician vanish, claiming her own name in lights.

First published in Australia, the book includes words and phrases that are unique to that country. For example, "chooks" for chickens and "kerb" for curb. Also, many unfamiliar spellings, such as "learnt" and "spoilt," may temporarily stall students, but they will quickly accept the slang and vocabulary. The content is enjoyable for its original play on words and ridiculous to absurd situations. Part of the book is written in rhyme, part in the form of short stories or vignettes; a few picture-story puzzlers are also included. Black-and-white drawings lend a comical and almost silly element without adding any integral meaning to the stories. Intended to entertain, children will appreciate the light, nonsensical touch of the pictures.

Nonsensical phrases that are quirkily humorous make up many of the selections, providing good fun. Many of the stories are written in short, choppy sentences, but manage to convey the message of a given tale.

Davis, Maggie S. *The Best Way to Ripton.* Illus. by Stephen Gammell. New York: Holiday, 1982, unp. (Beginning)

A jaunty old jalopy driven by an eerie old man in dark glasses comes bumping along a country road. As he nears a fork in the road, the driver happens upon a farmer-pig raking his fields. Abruptly stopping his car, he asks the pig for the best way to Ripton. Farmer-Pig simply tells him, "The best way is the safe way . . . and not to go through 'Crying Hollow Junction,' " and proceeds to tell him why not: A wolf who lives there will season him smartly and cook him in stew. The pig then asks the man, "Do you believe it?" Accompanying this scene, pencil illustrations depict a ghastly wolf in a cook's hat, busy at work.

An odd assortment of objects and figures float across the pages— apparently unrelated to the text. For example, there are fish in the sky, airplanes hovering near the ground, and straggly, leafless trees with roots exposed and protruding into the air.

Appreciative of the pig's advice, the old man thanks him and asks another way to travel to Ripton, only to receive the following absurd reply: "Take the smooth way, but not Deep Tumble Highway where the road is so rough the car will destruct and you will probably end up on the moon." Annoyed and exasperated, the old man begs for exact directions, but Farmer-Pig has more to tell about all the wrong ways to get to Ripton.

Pictured almost as if dancing or strutting, the pig seems to be enjoying his ridiculous replies to the old man, who by now, has removed his dark glasses and is angrily shouting at the pig. But the pig is not put off by the old man's impatience as he kneels down to direct him further. When he tells the traveler not to take Snail-Paced Lane, the old man climbs on top of his car and delivers his own explanation of why he shouldn't go by that route, matching the pig's nonsense.

> Square down the middle of Snail-Paced Lane, a tottery mule pulls a wagon. He can't hear me honk because behind me on a bus are seven merry minstrels making music. I want to get to Ripton—but I don't get to Ripton—that is, I can't get to Ripton—till the snow falls! DO YOU BELIEVE IT?!

The pig believes it, and when his missus calls him to dinner, he tells the tired old man that he missed Ripton ten miles earlier. He ends up taking him home with him—piggyback.

Gammell's sketchy pencil drawings enhance the cleverness of this humorous tale and complements the exaggerated text. All in all, it's an amusing yarn, well told, with a wacky, almost bizarre, yet sophisticated flavor that will not be lost on able youngsters. The author provides readers with an escape into hilarity, offering comical, wry, dry wit with fun-poking slapstick humor. The characterization is cunningly developed with an accent on the games played by Farmer-Pig. His wild imagination and nonsensical responses sorely try the patience of the old man. All ends well regardless of the perplexity the old man must endure. Beginning readers with a keen sense of humor should respond to this unusual story.

Demi. *The Adventures of Marco Polo.* Illus. by author. New York: Holt, Rinehart & Winston, 1982, unp. (Beginning)

Packed with pictorial highlights of Marco Polo's lively trips to and from China in 1271, this tiny treasure contains a wealth of information for the very young child.

When Emperor Kublai Khan of China requests holy oil from Jerusalem as part of his study of different religions, Marco Polo is invited to accompany his father on this venture. A wide red line shows the route they take to obtain the oil before they return to China. Demi focuses on events, customs, animals, art, inventions, people, and plants they encounter along the way. Each small, brightly colored illustration is clearly labeled—carpet makers at work, oil gushing from the ground surrounded by people on camels, poisonous waters, mountains, unusual sheep, and zebu.

A savage gang of armed robbers is seen casting spears across the pages at Marco Polo's caravan as some travelers fall helplessly from the galloping camels. The travelers are plagued by blowing, biting sand and unbearable heat before they enter Kerman. Miniature illustrations of Khan's soldiers on horses, natural resources, such as cotton bolls, and minerals, such as jade, are depicted, as are skeletal remains of those people who did not survive the harshness of climate or invaders.

The holy oil is finally presented to the Kublai Khan, who is shown ensconced upon his throne surrounded by an army of soldiers with shields. Marco and his troop see many notable inventions credited to the Chinese: the compass, the spinning wheel, paper, kites, gunpowder, and the water clock.

Over the years, Marco witnesses many more unusual sights as he is sent on other missions by Khan. Some of these are comical, such as the dragon dance celebrating the Chinese New Year, devil dances, and acrobats in action.

Elsewhere, in a battle, Marco victoriously captures some elephants for Khan, and he uses Italian slings in another battle on the desert. Khan generously rewards the young explorer with a prestigious voyage on the Yangtze River before pronouncing him the governor of Kinsai. Finally, after several other fruitful adventures, Marco Polo returns home to Venice, much older and wiser and a hero.

Demi provides young readers numerous historical essentials by breezily illustrating them against a white background. The book cleverly incorporates important events of the explorer's travel with many incidental but interesting items of information that are all clearly labeled. Very young children can easily follow Marco's route, share his adventures, and gather a significant amount of new information.

Although the text is limited, the language is not. Rather, not unlike biographies for older children, the book acquaints young children with a factual, yet delightfully diverse, account of Marco Polo using whimsical illustrations for a historical topic. Endpapers contain maps of the entire 24-year-long journey while the inside of the book details segments of the route.

Demi. *Demi's Find the Animal ABC: An Alphabet-Game Book.* Illus. by author. New York: Grosset & Dunlap, 1985, unp. (Beginning)

This imaginative approach to an alphabet book combines a game of finding the hidden animal with letter recognition, thereby keenly exercising children's powers of observation and visual discrimination.

Each letter of the alphabet, upper- and lowercase, is located in one corner of the page along with a small framed animal and the challenge: Can you find this (elephant, unicorn, etc.)? The reader must discover the identical animal in the larger design, which contains a multitude of animal shapes in differing sizes and postures. Every other two-page spread is colorfully illustrated. Sometimes the pages show a giant shape of an animal filled with a tiny shape of the same creature. For example, a black-and-white double-page spread sporting a crafty old alligator hides a tiny alligator exactly like its larger brother next to the letter A. For the letter B dozens of brightly colored exotic birds are perched on telephone lines. Three haughty camel shapes are filled with camels for C. Similarly, giraffes and foxes are interspersed on two pages that require those animals located to be animals not commonly found in alphabet books. For example, ibis, jaguar, vole, X-ray fish, and yak playfully scamper across the pages. The nine-banded armadillo, representing the letter N, is perhaps a bit awkward for very young children.

Discovery of the animal is a treat in this amazing book, and for those perplexing puzzlers, solutions are in the back with red arrows pointing to the little animal to be located. Remarkable in format, this large, unique book is a joy from bright red cover to bright red cover that shows an elephant shape filled with many kinds of amusing animals from pink seals to purple elephants. Children will delight in "studying" the pages in an attempt to find the many frolicking creatures. This atypical alphabet requires diligent discernment and identification. As an added challenge, a tiny cat is hidden somewhere in the book. However, since there is not a specific "cat" page, children must search every page to locate it.

---

dePaola, Tomie. *The Mysterious Giant of Barletta: An Italian Folktale.* Adapted and illus. by Tomie dePaola. New York: Harcourt, 1984, unp. (Beginning)

Known as the Mysterious Giant, a huge statue of a curly-haired, round-faced young boy stands in front of a church in the town square of Barletta. From this vantage point the giant overlooks the townspeople as they pass by in the course of their everyday activities—nuns and citizens coming to church for Holy Mass, children playing in the streets, and doves resting on the statue's shoulders. Living across the square from the statue, the oldest resident, Zia Concetta, draws comfort from the presence of the statue, which has been there for as long as she can remember. (Each evening Zia gazes at the giant from her window and calls, "Buona notte, Colosso—good night, Big One.")

One day, the boy-giant notices a drastic change in the people's usual calm manner. Frightened at reports of an approaching army bent on destroying their town, the townsfolk are scurrying around packing their belongings and preparing to flee Barletta. In desperation, Zia tells the boy-giant how much the townspeople love him and asks Colosso to come down from his pedestal and help save the town. The statue obliges, and the two devise a plan.

Accordingly, Zia instructs the people to bring her the largest onion in town and then hide in their homes and not ask any questions. After Zia cuts the onion in half, the Mysterious Giant heads for the outskirts of the city, holds the onion pieces close to his eyes, and soon begins to cry. When the enemy soldiers approach and ask him what he is doing, the Mysterious Giant replies that the other boys in town won't let him play with them because he is too small. At the prospect of meeting the other inhabitants—supposedly larger than this giant-sized boy—the army flees immediately. The Mysterious Giant returns to Barletta where he resumes his former position in the town square.

DePaola's colorful contemporary folk art illustrations effectively support and complement this adaptation of the Italian folktale, one of many stories about the Mysterious Giant. The clever plan relies on the boy-giant's wit instead of his brawn, suggesting the use of one's intellectual capacities instead of force. The scheme to save the town, contrived by the two main characters, is not immediately apparent since it is not revealed in detail in the text. Consequently, gifted young readers have an opportunity to predict how the giant will put the onion to use.

Dolan, Edward F., Jr. *Animal Rights.* New York: Watts, 1986, 146 pp. (Advanced)

Believing that animals deserve proper treatment from humans, not because we are their superiors and thus responsible for their care, but because animals share our earth, Dolan makes a case for animal rights by describing, often graphically, the treatment of animals by scientists, farmers (mass production), hunters and trappers, caretakers in zoos, circuses, rodeos, and pet owners.

Historically, humans have used animals to meet their own needs—as pets and work animals—often ignoring animals' individual nature. Most religions imply compassion toward our fellow creatures, and the first animal protection laws were enacted in 1641. However, it was not until the nineteenth century that present-day animal protection societies, such as the Society for the Prevention of Cruelty to Animals, were founded and state and federal legislation was enacted. The work of Peter Singer, who compared the mistreatment of animals to human slavery, coining the word "specieism" (i.e., animals are frequently abused because they are of a different species), gave impetus to the view that animals have rights. Dolan describes basic animal rights, including the right to live their lives according to their basic natures, have good health, avoid pain, a humane death, and survival.

Dolan devotes three chapters to animals as subjects for scientific experimentation, describing such research as biomedical, drug development, product testing, and product extraction, as well as educational experimentation. Descriptions include the procedures and concomitant pain to the animals of commonly used tests. Examples described are the Draize test in which confined rabbits are usually not given an anesthetic when being tested to determine product irritation to the human eye, and the LD_{50} (lethal dose test) to determine what amount of a given product will result in the death of half of a group of animals within 14 days. Alternatives to animal experimentation include reducing the numbers of animals used, substituting such substances as bacteria, single-cell organisms, and human and animal tissue, and limiting educational misuse of insignificant and unnecessarily cruel experiments. The book also details the efforts of militant groups such as the Animal Liberation Front to free lab animals, as well as state and federal laws seeking better, more humane care.

Other, perhaps less obvious, areas of cruelty include factory farming, that is, raising large numbers of poultry, pigs, and cattle in confined areas where they are fed mechanically, deprived of their instinctive behaviors, and generally kept under stressful conditions before being brutally slaughtered. To counteract these farming practices, Dolan recommends buying traditional farm products, reducing meat consumption, and encouraging vegetarianism.

Dolan describes the cruelty of the steel jaw trap, the clubbing of fur seals, and the efforts of animal advocate groups to deter these practices. He refutes arguments that hunting assists in weeding out weak animals, thus preserving the best of the stock. He also presents figures that reflect the role of the federal and state governments in promoting hunting.

Traditional family events, such as circuses and rodeos, are revealed as placing restraints on animals by requiring them to perform acts against their nature, such as tigers who are afraid of jumping through flaming hoops, thereby bringing pain and suffering to the animals. Even zoo animals, often in crowded facilities without their natural habitats, are at risk. Abused pets and stray cats and dogs, often ill and starving, are another group of animal sufferers. Dolan advocates responsible pet ownership and lists a series of questions prospective pet owners should ask themselves before taking on the responsibility of an animal.

Dolan offers suggestions for what can be done to help mitigate animal suffering in most of the areas outlined in the book. Many of his recommendations could be implemented by adults, but some, such as contacting legislators and talking to friends about the effect of hunting and trapping on wildlife, are within the province of youngsters. Animal advocate organizations and their principal operations are listed along with a recommended list of further reading. The title is suggested for upper-intermediate-grade readers. The unsentimental realism depicted in the photos and described in the text, while not excessively cruel, may be overwhelming to very sensitive young readers. The value of the work to gifted readers who are often concerned with ethical issues is that it may develop an awareness of the issues involved in treatment of animals. The problems of inhumane treatment and experimentation are of concern to us all. Wherever information is presented on both sides of an issue, readers can evaluate and decide for themselves.

Drescher, Henrik. *Looking for Santa Claus.* Illus. by author. New York: Lothrop, 1984, unp. (Beginning)

Readers of this zany picture book will meet Blossom, a cow who jumps over the moon while "looking for Santa Claus." Drescher's portrayal of three preposterous mean sisters and their niece, Maggie, is reminiscent of the story of Cinderella and her ugly stepsisters. Pictured with outrageous hairdos, the obnoxious aunts make Maggie sweep and clean the house while they sit around munching chocolates and tossing the wrappers on the floor.

On Christmas Eve, the aunts' absurd cruelties reach a peak as they send Maggie out in deep snow to free Blossom, a cow, from the snow. After Maggie digs a path to the poor, imprisoned cow, Blossom invites her to climb aboard her back to go looking for Santa Claus. The book's wacky adventure is launched as we see the two of them flying high over a crescent moon in a dark, wintry sky. The flying duo leaps around the earth, studded with jagged pieces of continents and various identifiable landmarks such as the Statue of Liberty. They race by Russia where they acquire a white-bearded cossack; then they rescue a red-suited Swiss shepherd, who hangs onto them for his life with one of his sheep clinging to him. Finally, a sheik, picked up in Egypt and dressed in a Santa Claus suit fills the last seat on the cow's back. Along with these three Santa-look-alike passengers, Maggie and Blossom start their homeward journey.

As they gallop across the world, they notice the season's celebrations everywhere. Nearing the aunts' snow-covered house, they see smoke signals for help curling from the chimney. Blossom and her passengers dive head-first into the snow and dig their way to the door. Relieved and happy to see their niece again, the aunts give them a warm welcome, and they all enjoy their own festivity.

Blossom curls herself to form a sofa on which all of them crowd together and warm their feet by the fire. Then, as presents begin to tumble from the chimney, they rush outside to see the real Santa soaring away.

Drescher's captivating, joyful illustrations, using rich color and stimulating scribbles, successfully enhance the humor and enchantment of this story. Every page, brimful of bustling activity and excitment, delights the reader with little unexpected and appealing pleasures, such as a bird with a worm in its mouth on Maggie's tall broom, an owl on the top of an evergreen tree in Russia, and Blossom meeting a jet plane with passengers waving from the windows. The haphazard appearance of events and people is delightfully different from ordinary picture books. This imaginative story is written in a humorous style with a sophistication that young gifted children will treasure.

Du Bois, William Pene. *Gentleman Bear.* Illus. by author. New York: Farrar, 1985, 78 pp. (Intermediate)

Teddy bear lovers everywhere will delight in this unusual book about an English boy's lifelong relationship with his stuffed friend.

Lord Billy Browne-Browne was born into an aristocratic and eccentric English family in 1916. His father, Sir Peter, and his mother, Lady Betty, granted his every wish. When Billy takes too many tumbles down the great staircase, his parents decide on a teddy bear to cushion the child's clumsy falls. "Bayard" and Billy became close friends, the bear serving as Billy's confidant in all decisions and problems. Bayard goes where Billy goes: to the tailor for new suits just like his master's and to boarding school where Billy discovers five new friends who share his fondness for teddy bears. The six boys, known as the "Teddy-Bear Six," remain in close contact the rest of their lives.

Billy's athletic skill brings the two to the 1936 Olympics in Berlin where they march in the opening day parade, dressed identically. Winning third place in pole vaulting, Billy attributes his success to Bayard. Consequently, when Hitler congratulates the winners, it is Bayard's paw he shakes, amusing the crowd tremendously. That evening, Billy accidentally meets his future wife, also a member of the Olympic team, who falls in love with both Billy and Bayard.

Later, after the Teddy-Bear Six enlist in the RAF, each takes his bear with him on a dangerous mission to obtain aerial photographs. Bayard is wounded, but all survive with success.

When the teddy bear is "kidnapped" just before the Queen's ball, Billy, who has now been married for 15 years, becomes hysterical. A special party is held to invite anonymously the kidnapper, who turns out to be a boy who found Bayard in the street.

Bayard, who has become world-famous for his fame during the Olympics and the war, is an object of desire for millions of people who just want to touch him, hoping good fortune will come to them. People send teddy bear clothes to Bayard and old teddy bears to Billy, hoping their last years can be spent in comfort. By 1985, Sir Billy, who is communicating less and less, uses Bayard's daily suit of clothes to signal his preferences; for example, a red suit means Billy is not in a talking mood and a green suit that he is willing to play a game of billiards. The story ends after Sir Billy consents to being interviewed by a persistent reporter who has hounded him most of his life.

Written with tongue-in-cheek humor, *Gentleman Bear* is an imaginative and sophisticated story that middle graders and older children will enjoy. The large book appears to be a picture book about bears, but the reader will also find a stimulating story about a young boy's experiences as he grows into a man. This is a truly unique story that may awe readers by Billy's obvious dependence on his friend, even as an adult. But children who have shared an attachment for a favorite toy or blanket will appreciate the au- thor's mature treatment of this special bond. Du Bois has included heart- warming and colorful illustrations of Billy's life and his teddy bear. The story might be about any normal boy in England, except this one has a favorite teddy bear that greatly enriches his life. The overall acceptance of this relationship as ordinary seems preposterous, but is diluted by the reader's identification with Billy and his unwavering loyalty to Bayard. The format is picture-book size; however, the language is complex beyond the younger child's understanding with a sophisticated adult overtone.

Dunrea, Olivier. *Skara Brae: The Story of a Prehistoric Village.* Illus. by author. New York: Holiday, 1985, unp. (Intermediate)

The prehistoric settlement Skara Brae, "Village of the Hilly Dunes," on the Bay of Skaill in the Orkney Islands was uncovered in 1850 after a storm tore away its grass and sand dune coverings. Its four stone huts and various artifacts remained accessible until another storm, in 1924, destroyed part of the dwellings. At that time a seawall was constructed for protection, and an archaeological excavation unearthed six more stone dwellings, well pre- served in sand.

Skara Brae was settled in 3500 B.C. by Neolithic people in search of land and food. Initially, the inhabitants erected temporary shelters made of ani- mals' skins and lived off their grazing animals—sheep, cattle, and pigs—and other food, such as birds, eggs, fish, and wild plants obtained from the land and sea. After approximately a year, however, these New Stone Age settlers built permanent dwellings using the abundantly available stones. By piling up stones, they constructed small, square houses or huts ($12' \times 6$ to $9'$ wide interiors) with rounded corners. The houses were divided into functional areas such as bed, hearth, small cell (used either for storage or as a latrine), dresser, and even wall recesses for personal items. Refuse, called "midden," consisting of broken pottery, shells, bones, and other discarded items, were piled up outside the huts and served as insulation. This protective layer eventually mixed with the sandy dunes.

After several generations the settlers focused on social and ceremonial activities, including the probable construction of a communal burial mound (a "cairn"), and such crafts as clay pottery, jewelry making, and unusual carved stone balls, done by the men. Over the years the physical layout of the village changed because of the shifting sands that covered some huts, the growing collection of midden, and the rebuilding of some huts to increase their size. Finally, in about 2400 B.C. a severe storm devastated the village, forcing the settlers to abandon their homes and leave many of their belongings behind.

Soft, detailed ink and wash illustrations, sectional drawings of interiors of huts, and aerial views of the village complement the text and further serve to engage the reader's attention. In particular, the importance of stone is made visibly certain by Dunrea's drawings, meticulously showing variations in individual stones. The story is written clearly and simply, using only a few technical terms such as "corbelling" (overlapping construction), which are defined.

Based on facts learned during his visits to the archaeological site, Dunrea's account makes only a few assumptions about some of the materials and designs used in construction and whether or not the inhabitants built a communal burial mound similar to others in the area. The book gives young readers a rare look at a discipline usually reserved for older readers. As an introduction to a prehistoric period, the story of Skara Brae leaves thoughtful young readers speculating what happened to the Neolithic people who possessed the construction skills and ability to utilize available resources and create a vital community.

Ekker, Ernst A. *What Is Beyond the Hill?* Illus. by Hilde
Heyduck-Huth. New York: Lippincott, 1985, unp. (Beginning)

Through full-page paintings using muted earth tones and a series of questions, the vastness of the universe is explored. From the beginning readers are involved in the search for "what is beyond the hill?" as they join a boy and girl who are looking over a backyard fence asking the question. As the reader turns each page, a broader view of the world emerges accompanied by a brief statement acknowledging another hill or mountain and asking if the world stops there. After this horizontal view, each succeeding painting depicts a higher elevation to symbolize upward movement—familiar, soft, rolling hills of a pastoral scene, a busy town nestled in a valley, a sheepherder and his flock high on a hill in a foreign land, a steep, rocky, barren mountain with spiraling roads and tunnels, and on to the stars in the sky. Illustrations are effective as they parallel the concept of the unknown by becoming less detailed and more abstract with the final amorphous shapes of the stars.

By asking more questions than it answers, the book stretches the reader's imagination and encourages thinking about the vastness not only of our world but of the universe. For these reasons, it is recommended for gifted youngsters who need intellectually stimulating reading.

Epstein, Sam, and Beryl Epstein with Michael Salmon. *What's for Lunch? The Eating Habits of Seashore Creatures.* Illus. by Walter Gaffney-Kessel. New York: Macmillan, 1985, 48 pp. (Intermediate)

Who helps maintain the pristine serenity of the seashore by consuming dead fish, crabs, other forms of ocean life, remains of food left by picnickers, and just plain garbage? The majestic seagull. In addition to a diet of clams and birds' eggs, this magnificent bird scours the beaches and keeps them clean.

This book explores the eating habits of about 20 seashore creatures and the precautions they take to survive predators. Curious children will be fascinated by descriptions of unusual means of taking food, such as that of the sea squirt, which processes as much as 45 gallons of water a day in search for the plankton it needs to survive.

Winged hunters, such as the osprey, tern, pelican, skimmer, and heron, are skilled fishers that can spot fish from high above the water and dive down and scoop up their own lunch or food for their young. The heron seems to be setting a trap when it drops a feather into the water. An unsuspecting fish will swim to the feather only to be snapped up by the heron's sharp, long beak.

Children will also enjoy reading about the fiddler crab commonly seen scurrying here and there at the seashore when the tide is out and hiding in its burrow in the sand when the waves come in. These shy, swift creatures, which resemble sand-colored spiders, sport distinctive eating behaviors. The female eats daintily with both claws, whereas the male uses its one small claw.

There is also the clam's steadfast resistance to the prying beaks of the seagull, which continually drops the clam to break it, or to the strong arms of the starfish. Other seashore animals examined by the Epsteins include sandpipers, ducks, hermit crabs, scallops, mussels, oysters, snails, barnacles, jellyfish, corals, and worms. Each animal is illustrated with soft, intricate pen-and-ink drawings.

The book instills respect for these tiny complex creatures whose eating habits contribute to the natural preservation of the seashore's beauty. Everybody participates in a test of survival—whether a super scavenger like the seagull or a miniscule survivor such as the sea squirt. The uniqueness of the topic will appeal to the gifted child who has appreciation for nature and vulnerable creatures' survival habits.

Fadiman, Clifton. *Wally the Wordworm.* Illus. by Lisa Atherton. Owings Mills, Md.: Stemmer, 1983, 56 pp. (Beginning)

In this new edition of his 1964 *Wally the Wordworm,* Clifton Fadiman shares his love of words with youngsters based on his belief that children should read books with words that are challenging and fun to pronounce. Wally, a cartoonlike character with an expressive face, leads the reader on a loosely woven adventure through a dictionary. Standing upside down Wally discovers palindromes—words spelled the same way forward or backward. On a safari word hunt, he explores animal names. For example, Wally distinguishes the alligator and crocodile by the shapes of their snouts. Appropriate for an imaginary word hunt, Wally also meets fantasy creatures, including the centaur, chimera, roc, phoenix, Cheshire cat, and unicorn, all illustrated in a double-page spread.

Wally also enjoys onomatopoeic sounds and word riddles. His adventures draw to a close as he bores his way to Z, proclaiming that he will never tire of words and expressing pride in knowing so many words. The last few pages, bordered in rectangular sections, reminiscent of a picture dictionary, return the reader to a feeling of order after the frolicking adventure.

Every page is filled with either black-and-white sketches or colorful pastel watercolors suggesting the dynamic nature of words and illustrating the puns—Wally chewing on candy bar wrapper words—and visual interpretations of word meanings such as "repeat" written in colorful letters three times, and the large uppercase letters spelling "gymnastics" positioned on parallel bars.

This is a delightful way for gifted readers to increase their vocabularies. In addition, Fadiman's book may motivate young readers to browse through a dictionary independently, continuing to hunt for words, and thus adds a new purpose for a book otherwise viewed as a reference tool. The visual puns as well as the multisyllabic words offer a challenge to highly capable young readers. The book can be enjoyed individually or as a read-aloud.

Fisher, Leonard Everett. *Boxes! Boxes!* Illus. by author. New York: Viking, 1984, unp. (Beginning)

Boxes of many shapes and sizes (80 according to the author's notes) are accompanied by brief, rhythmic verse, one line per page. The boxes sport children's toys and familiar objects—colored pencils, jack-in-the-box, puppies—in bright rainbow hues.

Although the term *box* is used primarily as a noun to indicate a container, reference to "box a plant" illustrated by red geraniums in a cratelike box uses *box* as a verb. The shapes and sizes of boxes progress from simple to more complex arrangements and combinations—from boxes with a specific single purpose such as a heart-shaped box of Valentine chocolates to box kites. Finally, in the last double-page spread, all the boxes shown throughout the book are piled up in a room being entered by a child whose head is covered by a bright red box with two circles for eyes.

A concept book that can be used for color recognition and counting, *Boxes! Boxes!* is cognitively challenging because of the varied functions of the illustrated boxes. Even an ant farm is encased in a see-through box. Preschool and other early readers will delight in the sprightly tone and conclusion. After reading *Boxes! Boxes!,* some youngsters may discover other uses for these multipurpose containers.

Fisher, Leonard Everett. *Symbol Art: Thirteen Squares, Circles, Triangles from around the World.* Illus. by author. New York: Four Winds, 1986, 64 pp. (Intermediate)

The basis of early written communication, symbols and symbolic forms have continued to constitute a significant part of our universal language. *Symbol Art,* a collection of symbolic designs and their meanings and historical development, represents 13 systems of human thought and endeavor—astrology, astronomy, magic, chemistry, biology/botany, mathematics, weather, printing, business, business logo, shorthand, music, and religion.

To set the stage for this intriguing overview, Fisher starts by defining the meaning of "symbol." To this end, he provides descriptive examples (such as the American flag), presents a concise history of symbolic art, and emphasizes that all graphic design is based on variations or parts of three basic shapes—the square, circle, and triangle. Each of the 13 sections is introduced by a double-page spread consisting of a full-page brown scratchboard drawing followed by a page of text that links symbols from ancient to modern times in a concise history and explains terminology specific to that system. Wherever appropriate, Fisher has included examples from different cultures and religions, such as the Japanese yen, the British pound, the Celtic witch's foot, the Judaic symbol for God, and the papal cross.

Most familiar to intermediate-level readers are the musical notation, symbols commonly seen on weather maps, and many mathematical and astronomical symbols. Many youngsters can also identify some of the proofreader's marks in the section on printing, such common business symbols as those for copyright and percent, and logos of businesses.

A unique and well-designated presentation of symbols spanning the ages as well as most aspects of human endeavor, *Symbol Art* can be read and interpreted on different levels. Implicit in the graphics and text is the opportunity to make comparisons, to search for commonalities of visual expression across different systems, and to make the connection between ancient symbols and present-day representations of ideas and events. To interpret symbols beyond the literal level, readers must be able to deal with abstractions. Interested youngsters will find it a challenge to relate abstract symbolic forms to their referents.

Fleischman, Sid. *The Whipping Boy.* Illus. by Peter Sis. New York: Greenwillow, 1986, 90 pp. (Intermediate)

This imaginatively written story contains elements of truth from medieval times when "whipping boys" were retained at court to endure the punishment of a misbehaving member of royalty. Such was the case of Jemmy, a street ruffian. Young Prince Brat was a spoiled, spiteful, and deceitful boy who enjoyed watching Jemmy take his whacks, but he always was disappointed that his servant never cried out.

One night, when the prince is bored with his own mischievous antics, he arouses Jemmy from sleep to run away. The prince has never learned to read or write so he needs the orphan boy, who has learned these skills well from his required presence at his master's tutoring sessions. Feelings run high between the two, for each despises the other. As the prince's manservant, Jemmy must accompany him, even in this secret venture, for to disobey the prince is next to death.

The boys set out on a royal horse and immediately are approached by two well-known outlaws, Hold-Your-Nose Billy and Cutwater, who are not impressed with the arrogant young prince's demands that they unhand them. It is not until the men spot the king's crest on the horse's saddle that they are convinced that one of the boys must live in the palace. The renegades take the boys to their hut where they dine on the contents of the prince's picnic basket while the runaways are given stale bread and herring. When Jemmy has to write the prince's ransom note for him, the kidnappers conclude that he is the true prince and that the prince is the whipping boy. In his plan to save the prince, Jemmy persuades the outlaws to ask for a higher ransom than merely the prince's "weight in gold" and instructs them to send the message to the castle with the whipping boy (who is really the prince). Jemmy believes that he can easily escape the thugs and return to the streets and the sewer-life he knows so well.

To Jemmy's astonishment, the prince refuses to return to the castle and sends the horse instead. In spite of Prince Brat's foolish behavior, which initially complicates any attempt to escape from their captors, the boys finally get away. As they sprint through a forest, they happen upon a young girl who is looking for her dancing bear and she directs them to the river. Jemmy keeps trying to convince the prince to return home, but Prince Brat is adamant about not wanting to return to an "uncaring" father.

A potato cart serves as a temporary hiding place before Hold-Your-Nose Billy and Cutwater discover them. When Prince Brat is subsequently thrashed as the whipping boy, he takes his lashes in grim silence, surprising

Jemmy, who did not believe the boy had any integrity at all. They are rescued by the girl and bear, find the potato man again, and all travel to the fair. They find food, and Jemmy is warmly recognized by old gutter-buddies. The outlaws return and chase the boys into the sewer system, a familiar environment to Jemmy. All the while, the prince keeps confessing his feeling of friendship toward the resistant whipping boy. The two finally escape when the outlaws are attacked by rats. The prince insists that Jemmy return to the castle with him, as well as the girl, bear, and potato man. The king amply rewards the group and the two boys become close friends.

Rich in the contrasts between royalty and commoners, this story will entertain, excite, and endear its readers without eliciting moral judgment. Jemmy, the strong-willed, steadfast servant boy employs common sense in threatening situations, whereas the proud, self-centered prince assumes that his belittling commands are the solution to all problems. When his courage is openly challenged by the outlaws and the dangerous circumstances he encounters, Prince Brat is forced to examine his own feelings and put his pride aside. He begins to recognize Jemmy for the strong person he is regardless of his demeaning position in the castle. The boys' contrasting personalities and social status lend an added dimension to the conflict.

The story is full of action, adventure, and humor. The many black-and-white illustrations amusingly portray the people and events, thereby complementing this lively story. Intermediate-age children will appreciate the wit and humor and the boys' friendship that emerges from chaotic beginnings.

Folsom, Marcia, and Michael Folsom. *Easy as Pie: A Guessing Game of Sayings.* Illus. by Jack Kent. New York: Clarion, 1985, unp. (Beginning)

Appropriate for the young child who knows the letters of the alphabet, this appealing book uses analogous old sayings and new sayings—for example, "straight as an arrow" and "plump as a quail" to introduce the letters of the alphabet. Each letter appears on a separate page with an illustration and the first part of the corresponding saying. On the next page the saying is completed and accompanied by a pictorial clue to the alphabet letter. The entertaining illustrations are simple and cartoonlike. For example, on one page the letter M is shown alongside three children pulling on a rope in a tug-of-war with the caption "Stubborn as a. . . . " The next page pictures a mule at the end of the rope refusing to budge. The word "Mule" appears at the bottom of the page with the M highlighted in a contrasting color. In another case, a street roller is shown driving over a pancake to illustrate "flat as a pancake."

The overall approach is fresh, inviting, and nonsensical, striking a chord of merriment on each page. The authors' choice of "easy as pie" for the title demonstrates how simple it is to make up verbal formulas given an understanding of the fun of making comparisons.

Young gifted children will enjoy the challenge of trying to complete the saying before turning the page for the correct answer, as well as appreciate the play on words in the sayings. Many children will attempt to invent their own sayings.

Fox, Paula. *One-Eyed Cat.* New York: Bradbury, 1984, 216 pp. (Advanced)

Ned lives with his father, who is a minister, and his invalid mother in a huge, old house in the countryside overlooking the Hudson River. Surrounded by mountains and deep forests, Ned spends much of his out-of-school time exploring the countryside alone.

When he is 11 years old, Ned's favorite uncle brings him an air gun as a present. Deciding that his son is not old enough for this special gift, Ned's father puts it away in the attic; however, the same night, Ned sneaks up to get the gun and takes it outside to try it out. When he sees a movement in the dark, he automatically pulls the trigger, never knowing for sure whether or not he hit something.

Not long after this incident, a stray cat appears at the dilapidated house of old Mr. Scully, the man whom Ned helps after school. Mr. Scully explains that a cat like that has become wild and lives in the forest. When Ned leaves some food for the cat he notices that one eye is missing and immediately is convinced that this is what he hit when he fired the gun in the night. He consequently accepts a burden of guilt and responsibility for the wild cat, without confiding his secret to anyone.

Caught in a struggle with his conscience between doing the right thing and trying to keep his secret, Ned begins to tell little lies to cover up. Soon his schoolwork begins to suffer and his behavior at home becomes unpredictable. He finds comfort in talking with his mother in her room. She senses an anxiety about Ned but never pressures him. His father is busy with his church activities but tries to remain open and receptive to Ned's needs for attention and company.

Mrs. Scallop, the nosy, talkative housekeeper who cooks and tends to Ned's mother while his father is at the church, becomes a pest to Ned as she tries to pry, using special treats to get close to him.

Mr. Scully is the person with whom Ned feels most comfortable, and Ned, in turn, provides company for the aging neighbor. Over cups of tea Ned helps Mr. Scully sort through boxes of old keepsakes, listening to the old man telling him that this job is necessary at this time of his life to put things in order. When Mr. Scully has a stroke and is placed in a nursing home, Ned visits him and keeps him informed of the wild cat's whereabouts. Just before the old man dies, Ned tells him of his suspicion that he must have shot the cat's eye out. Mr. Scully, who is no longer able to talk, responds with a squeeze of his hand to let Ned know he understands.

Finally, Ned tells his mother about taking the gun and the cat. He feels that a tremendous burden is lifted from him when his secret is revealed. Their bond is strengthened when Ned's mother, who is again able to walk a little as a result of a new treatment for her crippling arthritis, shares an experience of guilt with her son about her running away from home for three months.

Fox's thought-provoking story will appeal to sophisticated young readers and certainly to the mature gifted child. Complex plot, rich language, and a heart-wrenching sensitivity combine to impart a mood of tender relationships without sentimentality. The gentleness with which the author describes the life of Ned's family creates images of warmth, security, and caring among the members in this small secluded setting. Ned is soon established as a very real and human character, and thus the reader can identify with Ned's guilt and his struggles with his conscience.

Frank, Rudolf. *No Hero for the Kaiser.* Illus. by Klaus Steffens. Trans. by Patricia Crampton. New York: Lothrop, 1983, 222 pp. (Advanced)

Fourteen-year-old Jan and Flox, Vladimir the shepherd's dog, are the only living creatures left after Russian and German troops have destroyed Jan's small Polish village in 1914. Jan's father and Vladimir have left to join Russian troops fighting the Germans. Eventually, the boy and the dog are discovered by German soldiers, who take them along and provide food, clothing, and shelter. Jan becomes close to Albin Rosenlöcher, calling him "Papa." Little Panie (master), as Jan is affectionately called by the soldiers, serves them well by his knowledge of the terrain and his keen powers of observation to detect Russian observation posts and other enemy activity. He frequently warns the soldiers of dangers and saves many lives, thereby earning their respect and awe. Jan's freedom to use his intuition is contrasted with the soldiers' obedient but unthinking behavior.

As the war accelerates and the German soldiers cross the countryside, eventually serving on both fronts, Jan sees death and destruction in the form of dismembered bodies and the suffering wounded. He questions the devastation of the land and the soldiers' requisitioning the last food and animals from poor peasants. The boy is concerned not only about the effect of war on people but also on animals—horses driven beyond their endurance.

Amid these experiences and conflicting feelings, Jan is instrumental in the destruction of a town after he spots an ambush and passes on the order to fire. After the battle, Flox recognizes among the wounded a dying Russian soldier—his former master, Vladimir. Before dying, Vladimir gives Jan some postcards from Jan's father, who inquired about his son.

Trying to find a way to honor Jan for his courage and brave assistance, some of the soldiers propose petitioning for a German citizenship for the boy. The officers also think that such an act would increase a lagging enthusiasm for the war effort. However, on the day of the scheduled ceremony to grant Jan's citizenship—even the Kaiser was scheduled to visit—Jan decides not to accept and disappears.

This antiwar novel, originally published in 1931, was publicly burned in 1933 when Hitler was in power. In 1979 it was republished in West Germany.

Most chapters begin with a commentary on the irony and terrible waste of war, adding a didactic dimension to this very moving story. The bloody scenes of battles and the aftermath are vividly described, making the work suitable only for mature young readers. However, the tone is not always grim, as, for example, when Papa Rosenlöcher takes Jan home on leave at Christmas. But any joy is short-lived when a telegram brings news of another death, and Papa suffers a heart attack after being humiliated by a superior when he prepares to rejoin the army.

Highly able, mature young readers will respond ardently to the important universal messages about the futility and devastation of war. Sensitive youngsters may be moved to tears at descriptions of the suffering endured and the poignant scene when Flox recognizes his former master and licks his hands as the man sits, head drooping, dying.

Several full-page sepia-toned drawings focus on Jan and the soldiers and are as realistic as photographs. As a story of a boy's courage, loyalty, and struggle to make sense of the confusing world around him, Frank's work is outstanding. Jan's decision not to accept German citizenship serves as an example of rational thinking and the use of free will against a backdrop of emotionally charged propaganda.

Freedman, Florence B. *Brothers: A Hebrew Legend.* Illus. by Robert Andrew Parker. New York: Harper & Row, 1985, unp. (Beginning)

Seth, a wheat farmer, lived long ago in Israel where he had two sons, Dan and Joel. Thus begins a lovely legend about the beginning of Jerusalem.

As young boys, the two sons begin helping their father plant and harvest the wheat, taking time to play in the stalks while watching the crops grow. When Seth gets old and ready to die, he divides his land between the two brothers, and each builds his own house. Joel marries and has sons to help him with the wheat; Dan remains single. Both remain close and visit each other. When Joel has an unproductive year because of severe drought, he turns his thoughts to Dan, who has no sons to help him. He decides to take some wheat to Dan in the night and leave it on his threshing floor. At the same time Dan entertains similar thoughts of his brother. Knowing he has more mouths to feed, Dan also brings wheat. In the morning, the brothers, unaware that wheat has been brought to each of them by the other, notice their ample supply and realize that each could have given more wheat to the other. This realization prompts the brothers to repeat their unselfish activities the following night. Finally, Joel's family volunteers to help him in order to take more wheat to Dan. However, Dan is also bringing more wheat. This time they meet in the night and embrace in happiness. A soft voice surrounds them, praising their brotherly friendship.

After hundreds of years, the city of Jerusalem begins to develop on the spot where the brothers' farms once were, and Solomon's Temple is subsequently built where they had met in the night. When the Temple is completed, the voice formerly heard praising the two brothers sounds again as the story ends.

Freedman's text is brief, using simple sentences to convey a deep message of brotherly love and sharing without rivalry. Parker's pen-and-ink drawings combined with subtle watercolors enhance each page of the book. Wheat fields and harvesting are depicted in golden yellows and browns, and deep blues color the many starlit night scenes. Peach and pink gloriously portray sketches of Jerusalem and Solomon's Temple.

This warmly written straightforward tale holds appeal for young children and evokes deeper feelings in gifted youngsters who can understand the depth of the brothers' relationship and the significance of this universally meaningful legend.

Freedman, Russell. *Children of the Wild West.* Photographs. New York: Clarion, 1983, 104 pp. (Intermediate)

Black-and-white photographs enhance this story of children and their families traveling west in the early days of the nineteenth century. The author explains how photographs were laboriously developed during frontier days of limited technology and crude processes. Covered wagons served as darkrooms, camera equipment was bulky, and action photographs were unheard of until the 1880s. However, people hoping for a photograph of themselves would remain absolutely still for this lengthy procedure.

Traveling west from Missouri in a wagon train in the 1840s was harsh and often seemed unendurable, as depicted in Freedman's account of daily occurrences and hardships encountered along the way. Life is characterized by long days beginning before dawn filled with countless activities, including those necessary to prepare for night, such as feeding the livestock, cooking meals, and circling and securing the wagon train for safety. The reader is drawn into the activity of riding on the bumpy Oregon Trail, battling insects, dust, heat, and cold and possible enemies. Every family possession was carried in the wagon, including all supplies. However, as rivers and streams were crossed, many cherished possessions had to be discarded to lighten the load. People succumbed to severe weather conditions or illnesses, and oxen and mules died from exhaustion or were slaughtered for food when supplies ran low.

Although the smallest children and their mothers usually rode in the covered wagon, some pioneers had to finish the trip by foot or horseback when wagons were abandoned. Six to eight months of treacherous travel claimed the lives of many children, but those surviving welcomed the rich valleys of Oregon and California with the promise of hope and freedom. The discovery of gold in California also lured many of the frontier people, who rushed to the coast, disregarding the possibility of settling on the plains.

The American Indians encountered along the Oregon Trail are also introduced, always in a positive and realistic manner, and their lifestyles, customs, and relationships with the settlers are explored. Excellent photographs depict Indian villages and children.

Gradually, sod houses were built to house families on the plains. These homes became more comfortable as pioneers learned how to reinforce and decorate them. Soon frontier towns sprang up to accommodate trading of crops. Eventually, cities developed as schools, churches, and stores were built. The country school, in which students of all ages were taught in one room by one teacher, will interest children in making comparisons with their school experiences today. Many children could attend school only part time because they had to devote long hours to helping their parents with various tasks on the farm. Freedman describes many of these responsibilities, some humorously. Regardless of their rugged life-style, pioneer children enjoyed parties and games, such as races, picnics, ball games, dancing, and special celebrations, most of which were held on weekends.

This attractive book, which includes a table of contents and index, acquaints today's children with the character-building experiences on which this country was built, emphasizing the strength and courage of pioneer people. It is an excellent account of a particular part of American history, portrayed with an honesty that enriches the literature of children both young and old. Gifted children with an interest in our country's heritage will appreciate the authenticity of this presentation.

Frost, Robert. *A Swinger of Birches.* Illus. by Peter Koeppen. Owings Mills, Md.: Stemmer, 1982, 79 pp. (Intermediate)

In an introduction by Clifton Fadiman, Robert Frost is remembered as a poet who preferred to "say" or "talk" his poetry rather than recite it, thereby conveying meaning through his voice, tone, hesitations, and so on. Telling us that good poetry is the shortest way of saying something complicated, Fadiman classifies Frost's poetry as "good," meaning much is said with few words.

This collection of 38 poems includes some familiar ones, such as "The Road Not Taken" and "Stopping by Woods on a Snowy Evening." Others are less well known—"Canis Major" and "A Peck of Gold." The book also contains "The Gift Outright," "The Pasture," "The Last Word of a Bluebird," "Fire and Ice," "The Runaway," "Tree at My Window," "Departmental," "A Passing Glimpse," "Mending Wall," "A Young Birch," "Now Close the Windows," and others.

All poems, simply written in enriching language, deal with the earth and its treasures and the feelings they evoke. Grouped according to season, from one early spring to the next, the poems begin with "Birches" and end with "A Patch of Old Snow." Each season is depicted in full colors with every poem gloriously illustrated. Koeppen's exquisite detailed portrayals of paths and meadows invite the reader to come into the book. A glossary clarifies less familiar words.

This superb volume of large, picture-book size provides an excellent selection for elementary age and older children. For younger children who may be meeting Frost for the first time, the poems enlarge their appreciation of fine poetry. Older readers, in turn, will grasp Frost's nostalgia and romanticism and thus share with the poet the harmony and inner peace that permeate his work. The young gifted "poet" or those who particularly enjoy the deep meaning and language of poetry will find Frost a favorite.

Gallant, Roy A. *Lost Cities.* Photographs. New York: Watts, 1985, 64 pp. (Advanced)

Seven chapters that are abundant in archaeological information about the lost cities of Crete, Mycenae, Troy, Pompeii, and Chichén Itzá constitute this highly readable volume. A description of how cities became "lost"begins with the destruction of Helike and St. Pierre and ends with the eruption of Mount St. Helens during our time.

A discussion of the island of Crete, in ancient Greece, begins with an account of the myth of Theseus and the Minotaur. Throughout the centuries many scholars have written of the legend, including Sir Arthur Evans, who searched for the legendary home of Minos and the Minotaur. In his pursuit, Evans' workers uncovered the Minoan palace that Gallant describes in meticulous detail. Gallant concludes that the apparently peace-loving Minoans were probably destroyed by volcanic explosion.

In his discussion of the city of Mycenae, known as the city of gold, Gallant tells of how archaeologists unearthed artifacts made of gold, in much the same way plastic is used today. Describing the Mycenaeans as a strong and powerful civilization, Gallant can only speculate as to their disappearance.

The author provides a wonderful story of the history of Troy and gives an extensive coverage of Pompeii's destruction and the devastation left in the wake of Mount Vesuvius's eruption. Gallant's thorough and fascinating account of this disaster makes one wish to visit these ruins firsthand.

The readers' travels bring them closer to home with a description of the Mayan civilization in southern Mexico. The mystery surrounding the end of the Mayan culture still remains unsolved, encouraging young intellectuals to find out more about the resourceful people that once made up this civiliza-tion. In conclusion, Gallant lists several other ancient sites, such as Atlantis and Stonehenge, accompanied with explanations and speculations as to their origin.

This excellent resource contains a table of contents, index, and a bibliogra-phy for further investigation, in addition to black-and-white diagrams, maps, and photographs. Using sophisticated language unique to describing ancient civilizations, the author appeals to the gifted child's ability to analyze and deduce conclusions. In addition, gifted children will be drawn to learn about ancient and medieval civilizations and try to seek underlying answers to explain the rise and fall or disappearance of these cultures.

Gardner, Beau. *Guess What?* Illus. by author. New York: Lothrop, 1985, unp. (Beginning)

Given visual clues and no text, readers are invited to guess which animal is being represented. For instance, parts of a commonly recognized farm, zoo, or wild animal—a rooster's tail, a peacock's feathers, a skunk's tail—are illustrated in bright, bold shapes on each right-hand page. On the verso, the entire animal appears in dark gray against a lighter gray background with the detail outlined by a narrow white rectangle. The animal is identified in small white type in the lower left corner of the page. Brilliant illustrations using only a few contrasting colors, such as red, blue, and yellow and pink and orange against yellow, highlight the featured details.

Without textual clues, readers must visualize part-whole relationships to identify the animal creatures in this puzzlelike format. "Answer" drawings are clear enough that even preschoolers who have a recognition knowledge of many animals without yet being able to read can interpret and synthesize the visual clues and arrive at the correct answer. Very young children will enjoy the colorful challenges as they stretch their imaginations.

Gardner, Beau. *Have You Ever Seen . . . ? An ABC Book.* Illus. by author. New York: Dodd, Mead, 1986, unp. (Beginning)

Original, humorous, and creative, *Have You Ever Seen . . . ?* is a striking alphabet book in which text and graphics assume almost equal importance. Showing bold, solid-shaped figures contrasted against crayon-bright colors, the pages seem to glow with a variety of brilliant hues. Upper- and lowercase forms of each alphabet letter are printed in stark white at the top of each page (the complete alphabet appears on a chart at the back of the book). Within the text, examples of words beginning with the featured letter stand out in uppercase letters. Thus, odd pairings of attributes, accessories, or actions combine to answer the question posed by the title in reference to each letter of the alphabet. Response phrases combined with the clever graphics are unique and funny, such as "a turtle with a tie?"

Young preschoolers who have not yet learned to read will be able to decode most words because of their familiarity and the clear and vivid graphics. This alphabet book is ideal for enriching preschoolers' expressive language as well as their imaginations and would also appeal to beginning readers who delight in the humorous aspects of unique word combinations. Stimulated by this exciting book, readers will want to use alphabet letters to invent their own personal answers to "Have you ever seen . . . ?"

Gardner, Robert. *Ideas for Science Projects.* New York: Watts, 1986, 146 pp. (Intermediate)

This unusual science-experiment book asks more questions than it answers and provides a wide range of projects and experiments bound to interest many readers. Gardner recommends a systematic approach to inquiry consisting of (1) researching a topic, (2) using the five senses to make observations, (3) employing trial-and-error experimentation, (4) controlling variables, and (5) designing an experiment so it can be replicated. Without providing a specific procedural guide for every project, Gardner encourages careful notetaking to record a statement of the problem, plan, observations, results, and conclusions. At the same time, he warns readers that not every project will conclude as anticipated but that the process is what is important. Gardner also provides a guide for preparing science fair reports and displaying materials and includes names and addresses of national science competitions.

According to Gardner, some of the experiments and projects in the book (projects are of varying levels of difficulty) are meant to motivate further inquiry; others are sufficiently detailed for the young reader to follow. Each chapter focuses on one area of science: experiments with water, astronomy, light and optics, chemistry, physics, heat, electricity, psychology, botany, and zoology. Readers are encouraged to expand their interests by trying projects in several areas.

Within each chapter, subheadings indicate the particular projects. Among the detailed discussions of experiments in the chapter on chemistry, for example, are experiments to determine how much oxygen is in the air, finding natural acid-base indicators using fruits and vegetables, and estimating the maximum volume of an ion. Readers are also given opportunities to design their own projects, such as devising a method for separating the components of a mixture and finding out how to identify samples of metals. In the chapter on heat the reader is exposed to research about caloric mass and challenged to experiment with measuring the temperature of a flame and to investigate heat loss, surface area, insulation and R values. However, adult supervision is recommended.

The chapter on psychology includes optical illusions and observing a person during REM sleep and explains how to determine physical condition (using the Harvard step test) and a person's reaction time, calculate power, and measure the strength of muscle pairs. Some of the more unusual projects in the chapter on plants deal with how to separate plant pigments and clone plants. In the chapter on animal science, readers have an opportunity to apply many observational skills when conducting the experiments. Some of the suggested projects involve observing and feeding birds, preserving animal tracks, collecting and preserving spider webs, observing the life cycle of mealworms, studying the gulping rate of goldfish under different water temperature conditions, and examining the behavior of various insects.

Ample safety cautions printed in boldface type appear throughout the text as readers are warned not to handle hot objects, to be careful with flames, and not to look at a laser beam. For initial emphasis, there is a "Safety First" page in the introduction. Black-and-white drawings and diagrams enhance Gardner's explanations of apparatus while illustrating size and other relationships. The book is particularly valuable for gifted readers, as the level of questions stimulates further inquiry, asking readers to go beyond the information given them to design their own experiments and arrive at their own conclusions. Answers are not always apparent, nor are they directly provided. Most intermediate-grade youngsters seeking ideas for science projects will find a wealth of ideas and questions to guide their explorations.

Gardner, Robert. *Science around the House.* Illus. by Frank Cecala. New York: Messner, 1985, 123 pp. (Intermediate)

Materials commonly found at home—in the kitchen, basement, or garage— form the basis for simple experiments that demonstrate basic principles of physics. Readers are directed to use straws, paper clips, and other household materials to try out balances, measure the stickiness of liquids, such as soapy water, alcohol, and cooking oil; compare densities of liquids and solids, and weigh solids, liquids, and air. Other investigations focus on evaporation, condensation, humidity, and air pressure. Galileo's questions about falling objects, pendulums, and the law of inertia are examined in an easy-to-comprehend manner that relates examples of each scientific law to everyday experiences, such as moving forward in one's seat when a moving vehicle suddenly stops. Newton's laws of forces and accelerations are introduced by using a carpenter's level as an accelerometer. Readers are shown ways to reach the ceiling by lifting objects into the air with such forces as air blown through a straw, a vacuum cleaner, and an electromagnet. Readers are encouraged to analyze images in mirrors, bending light, rainbows, and shadows.

In contrast to many science experiment books that begin with lengthy explanations, Gardner's volume gets the reader's attention immediately with a brief introduction that usually includes a question to make the reader start thinking. For example, readers are asked if they know where their center of gravity is, what their reaction time is, how far away a storm is, what keeps an airplane in the air, and other similar questions that often intrigue children. Specific answers to most questions are not provided. Rather, these and other questions are explored through hands-on constructions and manipulations explained in clear text and diagrams. Scientific terminology is explained in familiar vocabulary and by relating physical phenomena to experiential background. In addition to scientific information, young readers are encouraged to use caution and to respect the rights of other household members when working with materials.

The particular value of this book to gifted readers is that results and conclusions are not explicitly stated, allowing readers to use their own thinking skills. Also, the experiments and demonstrations provide many hours of challenge and fun.

Garfield, Leon. *Fair's Fair.* Illus. by S. D. Schindler. New York: Doubleday, 1981, 32 pp. (Intermediate)

On a cold and snowy night, two orphans—a boy and girl—are brought, separately, by a huge dog to a mansion where their lives will be changed forever. However, before arriving at this mysterious haven, Jackson and Lillipolly must first undergo a test of endurance. A key, found under Growler's collar, begins the long, patient, and trying task of finding the door it will fit.

Finally, the dog leads Jackson to the house where Jackson finds Lillipolly, who had been brought there previously in the same manner. After sharing their stories that explain their unusual journey to the mansion, the children discover that they are mysteriously being provided food and warmth while they are sleeping. They, in turn, keep the house polished and sparkling, anxiously waiting for the inhabitants to "come home for Christmas."

However, after a while the food stops arriving, and Jackson and Lillipolly once again experience hunger. When six mince pies suddenly appear, they decide to save them to eat after dark, but their generosity is tested as six carolers arrive in the freezing snow. Consistent with their kind nature, the children give away the pies.

Returning to the fireside, Jackson and Lillipolly encounter two men who appear to be burglars. When the children tell the men that the owners of the house will be coming home for Christmas, the men discard their disguises and reveal their true identity as the mansion's owner and his lawyer. It's a relief to learn that the master had planned the whole episode to find two homeless children who were kind, patient, brave, honest, and generous to live with him. Without realizing it, Jackson and Lillipolly had proved their worth just by doing what came naturally to them. As the story progresses, "fair's fair" is the expression used by everybody at some time.

English phrases and customs season this story, which unfolds shortly before Christmas in a quiet village. The reader is drawn into the deep snow-covered streets with Jackson and can almost feel the icy flakes floating down. The silence of the snow piling up enhances the reader's desire for Jackson to hurry and find a warm, comfortable place to stay for the night. The little village is dark and closed into itself. The magnificent illustrations dwarf the characters and portray the grandeur and opulence of a world unknown to them. Schindler's illustrations are so full of feeling that they could almost stand alone to tell the story.

Despite overtones of sentimentality, Garfield's theme is fresh and significant, conveying the message that genuine benevolence is rewarded in time. Although most children who read the book may not really identify with the orphan characters and may perceive Jackson's and Lillipolly's goodness as trite, this tender and meaningful story leaves readers to make the judgment concerning reality. Through his use of foreshadowing, Garfield introduces young readers to a popular mystery story technique and weaves an intriguing plot that will stimulate creative thinking in gifted readers, encouraging them to mentally elaborate on his original ideas in this story.

Geisert, Arthur. *Pigs from A to Z*. Boston: Houghton Mifflin, 1986, 64 pp. (Beginning)

Hidden letter forms and frolicking, slender pigs engaged in building a treehouse make this an unusual alphabet book that can be read with renewed enjoyment many times. Each alphabet letter accompanied by brief text is printed on a creamy white page followed by large, full-page black-and-beige-toned, complex, detailed etchings. Through concise text of only a sentence or two per page ("K is for kicking over the nail keg. A small catastrophe.") and illustrations, a story is told of seven skilled, self-reliant pigs that, after finding the ideal spot, build a multilevel treehouse and then return to the comfort of their parents' home, weary from the day's work.

Each illustrated page contains seven pigs, five letter forms of the leading letter, and one each of the preceding and following letters. Each illustration shows the pigs engaged in either working on the treehouse or at play or rest. Chopping wood and transporting lumber over a gorge and through an eerie forest are just a few of the exciting events. To relax in between the construction, the pig siblings play hide-and-seek, float on a river, play improvised musical instruments, play a game of croquet, and find time to nap. While some of the pigs and letters are obvious, others are more obscure, and it takes considerable scanning to locate all figures. A key in the back of the book reveals hidden letters.

Hidden figure puzzles are not new, but Geisert's etchings of pigs with humanlike expressions on their porcine faces have a fresh, intriguing appeal. Discovering the hidden letter forms and concealed pigs demands both visual discrimination and spatial relationships skills and perseverance. Not every child will want to spend the time necessary to locate every pig or letter form; however, many will delight in persevering until they have uncovered all of the puzzles. Finding each alphabet letter is tricky enough; the additional challenge of locating all seven pigs in each scene is a special treat. Developing flexibility of thought, youngsters use divergent thinking to explore visually the possible hidden locations of the pigs and letters. This visually puzzling alphabet book should appeal to both beginning and more experienced readers.

Gerrard, Roy. *Sir Cedric.* Illus. by author. New York: Farrar, 1984, unp. (Beginning)

Gerrard's epic poem of Cedric the knight is rewarding reading both in terms of text and illustrations. Designed in a picture-book format, this book appeals to older children in style and content and to young audiences because of its humorous illustrations of small, rotund people with rather oversized heads.

Sir Cedric was a good and highly respected knight. He is seen astride his long-legged white horse against the background of his castle and clumps of daisies. So far, life has been rather predictable, but now Cedric is ready for more exciting adventures.

Cedric dresses himself and his fine horse, Old Walter, in impressive armor and bids castle members farewell as he departs, taking along some cucumber sandwiches. Along the way he meets country people of similar appearance. They are walking with a pig as large as they. Eventually, Cedric nears a clearing and encounters Black Ned, the wicked knight. Black Ned has a pleasing princess, named Matilda, locked in his tower with plans to marry her. But Matilda does not share his desires and would rather die. Responding to Black Ned's challenge to an on-the-spot duel, Cedric knocks Black Ned from his mount into a stream and rescues Matilda. The two soon become smitten with each other, and when he delivers her home, Matilda's parents, the King and Queen, are happy and relieved to see her alive again and invite Cedric to celebrate her homecoming with them.

Soon a marriage proposal and a feast follow, but during the festivity, news is brought that Black Ned is gathering an army to fight for Matilda. When the guests demonstrate their anxiety by starting to leave, Cedric jumps up on the table to command their attention. He instructs them to take up their arms and follow him to stop Black Ned once and for all. He leads the group through beautifully depicted forests and valleys.

In the ensuing battle, Cedric wins, and they all have tea—such is the custom. The humane knight sets Black Ned free, but not without dire warning to change his wicked ways. Sir Cedric and Matilda marry and live happily forever after, of course.

This rhythmic epic, while seemingly telling the usual story of good winning over evil, uses well-written, rich language. The droll expressions of the people and the tongue-in-cheek humor will be particularly appealing to the sophisticated picture-book reader.

A thread of humor is woven through the text accentuated by the exaggerated proportions of the characters, which are sure to delight the imagination. Illustrations are breathtakingly beautiful with a medieval flair, particularly the intricately drawn borders surrounding each page. Flowers and decorations are abundant, and the quaint little people sport droll facial expressions. The color is magnificent and the attention to detail is meticulous. Rhyme is pleasantly consistent except for one varied verse. Poems and illustrations are pleasantly appealing and make the book a study in satisfying literature.

Gibbons, Gail. *From Path to Highway: The Story of the Boston Post Road.* New York: Crowell, 1986, 32 pp. (Beginning)

Readers are introduced to aspects of temporal change through the story of the Boston Post Road connecting New York City and Boston, from its beginning as an Indian trail to its current stage as a four-lane highway. The chronology of this important traffic artery is related through a brief text consisting of a paragraph per page and appealing, colorful American-primitive-style illustrations depicting the passage of time through the changing seasons as well as different modes of transportation and architecture. Horses, stagecoaches, and other types of vehicles move from left to right along the path, thereby naturally leading the reader's eye to the next page. A simple map indicates the three separate branches of the Boston Post Road, as well as Boston, New York City, and other cities along the routes.

The primitive paths trampled by the feet of Indians and colonists became known as "roads" in the 1700s when colonists used horse-drawn carts and wagons to travel between settlements, and stagecoaches shorten the trip between Boston and New York City. With the Revolutionary War in 1775, routine use of the post roads is halted so soldiers and equipment can be transported. After the war, the road undergoes many improvements—roadbeds are strengthened and turnpikes are installed. Roadside inns also spring up, offering comfort to weary travelers. Using parts of the southern road, the train, in 1850, begins to rival the road as a transportation mode. However, by 1920, with the invention of the automobile, the road, now paved, assumes its former importance, eventually becoming a four-lane highway. A list of famous travelers adds interest.

Although the text is sparse and hence does not contribute significantly to the concepts conveyed by the brightly colored illustrations, the book offers a challenge for young beginning readers who are developing temporal concepts. Understanding that it took two weeks to travel between New York City and Boston on horseback in the late 1600s compared to less than one day on today's super highway requires the ability to integrate information about time and method of transportation. The story allows able young readers to identify the consequences of road improvements over time. The book is most appropriate for being read with an adult companion who can supply more information and encourage the beginning reader to make associations between the facts presented and the child's own experiences.

Gibbons, Gail. *Up Goes the Skyscraper!* Illus. by author. New York: Four Winds, 1986 unp. (Beginning)

A skyscraper is under construction in this tall, thin volume for young children, who are invited to take a close look at the piece-by-piece building of the giant structure.

Gibbons starts out by explaining the reason for building a skyscraper—to allow many people to live and work in a limited space on a city block. After a site survey, the steps necessary before the foundation can be built are illustrated. Plans are drawn, one page of the book showing a blueprint with labels and definitions for each major part of the building. Next, a temporary wall is built around the construction area with little windows for interested passersby to watch the people at work. Later, heavy equipment is brought to the site, each piece carefully labeled and accompanied by a clear description of its function.

Gradually, the reader sees how skeletal steel framework is assembled as each new column and beam is set in place. Thanks to effective, yet simple, illustrations, readers can see tower cranes at work high above the foundation and men and women at work on every level of the structure. In fact, the book appears to grow taller as the reader turns the pages and the skyscraper reaches high against a bright blue sky.

As fireproofing and wall sections are added, we see workers inside the building carrying out their specific jobs—electricians, carpenters, plumbers, heating-cooling specialists, and elevator installers.

At the "topping out," the last piece of steel is added. The traditional evergreen is placed on top for good luck and a celebration is held. But inside, the finish workers must complete their jobs before the skyscraper is completely done. This also includes interior design and decorating and the addition of safety features such as sprinkling systems. Finally, when the temporary wall is removed, the skyscraper is open for business.

Gibbons illustrates a complicated building process with clarity and encourages gifted children to employ higher-level thinking skills of analysis and synthesis. Sharpening children's powers of observation and awareness in this manner will help them utilize the information whenever they see an actual skyscraper under construction. The emphasis on the planning, construction, and completion of a skyscraper illustrates the interdependency of the individuals involved in this monumental feat. In addition, the author manages to incorporate an aesthetic element by showing that the building of a skyscraper is architecturally a work of art.

The brightly colored pages are filled with crisp, clear illustrations and definitions, making a glossary unnecessary. Technical material and vocabulary are brought down to a low reading level without losing their complexity.

Giblin, James Cross. *Chimney Sweeps: Yesterday and Today.* Illus. by Margot Tomes. New York: Crowell, 1982, 56 pp. (Intermediate)

More adventuresome than an ordinary history book, *Chimney Sweeps* details an old European profession in a delightful and informative story.

Before exploring the historical aspects of chimney sweeping, Giblin introduces the reader to a day in the life of a contemporary chimney sweep in America. Today's "sweeps" retain their black top hat and tails but use cleaning instruments more advanced than those of nineteenth-century England. Instead of today's vacuums and extension rods, small young boys, called "climbing boys," actually scuttled up the chimney, removing soot as they worked their way to the top.

Chimneys, a sign of wealth in the 1100s in England, resulted from Queen Elizabeth I's influence. People wishing to appear prosperous and affluent, placed false chimneys on their roofs until King Charles II taxed them, causing their instant removal.

Architecturally and economically, chimneys proved to be effcient and worthwhile, and construction spread to other countries. In time, the realization that chimneys required proper cleaning led to the emergence of the chimney sweep.

Superstition surrounded the chimney sweep in early times. Their attire of black hat and tailcoat, obtained from undertakers, is still a mystery. Some suggest they wore these clothes to gain respectability; others claim it was to obscure the soot inevitably encountered. Symbolic of the long winter season, chimney sweeps followed the character representing spring and summer in the May Day parade in old England. Sweeps were also believed to bring good luck because their potentially dangerous profession resulted in few accidents.

This view was enhanced after a sweep almost fell from a roof and was saved by a young lady, creating the custom in England for a sweep to kiss the bride as she leaves the church. In another incident, a sweep rescued the king from his startled horses and won respect for the profession once again.

As London's population rapidly increased, houses became taller and narrower, resulting in smaller chimneys. Thus, chimney cleaning became more difficult, yet still necessary, because of the danger of fire from soot buildup. Small boys, called "climbing boys," were used to clean soot from these newer chimneys. Children were widely exploited for this purpose and received very little compensation. After years of service, these boys could scarcely do anything else, for their health and growth were retarded. Many ended up on the streets.

Giblin devotes a full chapter to the typical daily experiences of the climbing boys. The treatment, lack of care, and disrespect for their young lives are described in detail, from the early hours of dawn to late at night. Many were orphans, and some were offered as sweeps by parents too poor to care for them. In the 1800s, a thorough investigation of this unlawful practice resulted in preventing children from working as chimney sweeps.

A device, invented to replace the boys, successfully cleaned most of London's chimneys; other chimneys had to be reconstructed to accommodate the new instrument. However, since this was expensive, children continued to serve as climbing boys until a law was passed in 1875 to protect them.

Excellent black-and-white photographs and diagrams, some humorous, complement the text, illustrating the activities of chimney sweeps. The poem "The Chimney Sweep" by William Blake lends a fitting touch to the conclusion of the book.

Giblin deals with an unfamiliar topic in an entertaining way, motivating readers to seek additional information about customs and habits in old England. Gifted children who are interested in this period in history will be stimulated by the quaint folklore surrounding this unique profession of long ago.

Giblin, James Cross. *Walls: Defenses throughout History.* Photog. and illus. by Anthony Kramer. Boston: Little, Brown, 1984, 113 pp. (Advanced)

Beginning with prehistoric times when walls were constructed of mammoth bones, this book offers a history of walls throughout the ages. Included are ancient walled cities, such as Jericho, and the Western Wall in Jerusalem, which partly remains today, a sacred place in Jewish history.

Advancing to another famous wall, the Carcassonne Wall, Giblin points out that the legend surrounding this construction is, after all, untrue. According to legend, after Charlemagne's five-year siege, the food supply of the city of Carcassonne had dwindled to practically nothing. An old woman, Dame Carcas, decided to roast a pig, stuff it with grain, and lower it over the wall for the enemy to see. When she shook the pig, the grain scattered, implying the food supply was still abundant. Seeing this, the army abandoned the city. The grateful inhabitants named the city for Dame Carcas.

In his review of the well-known Great Wall of China, the author explores the events that led to the construction of this archaeological wonder, emphasizing the magnitude of the task and the labor, materials, and time involved.

In a chapter on castle walls, Giblin explains the construction of "motte-and-bailey" castles where a huge artificial mound with a palisade of wooden logs around the top of it is surrounded by land and water. Other types of castle designs include the "square keep," which is like the Tower of London, where stone replaced wood for durability and strength. The "shell keep," which is like Restormel, an English castle, was also made of stone, but with a circular design with buildings inside them.

The description of castle walls used as fortresses is followed by a discussion of walls built to withstand artillery fire. Included are descriptions of famous artists' designs, such as those of Leonardo da Vinci and Albrecht Durer, that modified the shape and height of castle walls but were economically unwise to build. Instead, the "bastion," designed by Italian engineers, became the major fortification defense of castles worldwide.

Evolving from bastions, military forts were later built in Canada and the United States, including Fort Ticonderoga, Fort McHenry, Fort Sumter, and Fort Pulaski.

As a further sophisticated development, forts were built underground to escape destructive fire artillery. Known as "trenches" during World War I, these "walls" evolved during World War II to the Maginot line—a wall of fortifications between France and Germany—of elaborate design. Giblin also explains the purpose of the Berlin Wall and some of its effects on Germany. Giblin concludes with a proposal that a wall be built some day in space composed of satellites. The possible results of such a wall in time of war are also explored.

Walls is an excellent introduction to some of the most fascinating constructions in the world. With its chronologically proceeding historical background, Giblin's well-researched subject will inspire many readers to learn more of particular walls. The many well-captioned black-and-white photographs introduce readers to views of constructions usually not seen in other works. Vocabulary unique to each type of wall is well defined in the text and in the glossary. A bibliography and an index are also included.

Gilman, Dorothy. *The Maze in the Heart of the Castle.* New York: Doubleday, 1983, 230 pp. (Advanced)

Grieving the loss of his parents who mysteriously have died, Colin, a 16-year-old boy, seeks a way to rid himself of his sorrow and anger. His search for meaning takes him to a castle behind whose walls awaits a maze so complex that the teenager's life will be changed forever if he decides to enter. Colin accepts the challenge and approaches the castle with a positive, expectant spirit, aware of the great dangers and hardships he will encounter on his way to the faraway land of Galt, known as Utopia, at the end of the maze.

The Grand Odlum, the wise old man who is the keeper of the maze, tells Colin he must keep the sun in his heart and guard against darkness. Bidding him farewell, Colin enters the maze of very high stone walls—a place without time. After many unsuccessful attempts to find his way out, Colin eventually stumbles upon a group of people whose grayish-green skin matches the thick walls and foliage of the maze. They inform Colin that there is no way out of the maze. Some of them have been trying to find an exit for a long time, but have finally resigned themselves to dying in the maze. Their routine celebration of their misery astounds Colin, who does not accept this fate but persists in finding an escape. Upon his request, the people form a human ladder to the top of the wall and pull each person up. Colin is elated at the successful accomplishment of this task, but his helpers feel compelled to return to their maze, having given up a better life long ago.

Colin continues exploring the top of the maze walls until he finally jumps down to the harsh desert country below. He soon meets a young boy who has been cast out to die by the evil Talmars, who live in a kingdom inside the cliffs. Colin provides food and drink for his new friend, Zan, who relates the cruel punishments suffered by the slaves within the walls.

When Colin and Zan are captured by the Talmars, they find a way to escape and take several prisoners with them. They soon face the king's men again, and a fierce battle ensues. Unknowingly, Colin kills the king with his slingshot. The prisoners are released from the torture chamber, and Zan is made king. Colin knows it is time for him to continue his travels alone, and the people generously give him provisions for the journey. Soon afterward, he is approached by a mysterious young girl who claims she is Zan's sister and wishes to accompany him. It is not long before Colin finds himself enamored of Charmian and she of him—or so it seems. Later, when she becomes a bitter enemy, Colin is mystified, and finally, heartbroken.

Deserted, Colin travels on, but is finally overcome with cold and exhaustion. Having fallen asleep, he awakens in an underground community to which he has been taken by the Despas, the cave people. The Despas have come through the maze also, but have not continued their quest. Colin remains in a state of exhaustion and sleepfulness for weeks before he realizes that the Despas are giving him drugged tea to keep him there. The Grand Odlum's warning to protect himself against darkness rings in his ears. Colin learns he cannot leave of his own free will. Finally, he temporarily stuns the people with sunlight when he quickly removes the heavy animal skins that cover all entrances to the outside.

After escaping, Colin wearily resumes his journey. He soon enters "bandit country" where he meets Raoul and his sister, Serena, who become warm, caring friends. The three travel together for a time, cautiously avoiding bandits in the forest. They part, with plans to meet in a village across the valley. Colin is captured by a bandit who keeps him in a cage not large enough for him to stand up in. Here Colin is fed only with food that is thrown to him by vicious and curious onlookers. Stripped of all dignity, near madness and death, Colin suddenly remembers the Grand Odlum, and his thoughts are strengthened once again. He begins to take charge of his thoughts, remembers the maze and all that has happened to him, and finally finds peace in his soul.

One day, Colin finds a fresh orange inside his cage and soon learns it has been brought by Serena, who plans his release. Colin insists on the release of his only friend, a huge mountain lion in a nearby cage, refusing to move until the lion's rescue has been promised. Gayno, his keeper, has decided to kill Colin before a crowd of people, but Serena arrives in time to save him. They escape to the hills knowing Gayno and his bandit followers will not stop until they capture them. Magically, they are protected by a mysterious closing together of the trees and, finally, enter the land of Galt, where peace reigns.

Gilman has written a superb story of a young boy's courageous adherence to his beliefs and values. Characterization is strong and memorable. The plot is involved, suspenseful, and moving, culminating in an exciting conclusion. Colin's willingness to accept the challenge of the maze and all that lies between it and Galt is courageous, indeed. Readers share his emotional pain when he is rejected by the evil Charmian, experience his distress while held captive like an animal, and rejoice with him when he finally reaches Galt.

Goble, Paul. *The Great Race of the Birds and Animals.* Illus. by author. New York: Bradbury, 1985, 32 pp. (Intermediate)

Paul Goble's fantastic folktale of the relationship between humans and animals begins with the amusing statement that buffaloes used to consume people and proceeds to explain this phenomenon. The Creator designates the crow to summon all creatures to the hills where he organizes a race between man and the buffalo. The judges of the race will decide the winner; if the buffaloes win, they may continue to eat man. However, if man wins, he will hunt and eat buffaloes and have dominion over all four-legged animals.

The Creator instructs the participants to choose sides—two-legged creatures against four-legged creatures. With the call of the wild wolf and the coyote, the race is on. The fastest runner of each side is set in competition to decide the fate of man once and for all. The blue sky is filled with birds flying high and fast, except the lagging magpie, who lands on the buffalo's back. The birds soon stop for water but ingest too much and drunkenly fall asleep. Buffalo and man race on, with the magpie getting a free ride. Gradually, various animals drop out of the race and begin to establish the habits they have today.

Buffalo and man continue the race for days, with man finally showing fatigue while the buffalo charges on, though exhausted. When the buffalo nears the finish line first, the crowd cheers for the four-legged obvious winner. Then the magpie shoots into the air and across the finish line first, declaring two-legged creatures the winners and, finally, man's dominion over the buffalo. As a result of the race, man only hunts and kills the buffalo for necessary food; the magpie's feathers become a symbol of pride and honor, and Indian legend has it they are beautifully colored by the sun's rays; finally, dust from the race creates the Milky Way.

Goble's clear, clean designs are breathtaking in all their splendor. Rich, colorful illustrations spread across the book's pages, invoking the rhythm of the running buffaloes throughout the book. By means of his powerful illustrations, the author presents a magnificent symbolism of the proud, earth-loving Indians. A touch of humor is supplied by the ingenious magpie who rides on the buffalo's back to win the race.

Gifted young children will enjoy the race, while older readers can interpret the author's intent behind depicting humankind's rule over all creatures and the interrelationship of all living things.

Goffstein, M. B. *Artists' Helpers Enjoy the Evenings.* Illus. by author. New York: Harper & Row, 1987, unp. (Beginning)

Abstract, clean lines on a muted, shaded background surround a small group of chummy different-colored crayons aptly named Blanc, Noir, Gris, Bistre, and Sanguine (their names correspond to their color). Known as "artists' helpers," the crayons are shown holding hands as they stroll across the pages at the beginning of the book. The significance of their names is explained when the five friends discuss the importance of sticking together in different situations. For example, they must be careful to hold on to Sanguine in the desert (his darkish-red color is close to the color of sand); similarly, Gris could easily be lost in the gray twilight of dusk; a close watch must be kept on Noir and Bistre in the blackness of night; and against the whiteness of snow they must make sure they know where Blanc is.

As a typical day advances toward evening, the crayons leave the artists' studio and head for a café where they engage in lively conversations about such artists' terms as "shading" and "outlining." After an evening of singing and movement, the crayons go home—some to their families, some to empty dwellings. Once, when the crayons are invited to a masquerade ball, they disguise themselves as each other and have a merry time dancing.

The theme of this picture book may prove too subtle for even gifted young children to read alone; however, if an adult reads the story aloud, the creativity of the little story can be enhanced as perhaps the author intended. Early clarification of the French names for the crayon colors will help children enjoy the illustrations more. The theme of this otherwise simple story is unique and sophisticated.

Goffstein, M. B. *School of Names*. Illus. by author. New York: Harper & Row, 1986, unp. (Beginning)

Deceptively simple in appearance, the book deals with humankind's need to feel a relationship with the other inhabitants and elements of the world. The brief work is told in the first person from the narrator's point of view. In the first section, the narrator explains the need to attend the "School of Names" to learn the names of the stars, plants, ocean life, rocks and minerals, continents, oceans, islands, mountains, and other geographic features. In the second part, readers are told they need to know the names of animals to be able to recognize and greet other life forms by name. Delicate, almost childlike in simplicity, the soft, earth-toned colored drawings enhance the large-print text.

Many gifted children possess a special sensitivity to the beauty and importance of the natural world. These readers will understand the book's subtle message about human's relationship to nature, a theme that might go undetected by less capable readers. In addition, intellectually curious children can relate to the narrator's quest for knowledge. School-age youngsters should be able to read the book independently, but younger children might benefit more from sharing it with an adult.

Goodall, John. *The Story of a Castle*. Illus. by author. New York: Macmillan, 1986, unp. (Intermediate)

Goodall's picture book depicting the construction and subsequent changes and modification of a castle is beautifully accomplished. Elegant in format, half-pages are inserted to reveal both dramatic and traumatic events in the castle's history that spans several centuries.

To start the chronology, the title page shows William the Conqueror and his barons trudging to the top of a hill followed by a double-page spread featuring the Normans at the top of the hill selected to become the home of a castle in 1170. After a half-page turn reveals the start of the castle's construction with supports and framework being installed, subsequent pages show needed supplies being carried in. Next, a half-page gives a view of the inside of a private room where a family is enjoying a minstrel's music by a roaring fire. The kitchen is shown next, bustling with preparations for a banquet to be held in the great hall. A presentation of surrounding stables and gardens gives readers an idea of the vast area the castle's grounds covered, for these storehouses and ornate botanical prizes were enclosed within the castle's walls.

The prevailing peace and tranquility is brought to an end by the Civil War in 1644 as Cromwell's Roundhead troops attacked, sacked, and murdered the people. Goodall's illustrations depict this destruction and its aftermath with a half-page turn.

Continuing the book's unique format, a spacious double-page spread shows the owners surveying the damage and beginning to rebuild and re-store. Soon, the castle is reopened with a large party. Ladies in bouffant dresses of the times and gentlemen with powdered wigs all dance merrily within the castle walls. Once again, the grounds are grandly landscaped, a fitting background for croquet games and receptions. Gloriously painted pages exhibit a stately dinner party and a royal ball in progress.

In another chapter of its diverse history, the castle becomes a haven for the wounded in battle during World War I when Queen Mary makes a tour of it. Eventually, normal life returns and we see children coming home for the holidays. However, the next war again adversely affects life in the castle as it is claimed for a fortress. A half-page shows a small school in session for a group of children. Later, a huge tea party is held for the Queen's coronation before the owners finally are forced to open their home to tourists in an effort to help pay for maintaining this aristocratic legend.

Through this wordless book, Goodall effectively presents a stunningly illustrated portrait of the life of a noble building involving a variety of historical events from the 1170s to the 1970s. He allows us to visually experience the changes that took place in the palace and requires his read-ers to make intense observations and draw meaningful conclusions using analysis and synthesis. Older children will appreciate the quality of story and its rich, vibrant paintings.

Graham, Ada, and Frank Graham. *Busy Bugs.* Illus. by D. D. Tyler. New York: Dodd, Mead, 1983, 64 pp. (Intermediate)

This superb book details the activities of several insects, with a special focus on certain body parts and their unique functions in the insects' busy lives. With an emphasis on survival techniques, food gathering, and mating signals, each insect is described in one to three pages accompanied by stunning black-and-white close-up illustrations.

The reader can view the mud dauber wasp carefully packing her nest with paralyzed spiders to provide food for her young once the eggs are hatched. Messages between field crickets turn out to be courting calls picked up by the ears on the female's knees. Two industrious burying beetles are pictured at work on a dead animal many times larger than they, and the dragonfly's flight speed at 60 miles per hour explains its darting movements over water.

Children will recognize many of the insects, but several will be unfamiliar, such as the honeypot ant and the caddis fly. Readers learn that the firefly's lovely lights in the night are really signals flashed to her mate. By controlling the number of flashes and the brightness, the firefly ensures that each of these signals has a special meaning to the receiver.

The tiny leaf miner is magnified several times inside a leaf wall, whereas to us the only evidence of its existence is normally the markings it leaves on a leaf. The familiar housefly is also magnified—as a close-up—to emphasize its huge eyes.

The book exquisitely examines scientific information in an entertaining manner. The text is informative and fascinating for older readers; very young children will be curious about the intricate illustrations of these insects. Children will be encouraged to use their analytical skills to make comparisons among the different insects observed. A list of scientific names of the insects appears at the back of the book.

Greenfield, Howard. *Marc Chagall: An Introduction.*
Reproductions. New York: Overlook, 1981, 168 pp. (Advanced)

This biography of Marc Chagall, based on Greenfield's personal encounter with the artist, is an absorbing account of the life of one of the greatest painters of our time.

The story begins in the small Russian village of Vitebsk, where Chagall was born and spent his early years with his poor family. In spite of poverty, they were happy, and Chagall received much love and attention as his family felt there was a special quality about the young boy.

Chagall first became interested in art by copying other people's drawings. He knew at an early age that he wanted to be an artist and thereby share the beauty he saw as well as create his own interpretation of the world around him. At first, his family rejected his wish to study art, but they soon realized that the talented youth must have the opportunity to study with masters.

After receiving permission to study in Saint Petersburg—Chagall was a Russian Jew and, therefore, not allowed to travel freely—the young painter was to endure severe hardships, such as going without food, clothing, and at times, shelter. To Chagall, such struggles were worth it, and his dedication continued to inspire him.

Although aware of his great talent, Chagall understood that he needed to learn more about painting; in fact, he is depicted as being quite humble. To be truly happy, he must paint in his own way even though he craved acceptance from the art world.

Chagall eventually met Bella, his love and an inspiration, whom he married after he had established himself as a painter in Paris. Here, stimulated by the greatest art in the world, Chagall truly begins to paint in his own style. Chagall worked almost obsessively and was so absorbed in his work that nothing else mattered, including people. He did, however, establish a close friendship with the French poet, Blaise Cendrars.

When Chagall returned to Vitebsk, he saw his village as strange and unstimulating. His paintings from this period of his changed perceptions of his native town were to become some of the most famous he ever did.

Eventually, he marries Bella against her family's wishes since they did not see Chagall's aim in life as worthy. However, Bella is uninfluenced by their opinion for she deeply understands Chagall perhaps as no other.

Later, in Paris, Chagall was commissioned to illustrate Gogol's *Dead Souls* using the new medium he had just learned called "etching." This work, that took three years to complete, is some of Chagall's finest.

During World War II, Chagall, Bella, and their new daughter, Ida, were brought to America by the Emergency Rescue Committee. Chagall was warmly received in New York but always wanted to return to France. The sudden death of Bella so deeply affected Chagall that he was unable to paint for several months. A request from the New York Theatre Ballet to design scenery and costumes returned him to his work with passion, recalling his former work in Paris.

When the war was over, Chagall returned to Paris, a well-known and respected artist. He continued to paint with passion and concentration throughout his life.

Greenfield's portrayal of Marc Chagall as a dedicated artist is an inspiration to readers, particularly children with a desire to pursue art. The artist's unwavering pursuit of the only work that would truly make him happy exemplifies the challenge and reward of dedication to one's dream.

Chagall's work is depicted as unusual, unique, and even distorted, yet evoking happiness and delight in those who understand the joy the painter is sharing through his creativity. The language will stimulate and challenge the older, able reader, using a tone and respect sometimes reserved for adult books. The author writes with sensitivity, admiration, and knowledge of the painter. This biography will encourage young people to seek out Chagall's work, investigate his career further, and possibly stimulate them to examine the lives of other great artists.

Grey, Vivian. *The Chemist Who Lost His Head: The Story of Antoine Laurent Lavoisier* New York: Coward, 1982, 112 pp. (Advanced)

This biography chronicles the life of Antoine Lavoisier, the father of chemistry. From the beginning to the tragic end, when he was executed at the guillotine during the French Revolution, Lavoisier's life was full of conflict, trials, and tribulations.

Grey's biography presents the scientist's life in such clarity and detail that it can be understood by readers who do not have a technical or scientific background. She depicts Lavoisier's dedication and persistence without glorification or embellishment. Focusing on his achievements, Grey, at the same time, allows the reader a look into Lavoisier's personal life, which was filled with feelings of rejection. Lavoisier's naive and sometimes impulsive behavior balances the perfectionism and perseverance he demonstrated in his work, making him a more believable human being. Only when he gave up his life did this famous scientist give up his quest for knowledge and the betterment of humankind. Until that time, Lavoisier, a man of remarkable self-confidence, assumed people would believe him and that his life would be spared as that of a scientist necessary to the world, if not as a human being.

The first of 14 chapters describes Lavoisier's final days as he stands trial faced with austere judges whose minds seem made up even before Lavoisier makes his plea of innocence. This introduction to the spirited scientist captures the reader's attention and entices him or her to continue reading to learn about the events leading up to the chemist's execution.

A product of an eighteenth-century bourgeois family deeply rooted in the profession of law, the young Lavoisier was expected to follow the same career. He consequently received the necessary classical education and training for law, although a burning desire to become a scientist constantly tempted him away to attend science lectures at the university. In fact, he was so engrossed in intellectual pursuits that he allowed himself time for little else, including meals, until cautioned by his family to take better care of his health.

Although his interest was primarily in chemistry and the importance of exact measurement and scientifically based investigations and experiments—novelties during his time—Lavoisier took advantage of the opportunity offered by his father's friends to become involved in and learn mineralogical investigations.

As a young man, the extremely ambitious and hardworking Lavoisier made several unsuccessful attempts to become a member of the prestigious Academy of Science of France through his development of plaster of Paris and a street light system to make the city of Paris safer. The failure of the ultraconservative members of the academy to look with favor on the young, knowledgeable, but inexperienced scientist only challenged Lavoisier to try harder. His efforts eventually paid off when he became the youngest member ever to join the academy after his important discoveries involving Paris's water system and the development of a more efficient hydrometer to test water at its location.

In future years, Lavoisier's scientific endeavors included proving the Phologiston theory, devised to explain the burning of materials, to be unscientific—a discovery that went against the establishment and for which he encountered opposition, criticism, and hostility from other scientists. But eventually Lavoisier's discovery resulted in a new outlook on chemistry. Lavoisier's other pursuits consisted of mixing gunpowder and various experiments with oxygen and other gases. Perhaps most important was his development of the metric system and a single scientific system that allowed scientists to use a common language of substances and their interrelationships.

With his wife, Marie, who assisted in her husband's scientific work by illustrating and translating into other languages his discoveries, Lavoisier was involved in humanitarian causes all his life. These included projects to assist the poor, sick, and imprisoned—primary among these were tax system reforms. Both the Lavoisiers were so engrossed in their work that they were unaware of the political and social unrest in France preceding the Revolution. Due to his efforts to improve the tax system for the benefit of the poor and underprivileged, along with accusations that he allowed moisture to be added to tobacco, Lavoisier was sentenced to die at the guillotine along with his father-in-law. Herself later imprisoned, Marie Lavoisier continued her husband's work with the metric system and distributed copies of his work to scientists all over the world.

In this volume, the author has chronicled the complicated and complex life and professional career of a famous scientist while presenting a significant and identifiable story that allows readers a look at all sides of the events surrounding Lavoisier. The biography is objective, yet subjective, in describing Lavoisier's obsession with his work.

The black-and-white illustrations—reproductions, paintings, and etchings—help transport us back in time to the tumultuous French Revolution. Containing a table of contents and index, the book is an excellent biography and history book to place in the hands of gifted children. The portrayal of Lavoisier as an enthusiastic, persevering, questioning, dedicated scientist will be long remembered by readers of this book.

Hackwell, W. John. *Digging to the Past: Excavations in Ancient Lands.* Illus. by author. New York: Scribner, 1986, 50 pp. (Intermediate)

Drawing on his experiences as director and staff artist for archaeological expeditions in the Middle East, Hackwell describes the roles and daily routines of the members of an archaeological dig. Compared to the techniques of the nineteenth century, contemporary archaeology is a more systematic approach to uncovering the remains and treasures of ancient civilizations. Specifically, today's archaeologists are interested in learning about land usage, environmental influences, food preparation and storage, whereas earlier Western explorers were more concerned about finding treasures.

Typically undertaken by professionals during summer vacation months, an archeological expedition is usually composed of three teams—an environmental survey team, a site excavation team, and a dig support team—usually directed by an experienced archaeologist. Working together, the survey team members relate the past and the present by studying the current environment and its inhabitants as well as previous findings about the area. The site excavation team uncovers, through digging, remnants of ancient civilizations, such as cities, roads, and cemeteries. The importance of keeping accurate records is emphasized with a view to future expeditions because any disturbance of the area has a permanent effect. As a resource to the other teams, the dig support team provides laboratory and technical services for examining specimens, constructing maps and computer programs, developing film, and preparing publications and reports.

Among the specific stages of the excavation process, the author describes the process of preparing the surface, sifting soil, and marking and labeling locations of items discovered. The significance of information gained from pottery is told through text and sketches that include clear, full-page watercolors. Artifacts—from utilitarian items such as spindles and mortars and pestles to jewelry—are used to illustrate their importance for understanding the life of ancient civilizations. Coins are also singled out as having particular importance by providing information about ancient alphabets and the integration of other cultures through symbols and other markings on coins. In the Middle East, seals, including the valued king's seal, sometimes used for business transactions, can reveal information about the laws and business procedures of the times. Because human remains can provide evidence of a culture's religious and social customs, examination of burial rites and careful searching for personal items and parts of skeletons are among the methods used by archaeologists.

Hackwell does not glamorize the profession but he presents a realistic view of team members' work, including the inconveniences and sometimes hazards involved in working in remote areas. The vocabulary is demanding for young readers but not excessively so. Specific terminology, such as "balks" and "in situ," is defined in context as well as in the index. Watercolor paintings dramatize on-the-scene action, focusing on the professionals engaged in their work and thereby drawing the reader into the action. Many capable readers, including gifted children, are interested in archaeology. This accessible treatment of the discipline with an emphasis on scientific attitudes and the process of formulating hypotheses based on evidence is highly appropriate for such students.

Haugen, Tormod. *The Night Birds.* Trans. by Sheila LaFarge. New York: Delacorte/Lawrence, 1982, 138 pp. (Intermediate)

Jake, a young boy, struggles to cope with his emotionally ill father's behavior. His dad, Erik, is depressed and unable to resume his teaching career. Because of his illness, Erik avoids responsibility for household chores and frequently leaves their apartment for long walks. Jake's mother, Linda, who has given up her dreams of becoming a teacher to support her husband's education, is the breadwinner. In addition, she provides Jake with emotional support and a hopeful attitude that things will be better.

Adding to Jake's concerns are the fears instilled by neighborhood bullies—Sara, who tells Jake there is a murderer in the basement and that the old resident, Mrs. Anderson, is a witch, and her older brother, Karl, who pressures

Jake into shoplifting. Not only is Jake the recipient of mistreatment, but he also witnesses the beatings of other children by their peers. However, the bullies also demonstrate compassion; for example, although Sara threatens and scares Jake with her stories, she assumes a protective, comforting role when he is frightened and reveals a sensitivity through her tears as her brother is about to be removed from their home by the police.

As a result of all the turmoil and emotional upset around him, Jake is filled with fear and imagines hearing birds in the night, clawing at his closet door. If he does not lock the door, the birds sometimes get out and fly around the bedroom, frightening him. Whenever his dad has had a particularly bad day, the birds are restless.

Jake recognizes that his fears are imaginary when Mrs. Anderson, a kindly grandmother, not a witch, invites him in for a visit. At Linda's constant urging, Erik finally visits his doctor. He tries to return to teaching, but fails again. The story concludes with Linda consoling Erik with a promise of hope for the future.

The issues of a parent's emotional problems are viewed from the young son's perspective. At times, Jake assumes an adultlike role, as when he goes out to search for his wandering father and the day he reminds his dad that it is time to go home to do the laundry instead of extending their excursion. As Jake begins to take more control of his life and stops accepting everything other children say to him, he starts to rely less on his magical thinking and rituals, such as avoiding a brown spot on the stairstep to avert disaster.

The story is told in a simple, yet eloquent, straightforward manner. Gifted readers who are sensitive to the insecurities of others can empathize with Jake's problems with his peers and his emotionally ill father. Many gifted children are capable of understanding the reasons for human behavior; hence the book could serve as a starting point for discussions about the parent-child relationship and the sometimes cruel behavior of children.

Heller, Ruth. *How to Hide a Butterfly: And Other Insects.* Illus. by author. New York: Grosset & Dunlap, 1985, unp. (Beginning)

This tiny picture book is a visual treat for young readers. Focusing on familiar insects, such as the butterfly, Heller's beautiful illustrations will have readers turning the pages over and over again.

Enhanced by rich, colorful, and carefully drawn illustrations, rhyming facts about insects' camouflaging nature introduce new words to the young set, such as "imitates" and "depending." At the same time, children gain scientific information—for example, "Flies only have one pair of wings, while bees . . . you see, have two." An orange and brown butterfly seems to disappear on brown leaves when it folds its wings. A large moth with brilliant pink wing sections becomes almost undetectable on a tree's bark by simply folding under its wings. Similarly, an inchworm hustling across the pages is "lost" as a twig, while a proud praying mantis effectively hides in green and gold grasses. A grasshopper is shown with its wings spread out just before it pretends to be a piece of straw. Explaining that it is not an insect, the author calls attention to a little green spider and its subtle and various color changes that allow it to capture its prey.

Keen discrimination is required to discern the insects obscured against the background of their natural habitat. Recognition of some insects would depend on children's experiences as they use investigative skills to identify the insects. Even prereaders will be intrigued with the creatures' ability to hide themselves from predators.

Like Heller's other books of the same hide-and-seek format (e.g., *How to Hide a Crocodile, And Other Reptiles* and *How to Hide an Octopus: And Other Sea Creatures*), this tiny volume's brief text reveals respect for the younger primary reader with the inclusion of vocabulary often found in books for older readers. It is truly a treasure in design and content.

In addition to these books in the series, Heller offers volumes on the camouflaging habits of the polar bear, gray tree frog, and the whippoorwill.

Heuck, Sigrid. *Who Stole the Apples?* Illus. by author. New York: Knopf, 1986, unp. (Beginning)

Appealing to the beginning reader and younger children, *Who Stole the Apples?* is an unusually fine example of a rebus story—unusual in that each pictorial representation is uniquely different, whereas many rebus stories use the same illustration for each object. For example, a forest is made up of a variety of trees of different shapes and colors rather than a uniform, indistinguishable mass of vegetation. Illustrated in deep, vivid colors and simple small pictures of characters and objects, the text not only complements but also adds visual appeal to this enchanting tale about a horse searching for apples.

The story begins deep in the forest where a little gray horse discovers that all the apples have disappeared from his apple tree. He sets out to find the apples and soon meets a bear who is eager and willing to direct him to the apples. Together, the two animals pass many interesting places and people, including a chimney sweep.

The pair promise apples to everybody who helps them, including a captain and his crew who take them across the sea. Finally, their journey takes them to a parrot who informs them that the magpies have stolen the apples. A large, leafless tree with many branches emerges as the nesting place of several black magpies, each with an apple in its beak. When the birds see the horse, they open their beaks to caw, thereby letting the apples fall. As the horse and the bear return home, they deliver the promised apples to their friends.

Double-page spreads of brilliant color emphasize the story line and relieve the concentration otherwise required for the rebus text. The pictures vary, yet retain certain characteristics. They will intrigue a young child and entice him or her to stop and contemplate each one. Many children will also be tempted to count the animals and people along the way. This special little book with its unique format requires that children utilize high-level thinking skills and their ability to discern pictures and associate them with words to interpret the story.

Hodges, Margaret. *If You Had a Horse: Steeds of Myth and Legend.* Illus. by D. Benjamin van Steenburgh. New York: Scribner, 1984, 131 pp. (Intermediate)

Nine stories describing horses referred to in mythology and legends make up this unusual work. Derived from folklore of many countries, including Norway, Sweden, Persia (Iran), Ireland, Greece, and the United States, this collection of retellings is varied and full of adventure. The stories emphasize the importance attached to owning a powerful horse long ago. The animal signified speed and was used to accomplish dangerous feats.

In "Horses of the Sun," Phaeton learns that his true father is the sun god Apollo. He begs his father to allow him to drive his great chariot and white horses for one day through the constellations. Apollo is reluctant, yet feels compelled to grant his son's request, for Phaeton can barely hold the huge chariot in the sky. Phaeton finally departs but meets misfortune and dies. Apollo's horses bring the empty chariot home.

Another legend, "The Horse Who Built the Wall," is about a great black stallion who helps a stonemason build the wall around Asgard, a city above the earth, in exchange for the sun and the moon and the goddess Freya.

In most cases, illustrations depict each magnificent horse as prominent and ferocious. Children who are readers of mythology will enjoy these tales and may be particularly interested in the reference notes. For example, "The Ebony Horse," from *The Arabian Nights,* is about a mechanical horse ridden by a prince to rescue his princess from an unhappy marriage to the King of Cashmere. The stories are filled with action, usually a quest or challenge that must be overcome to secure success. This unique book will be a useful addition to standard mythology collections.

Hodges, Margaret (retold). *Saint George and the Dragon.* Illus. by Trina Schart Hyman. Boston: Little, Brown, 1984, 32 pp. (Intermediate)

The noble Red Cross Knight has been sent by the Queen of Fairies to slay the deadly dragon. He is accompanied by Una, a lovely and distressed princess and a dwarf. It is Una's land and people who are being destroyed by the dragon.

The way back is long and dangerous, and the travelers stop to rest at an old hermit's place from where the young knight can view the beautiful palace. Eager to proceed, he is cautioned by the hermit to first fight the dragon in the valley below. It is from the hermit that the young knight learns of his origin; that he was stolen as a baby by fairies and hidden in a farmer's field. Thus came his name George, meaning to plow the earth and fight the good fight.

Relieved that someone has come to save them, the farm people in the valley warmly welcome St. George and Una. Soon the huge, fire-breathing, raging dragon stirs and rushes toward the knight. The Red Cross Knight's attacks are in vain as the giant beast grasps both knight and horse in his claws and carries them away. As the dragon is wrapping his tail around the horse, the knight is thrown to the ground. Finally, the knight wounds one of the dragon's wings. Angered and frustrated, the dragon bellows fierce flames of fire, scorching the knight's face and heating his armor red-hot. The dragon roars in victory as the knight falls in defeat. Observing this, the princess thinks the knight has lost; however, a mysterious spring of water appears where the knight lies and he rises to resume battle, confusing the dragon.

The knight appears stronger in the next battle and manages to cut off the end of the dragon's tail. Incensed, the raging beast grabs the knight's shield in his claws. Unable to rescue his shield, St. George cuts off the dragon's claw. The heat and flames from the angry dragon's breath overcome the weary knight and he falls to the ground. As Una fearfully watches him sleep beneath an apple tree, healing dewdrops protect the youth. The next morning he rises, completely healed and ready to face the dragon once more. The dragon fears this completely restored person and rushes to swallow him whole, but the knight runs his sword into the dragon's open mouth and kills him.

When the king and queen learn of the dragon's death, castle gates open and bells spread the good news. The Red Cross Knight is honored with celebration and gold and gifts from the king. Reminding the king never to forget the poor, the knight immediately gives his gifts to them. They all assemble in the castle for more merrymaking and to hear the tale of the deadly battle again.

The king welcomes the knight to remain with them forever, and when the knight informs him of his vow to serve the Fairie Queen for six years, the king presents Una to be his wife and promises him the kingdom at the end of the service. Taken with the princess's beauty, St. George marries her. Yet, true to his promise to the Fairie Queen, the Red Cross Knight rides off for duty each time he is called.

Hyman's illustrations are lavish and rich in this version of an old legend. The borders of the pages display flowers and figures with a tapestrylike romanticism. In contrast, the action in the text is vigorous, and the illustrations complement this graphically, portraying a vicious dragon. Through vivid analogies and complex sentence structure, this tale challenges the gifted child and lends depth to the legend beyond merely echoing the elaborate illustrations. In addition, the gifted child becomes acquainted with the elements of tragedy and success through the knight's dramatic encounters. Gifted readers can identify with the persistence of the young knight's efforts to slay the dragon. Each time it seems that the battle is lost, the knight proves he will not give up and continues to persevere.

Hughes, Ted. *Under the North Star.* Illus. by Leonard Baskin. New York: Viking, 1981, 47 pp. (Advanced)

Various animals depicting a life of lonely survival in a cold, relentless environment populate the absorbing poems in this picture-book-size volume. From amulet to eagle, each verse characterizes a creature's struggle to survive and the continuity of life in the colder regions of the world.

The poems echo expressions of hopelessness amid a strong determination to survive. Each animal's relationship to nature expresses a sensitivity to this harsh environment. Illustrations show courageous, proud, and confident animals, yet desperation constantly lurks in the poems. Some animals are portrayed starkly, often crudely, such as the wolf. Others reign stately and regal, such as the moose.

Baskin's watercolors capture the mood, spirit, and uniqueness of each creature. Even though some of the illustrations emphasize the beast's fierceness, it is not fear but admiration of the animal that will linger in the reader's mind. The reader is stimulated to question what human beings can learn from the animals' ways of coping with hostile and almost death-defying existence.

Ample white space sets off each verse—some long, others short—and the superb illustrations of the animals lend an aesthetic quality to the book.

In this exceptional volume of poetry, author and illustrator equally contribute to a powerful visual, emotional, and intellectual experience that will hold high appeal for intelligent young minds. Each poem in this sensitive collection will have an enchanting effect on the reader, evoking a certain respect for the subject. Even without the magnificent illustrations, the animal can be pictured by the stimulating use of rich language.

Johnson, Jane. *A Book of Nursery Riddles.* Illus. by author. Boston: Houghton Mifflin, 1985, unp. (Beginning)

Refreshingly new and different for many children, these British riddles are attractively arranged, one riddle to a page with an accompanying illustration on the adjacent page. With an old-fashioned English flavor, each riddle points to a visual clue hidden in the full-page illustration. The solution is written in very small upside-down letters in the lower right-hand corner of the riddle page.

Especially rewarding when shared between an adult and a child, the book contains riddles that require some assistance for the younger child to interpret, such as:

> Four stiff-standers,
> Four dilly-danders,
> Two lookers,
> Two crookers,
> And a wig-wag.

A delightful illustration of children playing in a haystack with cows reclining in the distance and a friendly, but resistant cow ridden by several children hint at the solution. In another riddle:

> As I was going o'er London Bridge,
> I heard something crack; .
> Not a man in all England
> Can mend that.

The illustration depicts London Bridge and various active little figures sledding and ice skating around and under the bridge. The reader must focus on happenings in the picture other than the bridge to discover the clue.

The riddles are brief, varying in length from four to six lines. The language contains rich imagery and lively rhyme. Although some words, such as "stronghold," "filly-foal," and "comely," may be unfamiliar to many young children, they will not be lost on the gifted child who welcomes the challenge of interpreting the meaning of new words. Older children will also delight in such words. The riddles are tightly constructed, allowing even very young children with limited attention span the joy of discovering the few well-chosen words that tell a little story for the child's understanding.

Endpapers showing small wreathed pictures of each solution add a finishing touch to this exquisite volume. With the addition of illustrious paintings that capture the charm and loveliness of the English countryside, the book is masterfully produced.

Jonas, Ann. *Round Trip.* Illus. by author. New York: Greenwillow, 1983, unp. (Beginning)

Strikingly beautiful, *Round Trip* is an experience in optical illusions, using stark black-and-white silhouette graphics that reveal extraordinary discoveries for the reader.

The story relates an adventuresome trip to the city early in the morning before the world is awake and back home again at night. For the city-bound part of the trip, the reader holds the book in the usual way but then turns it upside down for the return trip. In this way, totally new pictures emerge because of the black-and-white reversals. For instance, on leaving home, the travelers pass through their dark, quiet neighborhood where a flock of birds flying high above the houses becomes the moon's reflections when the book is turned. Later on, farm silos are reversed to become factory smokestacks. Similarly, smoke curling from a train streaking across the countryside becomes dark puddles after a rainfall. The white, winding early-morning roads set against the black mountains become streaks of lightning across a night sky. A complex picture of power line supports that reverse to bridge supports is equally imaginative. Ocean waves become flocks of white birds against black skies, and marsh plants reverse to a nighttime fireworks display.

In the city, white highways become city searchlights, bridge supports become telephone poles, and lights in black skyscrapers are twinkling stars over white skyscrapers when the book is turned upside down. Similarly, the seats in a movie theater become the ceiling of a restaurant. At the end of their visit, the travelers watch the sun set, and the reader turns the book upside down to read about the trip home.

Some scenes in this unusual book are more difficult to discern than others, besides being less familiar, such as a subway that reverses to a parking building. Possibly frustrating for some, this book will delight gifted children in its fascinating and challenging format. The text is brief, but the overall design is well planned and novel. Readers are forced to make observations and draw conclusions from the excellent illustrations. The curious and precocious young reader will eagerly accept the challenge this book presents. However, some may be tempted to turn the book upside down several times before completing the trip one way.

Jonas, Ann. *The Trek.* Illus. by author. New York: Greenwillow, 1985, unp. (Beginning)

A little girl, with knapsack and bright red lunchpail in hand, kisses her mother good-bye as she goes off to school. Soon her imagination and seeking eyes transform a walk in an ordinary neighborhood into an adventuresome "trek" through a conjured-up jungle. (Luckily, her mother does not see what her daughter sees as she waves good-bye at the door.) Only the little girl can visualize the lush, tropical jungle's inhabitants. So, of course, can the curious young reader.

Lying in wait is a dark green alligator whose scales are actually the rock pattern on the walk. A tiger is hiding in the lilies, and huge gorillas emerge from the irregular shapes of the shrubbery. Along the way are lazy turtles of clumps of grass, a giraffe hidden in the rock design of a fireplace, and koalas perched in a tree. The girl stops to watch monkeys formed from the twists and turns of tree branches and porcupine bushes all in a row. Her imagination causes her to see water buffaloes crowded around the park's pond. Huge gray elephants sport clusters of green leaves, filled trash bags are bulging rhinoceros, and a princely camel adorns the top of a fence.

She meets her schoolmate and they continue on together, pretending bravery since only they can see the animals. A delightful treat awaits the reader at the open market where the girls point out a huge hippopotamus of watermelons, monkey faces on the coconuts, a pig in the sweet potatoes, and sea lions that are really a box of eggplants. When they pass the otherwise familiar coffee shop, a coat appears to be a moose, and as they near the school, the vines climbing up the walls look like pangolins. Finally, they stealthily creep into the school, safe and sound from all danger.

The last two pages of the book contain pictures of the real animals depicted on the imaginary walk. The reader can identify unfamiliar ones and begin the search for those missed along the way.

Brief text accompanies a colorful explosion of illustrations that leaves readers to employ their imagination to discern the shapes, both obvious and obscure. The girls are dressed in neutral khaki-colored clothes to minimize their presence while the reader's eye is drawn to the elaborate constructions. Some animals are familiar, many are not. Not all of them appear in a jungle, but the theme is intriguing and the underlying idea refreshing. After successfully using their visual discrimination skills in this book, imaginative readers will be tempted to explore their own everyday world with open eyes.

Judy, Susan, and Stephen Judy. *Putting on a Play: A Guide to Writing and Producing Neighborhood Drama.* New York: Scribner, 1982, 150 pp. (Intermediate)

Within two main sections, Playmaking and Getting the Show on the Road, individual chapters present extensive information ranging from the most elementary steps of preparing for acting to the more complex activities involved in writing and producing a play.

After stressing the importance of "warm-ups" and pretending exercises—including ways to use one's body for different movements, such as becoming a marionette, doing mirror images in pairs, clapping out rhythms, and acting out feelings—the Playmaking section continues to encourage the reader's imagination for theatrical pursuit.

Children are reminded to use their powers of observation to study people's behaviors and responses and their voices to practice inflections and modulations. Imaginative exercises, such as creating actions in different situations, help build children's self-confidence in performing. The section on pantomimes is particularly useful, combining pantomiming and poetry in some instances. Simple plays without scripts, such as puppetry, improvisations (role playing), and scenes involving two or more people, further encourage children to continue to explore their imaginations. The authors also devote several pages to how to develop a "reader's theater." There is also a chapter on media plays, for example, radio plays, video drama, television plays, and moviemaking that will inspire children who prefer such activities as animated plays. In addition, this resource contains ideas for how to create one's own play and how to decide the conflict to be included, the characters, dialogue, stage directions, and more.

Part 2 involves putting on a play, assuming the reader has written a script and is ready to produce it. The responsibilities of each member of the backstage cast are described, with instructions for each step related to casting, rehearsing, and presenting a play. Sets, props, costumes, and makeup receive equal treatment in this comprehensive work, which also contains suggestions on how to advertise a play, along with final notes pertinent to the last-minute activities on the day of the show. The book concludes with ideas on how to organize one's own theater company. A table of contents, glossary, and index are welcome additions to the text.

This excellent book offers many motivating ideas and instructions for how to produce a play. Perhaps more details on actual playwriting would have been helpful. However, the book is full of sound ideas on a topic that interests many gifted children. By enabling readers to produce a play, this book is a welcome addition to the imaginative minds of middle graders and older children eager to perform.

Kamen, Gloria. *Kipling: Storyteller of East and West.* Illus. by author. New York: Atheneum, 1985, 72 pp. (Intermediate)

Rudyard Kipling, long a favorite author of children's literature, particularly the *Just So Stories,* lived a memorable life characterized by both tragedy and success. The first five years of Kipling's life were spent in India where his British parents preferred to live. His mother loved the Far East countryside, but was concerned that her son, "Ruddy," was not learning proper English. Consequently, she and her husband, who taught sculpture and pottery at an art school in Bombay, secretly arranged to send young Kipling and his sister, Trix, back to England to get a better education.

Kipling loved the servants who cared for him and the vast beauty of India in the 1900s. Therefore, had he known of his parents' plans, he would have been deeply hurt. However, he believed the Kipling family was returning to England for a visit because his mother had never explained the purpose of the trip. When they arrived in England, the children immediately were taken to a couple's home to live and attend school. After a week, the Kipling parents left early in the morning while the children were still sleeping. Kipling's mother was heartbroken at this arrangement; nonetheless, she carried it through, thinking this was what was best for her children.

Kipling did not like his new Aunty Rosa and her bully of a son. Furthermore, she seemed partial to his sister, Trix, and soon began her tormenting practice of humiliating and criticizing the young boy for not being able to read as well as his sister. Much later it was discovered that Kipling suffered from a severe vision problem. As a result, Kipling spent most of his time locked up alone in the playroom with few toys. The only caring person he knew was his sister, and she was rarely allowed in his "prison." Gradually, Kipling withdrew into his own imaginary world, and as time went by even his memory of his parents became vague to nonexistent. As his letters to them were closely supervised by Aunty Rosa, he could not disclose the misery of his life. Finally, on receiving word of Kipling's near blindness, his mother came to England where she soon learned of the ill treatment her son had experienced. Before returning to India, she placed Kipling in a boarding school, where, under the care of a sensitive headmaster, he began to excel in writing.

Eventually, Kipling returned to India to see his beloved parents and take a newspaper job that he retained for several years. His later desire to return to London to pursue his writing among other professionals led him to meet his wife, Caroline, a U.S. citizen from Vermont. On visits to Vermont, Kipling became so enamored with the winter beauty and the privacy of the rolling countryside that he decided to stay. The newlyweds consequently built a home there named Naulakha that still remains today.

During this time a daughter, Josephine, was born to the Kiplings while Rudyard was busy writing *The Jungle Book*. Preferring solitude and openly critical of the townspeople's life-style, Kipling was viewed by the local townspeople as unapproachable and unfriendly. Finally, a serious dispute with Caroline's brother over money and property ended the Kiplings' pleasant life in Vermont. In the meantime, another daughter, Elsie, was born. The Kiplings returned to England where a son, John, was born. The family settled not far from Rudyard's parents, who now also lived in England.

A serious tragedy befell the family when on a trip to the United States to visit Caroline's parents, Josephine died after a cold wearisome journey across the Atlantic. Kipling was crushed and vowed never to return. Instead, the family spent many winters in South Africa where the author gathered rich sources for what later became the *Just So Stories*. Kipling was awarded the Nobel Prize in Literature in 1907.

Rudyard Kipling's children were very special to him and he maintained close communication, especially through his delightful and amusing letters. After his son was killed in World War I, Kipling wrote the poem "My Boy Jack." When Kipling died in 1936, his ashes were placed in Westminster Abbey where the remains of so many other eminent citizens rest.

Kamen's warm and carefully written biography of Rudyard Kipling discloses a childhood of sorrow and loneliness from which the author may never have recovered. Although his own family life was tightly knit and affectionate, Kipling did not seek out others beyond that secure environment. Yet he was able to provide the world's children with some of the most satisfying stories written. Perhaps the early circumstances of his life contributed an outlet in the imaginative literary work of Kipling's adult years. Events sensitively chronicled by Kamen in this biography will stimulate children to seek more information about Kipling and, most certainly, his works. The gifted child may identify with this beloved author's tendency to withdraw from a world he felt did not understand him and respect his vivid and sensitive imagination as expressed through his stories. Many gifted children search for biographies that present an authentic portrayal, one that includes the person's human frailties and the distressing events that occur in real life.

The book is beautifully illustrated in cream and brown watercolors, each surrounded with a richly detailed border of symbols and events that chronicle Kipling's life, both its pleasant and unpleasant aspects. A glossary and bibliography are included to assist the reader.

Kaye, Cathryn Berger. *Word Works: Why the Alphabet Is a Kid's Best Friend.* Illus. by Martha Weston. Boston: Little, Brown, 1985, 128 pp. (Intermediate)

Like other titles in the Brown Paper School Book series, *Word Works* uses eye-catching brown-toned line drawings, comic-book-style characters, and step-by-step directions to introduce and reinforce its theme. As if speaking directly to the readers, Kaye presents tantalizing tidbits of information and poses questions about word origins and oral and written communication to stimulate curiosity and develop creative expression. Questions include both open-ended questions for which there is no one correct answer and more specific ones. Answers to specific questions are organized on one page in the back of the book.

In the first of 11 chapters, Kaye entices us to explore the world of words. "There are a million words out there to choose from. Why should you use the same ones over and over again?" Based on this premise readers are invited to speculate about many aspects of language, including why there are so many languages and what would happen if we spoke a universal language. After this introduction, a brief history of written communication follows, including the development of picture writing, rebuses, and the Roman alphabet. Old English spellings are compared to contemporary English. Also, using plenty of illustrated examples of codes and ciphers the author shows how to create unique writing systems.

Continuing to use the technique of introducing a topic and then encouraging the reader to apply newly learned information, Kaye explains the structure of language—rules and conventions of grammar—and then invites readers to devise a new directionality for words on the page and suggests that they experiment with the familiar backward or mirror writing. Sign language, fingerspelling, and use of gestures are also presented as methods of visual communication.

In a chapter on stories, Kaye gives readers an opportunity to apply their writing skills by suggesting ways to start stories such as backtracking (writing the ending first). The author emphasizes the importance of being astute observers using all five senses to obtain information when striving to improve communication skills.

A chapter about poetry reinforces the notion that there is no one correct way to write poetry, thereby allowing readers freedom to be more original and creative in their writing efforts. Providing only a few pattern poems such as haiku and name poems, Kaye encourages readers to choose the form their own poetry will take. To involve young poets' feelings and experiences she recommends writing poems for special occasions.

In "Meet the Press," readers examine the parts of a newspaper and analyze articles to discern the five W's before learning to understand editorials by comparing fact and opinion articles. Both verbal and graphic creativity is encouraged in an activity involving a comic strip. First readers are to fill in blank balloons with appropriate conversation. Next, the dialogue is provided, but the cartoon drawings are left to the reader's imagination. The chapter continues with the inevitable suggestion that readers produce their own newspaper, this time as a collaborative effort among neighborhood friends. The chapter concludes with some thought-provoking comments about the meaning of a *free press.*

In the chapters "The Play's the Thing" and "Keeping Track of Me," the author suggests ways to keep a diary and write a story or play. Suggestions include listening, observing, and note taking as ways to find topics for playwriting. Keeping records of one's daily activities, taking down oral histories, and writing letters are recommended as strategies for finding out more about oneself and others. Finally, information about how to write radio plays, design sets, and improvise with props is included.

A chapter on the future introduces computers and their influence on society, changes in word usage over time and language as a reflection of societal changes, the influence of words on emotions, and censorship.

Concluding on a lighthearted note, the last chapter focuses on ideas for how to plan a word party, complete with creative invitations, word games, and even recipes for sign language and letter cookies. In the absence of an index, the detailed contents, organized by chapters and subheadings, assist in locating particular topics among the wide range of information, anecdotes, and activities presented in a somewhat loose format.

Humor and imagery are used effectively in this book to develop and reinforce ideas. For example, when urging readers to make a word pool—a collection of words written on small pieces of paper stored in a box to stimulate writing—the text depicts a *swimming pool* filled with words.

The book will appeal to intermediate readers by its mix of amusing illustrations and brief but interesting and unorthodox introductions to words, their history, meanings, and usage in a variety of written formats. Divergent responses are encouraged by what-if questions and other open-ended language explorations. Further, readers are asked to use higher-level thinking skills, such as analysis to examine story elements and synthesis to transform a classic story into a contemporary one. *Word Works* should encourage readers who enjoy expressive language activities to begin using more and more unique words to express their thoughts and feelings.

Kennedy, Richard. *Amy's Eyes.* Illus. by Richard Egielski. New York: Harper & Row, 1985, 438 pp. (Advanced)

Amy, a human child turns into a doll, and the Captain, originally a sailor doll, comes alive and leads a crew of animals in this unusual fantasy, which continually delights and puzzles the reader.

As a motherless baby, Amy is left with her sailor-Captain doll by her tailor father on the doorstep of an orphanage. Ignored and mistreated by the mean Miss Quince, Amy spends most of her childhood reading Mother Goose to her constant companion—the Captain—and finds her only other comfort in the kindly Miss Eclair. One day, while mending the "worn" Captain, Amy pricks his head with her needle, whereupon he comes alive. Fearing that Miss Quince suspects his new identity, the Captain, now nearly a grown man, leaves, promising to return or send word of his whereabouts. Grieving over the loss of the Captain and the sudden departure of Miss Eclair—dismissed for aiding the escape of the Captain, whose letters are intercepted by Miss Quince—Amy withdraws until she becomes a doll and is placed in a shoe box.

Later, the Captain, having inherited from his former captain a ship, the *Ariel,* reclaims Amy and takes her away, carrying her inside his coat. The Bad Sister, alleged sister of the ship's former owner, accuses the Captain of having murdered her brother and demands half the gold sought by the Captain in accordance with a pirate's treasure map. To ensure her fortune, the Bad Sister boards the *Ariel.* However, because of her reputation as a witch among sailors, no crew is available for the voyage. Consequently, Captain brings toy animals to life—no sailor dolls could be found in local toyshops—by reading Mother Goose and pricking their heads with a needle. He had created Skivvy, a sailor who studies and ponders the meaning of biblical passages, in a similar manner by reading the Bible over long underwear stuffed with laundry. Captain and Amy in her doll form finally set out with a crew of cats, monkeys, squirrels, and other assorted animals, including the rebellious Davy Duck, who steals the Captain's Mother Goose and plans a mutiny supported by his own ducks, made of the ship's "duck" cloth. Not knowing that his first mate, Mister Cloud, had promised the *Ariel*'s former owner to look out for Captain, Captain is suspicious of Mister Cloud's actions and intents. Consequently, through a series of humorous conversations, each man believes the other is in love with Bad Sister.

Davy Duck betrays Captain as his glowing pipe at night reveals the *Ariel*'s location to the pirate Goldnose, who, eager to find the buried treasure, is following closely in the *Locust.* Skivvy, reading the Book of Revelation, uses numerology and ponders the Mystery of the Beast. He becomes obsessively fearful about their fate and warns the Captain to turn back.

Undaunted in his search for pirates' gold, the Captain locates the position of the sunken ship, cuts off the button eyes of Amy, puts them in a bottle, lowers it into the sea, and brings Amy to life so she can describe the whereabouts of the gold.

The bottle breaks, and Amy's eyes are swallowed by a fish. The Golden Man—a sailmaker on the sunken pirate ship who has been marooned on the island near the buried treasure—nearly drowns trying to rescue Amy's eyes. The Captain understands his longing to find the gold after the Golden Man is revealed as Amy's father and the Captain's creator.

In the meantime, miles to the south, Mama Dah-dah, an old black woman who is known as a wise healer, routinely feeds fish to an albatross. One day she discovers Amy's eyes as the albatross picks them out of a fish. Mama Dah-dah recognizes what had happened, and the albatross brings Amy's eyes to the *Ariel.*

Finally, in a fierce, bloody battle with Goldnose and his pirates, the Captain dies. As he lies dying in Bad Sister's arms, an albatross brings Amy's eyes. Bad Sister sews the button eyes on Amy, who identifies Miss Eclair as Bad Sister. Skivvy, wounded, sacrifices his life to save the survivors of the *Ariel.* Everyone on the *Locust* is killed. In the end it is suggested that Amy's father and Miss Eclair might marry, and the albatross returns to Mama Dah-dah, who sees the battle and its conclusion in the albatross's eyes.

The plot is unusual and made further complicated by different viewpoints and occasional monologues by the narrator. To realize and appreciate fully subtleties of meaning and characterization, readers are expected to note and reflect on various elements in order to reconcile actions and events. The story's construction and plot consist of multiple layers of interpretation. Themes include conflict between good and evil as personified in the sweet Miss Eclair and the bitter Miss Quince and in the Captain and Goldnose. The importance and meaning of gold, not as something intrinsically evil, but as embodying the potential for misuse, is made explicit. Feelings of desertion and loneliness and the search for one's relatives pervade the story. Philosophical issues emerge when Captain and Skivvy ponder their fate as dolls-become-men, wondering if they have a soul. Each chapter is preceded by a Mother Goose rhyme, and biblical references, particularly from the Book of Revelation, are cited when Skivvy tries to prevent what he senses to be their impending doom. Upper-intermediate-grade gifted readers who enjoy fantasy and analysis and interpretation of complex plot and characterization will find this work challenging.

Kennedy, Richard. *Song of the Horse.* Illus. by Marcia Sewall. New York: Dutton, 1981, 32 pp. (Intermediate)

A young girl becomes as one with her horse, Spirit, when she takes him from his stable and releases him to run across the countryside. The girl's love for her horse, the oneness of their spirits, the energy of the horse, the fleeting landscape around rider and horse conveyed in a fast-paced rhythmic style—

all make it an exciting, almost magical ride. However, as soon as the girl returns Spirit to his stable, she reenters the reality of daily living. When her mother inquires about her ride, the girl responds without detail.

The story is told in the first person as a description of the action, using metaphor and simile and a rich language that appeals to the senses. This mythical quality of expression combined with the intense relationship between the girl and her horse make the realistic horse ride appear almost as an imaginary journey. The reader at times identifies with both the girl and the horse.

Black-and-white charcoal drawings spread across the pages and enhance the feelings expressed in the text. For example, the horse's leg muscles seem to stretch and gallop across the pages. The horse's endless energy is compared to that of a powerful train rushing through the countryside, carrying a fascinated passenger.

Appealing to the emotions and senses, the story offers an excellent example of dramatic, poetic writing in prose form, inspiring readers to examine relationships between humans and animals and to view ordinary experiences with greater depth. Kennedy writes with a captivating magnetism, carrying the reader along fancifully and returning to the real world.

Kennedy, X. J. *Did Adam Name the Vinegarroon?* Illus. by Heidi Johanna Selig. Boston: Godine, 1982, 51 pp. (Intermediate)

Alphabetically arranged, these 26 poems of animals—some of them familiar, others either extinct or imaginary—will appeal to divergent thinkers. Kennedy's collection of animal subjects covers a wide range from a bee, a snail, and a fly to a vinegarroon, an iguana, a minotaur, and a hippogriff. According to the poet, four creatures are fabulous, three are extinct, two are constellations, and the rest more ordinary. Pronunciation guides are included for the more difficult names, such as archcheopteryx and xiphosuran.

The author's creative and clever use of words results in pleasant rhyme and delightful surprises, such as in the poem of a bee. The skillful use of language primarily to entertain in the poem about a quetzal is in perfect keeping with Kennedy's conviction that "while a book of verse for children needs to be funny at times, it might as well, whenever it can, sneak in a little poetry."

Some of the full-page interpretive illustrations that complement each poem border on the bizarre by showing animals with exaggerated features and unbalanced proportions. For example, a scorpion, known as a vinegarroon, is pictured larger than a dog. However, the intricately detailed pen-and-ink drawings often lend human expressions and gentle softness to the grotesqueness of the almost cartoonlike creatures; for example, the illustration of the iguana is ugly, with a sly sort of expression that is both scary and humorous.

The prevailing sense of humor is reinforced in both text and illustration and will enchant gifted children of all ages who are capable of capturing the spirit conveyed in unusual illustrations coupled with the clever play on words.

Kennedy, X. J., and Dorothy M. Kennedy. *Knock at a Star: A Child's Introduction to Poetry.* Illus. by Karen Ann Weinhaus. Boston: Little, Brown, 1982, 148 pp. (Intermediate)

Selected poems by both well-known and anonymous poets will amuse and delight young readers while introducing a variety of poetry and verse. Selections include lyrics, limericks, haiku, concrete poems, and poetry as songs—some lesser known and a few recognizable, folk songs. Among others, poets include Ogden Nash, Langston Hughes, Walt Whitman, Eve Merriam, and Bob Dylan.

The contents are divided into four sections—"What Do Poems Do?," "What's Inside a Poem?," "Special Kinds of Poetry," and "Do It Yourself"—in which poems are further arranged into meaningful subcategories. For example, "What Do Poems Do?" suggests such poetic functions as "Make You Laugh," "Tell Stories," and so on. Selections are preceded by brief conversational style introductions that pose questions to involve readers by making them think without engaging in excessive analysis. Soft, gray and black illustrations add interest without detracting from the impact of the poetry.

Within the section "Special Kinds of Poetry," the Kennedys explain a parody and present a few examples for the enjoyment of readers. The "Do It Yourself" section offers practical suggestions for how to inspire young poets and get them started writing. An afterword to adults includes practical ideas for how to work with groups of children. The book also contains indexes of authors, titles, and first lines.

More than providing an anthology, *Knock at a Star* makes poetry seem like a natural mode of communication and contributes practical suggestions for how to understand and write poems. Selections can be read independently by most capable young readers, or an adult reader can participate in a child's reading experience by reading aloud. The topics and emotions covered fall within the realm of most children's experiences, and gifted youngsters will appreciate the humor and visual excitement of concrete poems whose words take the shape of their focus or content, as in the true-to-life honesty and humor of Phyllis McGinley's description of sisters who are always drying their hair.

Kitamura, Satoshi. *What's Inside? The Alphabet Book.* Illus. by author. New York: Farrar, 1985, unp. (Beginning)

More than merely an alphabet book, this visual interpretation of the alphabet challenges the reader in an enjoyable manner. The cover's bright red border surrounding a conglomeration of objects in what appears to be an alphabet box immediately tempts the curious to explore the unknown absurdity inside. The reader is rewarded by double-page spreads of humorous drawings and charming characters in brilliant colors. Using distorted perspective, Kitamura fills each scene with an array of unrelated objects, exaggerated in size and often related to each other only by their position in the alphabet. On each double-page spread there is a partially revealed visual clue to the letters on the next page.

The first pages contain various boxes, some partly open with familiar fruits peeking out. The letters a and b are found on two of the boxes. The next page reveals the contents of the boxes, showing apples and bananas with the words written on the box flaps. The adjacent page features trash cans and the letters c and d, followed on the next pages by a cat and dog, both in comical situations. Letters continue to be presented in unusual ways and in unlikely backgrounds. A woodpecker plays a xylophone nailed to a tree. Usually, there is no clue as to what the letters depict until the page is turned. For example, e and f on a city street represent an elephant and fire engine among a multitude of objects sitting on the sidewalk, obviously rescued from the fire. For g and h, a hippopotamus is playing a guitar, for o and p, an octopus plays the piano, and for q and r, using a quill, a rat is writing a letter in its hideaway. More obscure is the comparison of morning and night squeezed out of toothpaste tubes marked M and N.

The author's choice of items to represent the alphabet is unusual and unexpected. The book, which is a visual treat, is not appropriate for very young eyes, as the vocabulary and concepts depicted here are too advanced for the experiential backgrounds of most very young children. Both primary and intermediate readers should welcome the opportunity to read this visually stimulating alphabet book.

Kitamura, Satoshi. *When Sheep Cannot Sleep: The Counting Book.* Illus. by author. New York: Farrar, 1986, unp. (Beginning)

Woolly, a sheep, has difficulty sleeping one night and goes for a walk during which he engages in an assortment of nightlife activities, hoping to become sleepy. Woolly chases a butterfly, sees owls, ladybugs, and bats, and watches stars and fireflies. Woolly also picks apples and listens to grasshoppers. When he spots 10 flying saucers, Woolly becomes scared and takes refuge in a huge house with 12 windows and 13 doors. Inside, Woolly uses colored pencils to draw 15 pictures, each depicting a scene from the book. Feeling hungry, Woolly eats 16 peas, takes a bubble bath, and lies down in a bed. When Woolly finally visualizes his 21 "family members" and wonders what they are doing, he falls asleep, nodding off with 22 Zs.

Kitamura's droll humor is evident in the brightly colored illustrations that combine realistic details with the cartoonlike sheep. For example, the interior of the home is drawn with an unusual perspective—the reader looks down at Woolly cooking his peas on a range, surrounded by a countertop filled with miscellaneous condiments, utensils, a key, corkscrew, and potted plant. Finished with soft pink endpapers in the front and night-sky-blue in the back and drawings of Woolly on the front and back covers, the book is a visual delight.

A unique counting book, *When Sheep Cannot Sleep* challenges beginning readers to find some of the objects mentioned, such as nine grasshoppers camouflaged in the thick grass. Illustrations are accompanied by two or three lines of easy-to-read text. Unlike most counting books, the text rarely mentions a number word, so the young reader must be observant while scanning the illustrations to locate the objects to be counted. For those readers who are still puzzled, an index at the back of the book lists each number word, number, and illustration of the object to be counted.

Kitchen, Bert. *Animal Alphabet.* Illus. by author. New York: Dial, 1984, unp. (Beginning)

This elegantly designed book features a new twist in alphabet books. Its fine, heavy, glossy pages abound with animal delights for the small child. Each large, graceful, black letter of the alphabet provides an amusing prop for an animal. The richly painted creatures contrasted against an abundance of white background result in a textural, three-dimensional quality.

Kitchen has cleverly combined a part of an animal with the letter representing it. For instance, bewitching bats hang from the bars of the letter B, while the cunning chameleon curves around the letter C. There is a languishing turtle sitting atop the letter T, and a curious koala bear climbing the K.

Starting with the cover depicting a playful elephant with its trunk twined around the letter E, every page in this magnificent book for all ages is an exciting adventure. Each animal is carefully selected and realistically painted in subtle subdued colors that allow the letter distinct prominence.

The last page offers a list of the alphabet and the corresponding animal. Even some adults will seek exact identification of several of the animals. Truly a sophisticated feast in zoology, this outstanding alphabet picture book will provide an aesthetic pleasure to the young gifted child.

Knowlton, Jack. *Maps and Globes.* Illus. by Harriett Barton. New York: Crowell, 1985, 42 pp. (Beginning)

This introduction to the traditional elements of geography features a brief history of the invention of maps from ancient civilization. Readers are informed that early maps were merely scratches in the sand made with a stick, intended to help people locate food or water or find their way home. Later, Babylonian maps were drawn on clay and baked in the sun to preserve them.

The Chinese made maps from silk or woven reeds designed to help people find their direction at sea. These crude representations of maps were inaccurate and incomplete, however, leading to the erroneous belief that the earth was flat.

The reader is then introduced to the voyage of Columbus and his discoveries, as well as Magellan and his trip around the world to prove that the earth is shaped like a globe. These events lead into an explanation of the globe that even very young children can understand. For example, the concepts of latitude and longitude are clearly illustrated. The purpose of transferring a map of the globe to paper is clearly outlined, as the author also points out that the top and bottom of the planet become distorted in this process.

A section on "map language," the equator, and the hemispheres and how to measure distance on a map and understand scale, including the variations obtained from measuring different sizes of globes, is expertly presented. A discussion of latitude and longitude assists children in realizing where they are situated on earth. Geographic formations, such as mountains, valleys, deserts, and glaciers, are made easily understandable by diagrams of simple topographical maps. Children can see the mountains and valleys beneath the ocean and begin to recognize the magnitude of these natural phenomena by making comparisons to such land formations as the Grand Canyon.

Physical, political, and local maps are also introduced, along with explanations and illustrations that demonstrate the specific purposes of these maps. For example, four different maps of the state of Arizona are presented, including maps of counties, national parks and monuments, major metal deposits, and early stagecoach lines. At the end of this well-organized book, the reader is invited to investigate an atlas and accept the challenge of traveling the world.

Knowlton's lucid presentation will help many beginning able readers to understand difficult concepts. Illustrations are clear, bright, and geographically appropriate in color for a book of this type. Each new topic is introduced in capital letters, and captions with additional information underscore many of the illustrations and diagrams. This is an excellent read-aloud book to be shared with an adult and complemented by using a globe. This highly informative book is addressed to young readers in a personal style and format that involve them in the fascinating rewards of discovery.

Kramer, Stephen P. *How to Think Like a Scientist: Answering Questions by the Scientific Method.* Illus. by Felicia Bond. New York: Crowell, 1987, 44 pp. (Beginning)

Most youngsters demonstrate a keen interest in cause and effect, changes in plants and animals, and similar phenomena in the world around them. Little printed material is available to help very young children develop the questioning skills of a scientist. *How to Think Like a Scientist* aims at presenting the structured procedures used by scientists in an effort to encourage young readers to develop the thinking tools necessary for expanding and developing their own scientific thought.

To introduce the importance of answering questions thoughtfully, Kramer describes three situations; a question is posed about each episode and potential mistakes stemming from answering the questions incorrectly are discussed. In the first story, errors are made because of improper use of information (ignoring little brother's insistence that your neighbors are being robbed because you see a TV repair truck in front of the house and assume the men are doing their job—carrying out the TV). Other types of errors consist of relying too much on other people's answers, as in an incorrectly labled bowl of fish or responding to a question the way we want to view an outcome.

Kramer refers to five steps of the scientific method: asking a question, gathering information, stating a hypothesis, testing the hypothesis, and sharing the results. Application of these basic steps is illustrated by means of vignettes or stories. Through an example of chickens that produce more eggs when fed by a neighboring farmer while the owner was on vacation, readers are led step by step through the process of asking questions and establishing a control and an experimental group. A full-page chart, appropriately labeled and illustrated, clearly sets forth experimental and control group conditions. Finally, readers are encouraged to answer further questions using the scientific method.

Opening and closing with the old saying that a snake thrown over a tree branch brings rain, Kramer challenges readers throughout this book to answer questions and assumptions for themselves. For the most part, the sentence structure is simple; and relevant concepts are plainly explained by example and black-and-white sketches. An index makes for easy references. The book is appropriate for primary-grade readers who have not been introduced to the scientific method. The complex process of formulating relevant questions, organizing data, and gathering information through observations, while still demanding, has been made accessible to young readers in this book. Youngsters interested in pursuing science projects will find the work useful for developing the thinking processes necessary for conducting a valid experiment.

Kushner, Donn. *The Violin-Maker's Gift.* Illus. by Doug Panton. New York: Farrar, 1982, 74 pp. (Intermediate)

Traveling the same road each day to reach the marketplace where he sells violins, Gaspard l'Innocent, a violin maker, must always cross the toll bridge with his donkey, Anselm. Brusque and impatient Matthias, the toll keeper who inspects everything before allowing a traveler across, informs Gaspard there are no taxes on violins and lets him cross. Gaspard continues to the marketplace, sets up his booth, and starts to play his violins, hoping to attract a buyer. Sometimes the Duke of Entrecote stops to visit with Gaspard about his violins, discussing the sound that comes from the finest violins in the world—the sound of an imprisoned human soul. Gaspard's dream is to discover how to create this coveted sound.

It is at the marketplace that Gaspard rescues a baby bird from a very high and dangerous church wall, unaware that the bird is to change his life forever. Unsure of what to do with the bird, Gaspard decides to give it to the toll keeper, assured that it would receive good care. Later, when he decides to reclaim the bird because of maltreatment, Gaspard finds that Matthias does not wish to part with it, instead showing the bird's unusual beauty to onlookers for a price. Gaspard continues with his violin work and refrains from trying to see the bird again.

Soon, news of the bird's ability to speak and even predict the future reaches Gaspard, who does not believe the claims and, consequently, does not bother to investigate for himself. However, the townspeople suspect that Gaspard has made a profit from the bird in some way. Trustworthy and honest of character, Gaspard is upset at these accusations but continues to make and sell violins.

Matthias begins to travel with the bird and grow rich from charging people for the bird's answers to the many questions they have. When Gaspard learns the performers will appear at a local inn, he decides to attend. His sympathy is with the bird in such dire surroundings, filled with smoke and noisy, greedy people. Selectively, the bird answers questions, choosing to answer a simpleton, but ignoring a peasant woman.

Gaspard notices the change that has come over Matthias, sensing narrowness of mind and a selfish disposition. Still, he believes Matthias means well and that he is caught up in the quest for fortune. When Gaspard leaves the inn, he reveals to his donkey his observations of the bird's exploitation and what he would do if he owned it. After much speculation, Gaspard concludes that the bird must be set free. Justifying this opinion to himself, Gaspard secretly rescues the bird and returns with it to his hut. Eventually the bird discloses its origin to Gaspard: how he came to fall from a nest on a low-flying cloud and was deposited on the church wall. Finally, before he flies away, the bird offers a secret ingredient needed to make violins that sound like human voices.

This fascinating tale commands attention with its wonderfully written abstract tone that may appeal only to the intellectually gifted. While not exceptionally strong, characterization is consistent; Gaspard remains a sincere, honest person regardless of his success late in the story. He continues to make violins as skillfully and lovingly as ever.

The illustrations are mostly pen-and-ink drawings and quaintly depict the events in the story. The language is very analogous, rich, and satisfying. The reading is thought-provoking and rewarding to the child who reaches for a more original and unusual content in books.

Langton, Jane. *The Fragile Flag.* New York: Harper & Row, 1984, 276 pp. (Intermediate)

Recognizing the implications of the President's proposed peace missile, a nuclear weapon to be launched in space, and the failure of the peace march her parents had joined to gain recognition, Georgie Hall, fourth grader in Concord, Massachusetts, becomes interested in national events. The President invites all children to write him a letter explaining what the newly designed, ornamental, glittering presidential flag means to them. In advance it has been decided that only letters favorable to the peace missile and those describing the child's state in positive terms will be chosen after careful screening by a presidential aide.

Fifty children, one from each state, are to be invited to the White House as official flag bearers. Influenced by her family's comments that the American flag belongs to everyone and by her feelings on seeing the old, faded flag taken down from the attic, Georgie decides to enter the contest. While composing her letter, Georgie experiences a vision blending past history—Concord minutemen, Henry Thoreau—and a scene of horror of nuclear devastation, ending when she extinguishes the fire burning the flag.

Having missed the deadline for mailing her letter but believing in the importance of convincing the President that he is wrong about the peace missile, Georgie resolves to deliver her letter in person. Accompanied by her adolescent sister and her 12-year-old brother; Robert Toby, grandson of President Toby; and best friend, Frieda, who later demonstrates great leadership skills, Georgie sets out on the 450-mile trip to Washington carrying the flag on a mop handle.

Carrying backpacks of provisions, the children walk during the day and sleep on side roads at night. Word of their mission spreads, and more children—even a baby accompanied by his older sister—join them by the hundreds. Realistic aspects of the march, such as homesickness, dirt and grime, heat, quarrels, and being frightened by motorcyclists, are described, as are the adventuresome highlights of the trip. During these events, Frieda proves her leadership skills as she keeps order and establishes rules of conduct, even scolding a youngster for swearing. Soon the marchers gain national media attention and become known as the Children's Crusade. In each town the children are welcomed by community groups.

The crowd of 16,000 finally arrives in Washington on the Fourth of July. As arranged by Robert, Georgie replaces a carefully screened flag bearer and reads her letter pleading for peace. As the President hears her message and gazes on the crowd, he suddenly has a vision of nuclear devastation and promises to stop the launch of the peace missile.

The story—Langton refers to it as a fable—deals with the issue of disarmament not by addressing specific facts but by presenting the protest action taken by children. The children are portrayed as competent, steadfast individuals—adultlike in exercising discipline, planning, seeking, and attaining their goal, yet retaining their childlike qualities. Probably for fear that inspired young readers may follow Georgie's plan, Langton ends the book by discouraging anyone from starting out along the highway—"even to save the world."

Gifted youngsters particularly should relate to the tenacity of the young protagonist. The story will stimulate thinking and discussion about what measures and risks one is willing to take to support a belief.

Lasker, Joe. *A Tournament of Knights.* Illus. by author. New York: Crowell, 1986, unp. (Intermediate)

Details about knights, armor, and medieval tournaments are interwoven in a simple story about a young boy who must prove his bravery to his father by jousting against an older, experienced knight in a medieval tournament. The rituals and preparation for the tournament, the fitting of armor, and the roles of the lady spectators add authenticity to the story.

Hoping to obtain horses, armor, land, and peasants, Sir Rolf, knight-errant, came to participate in a tournament arranged by Baron Orlando to honor his son, Lord Justin, who has recently been knighted. At a banquet the day before the opening of the tournament, Justin and Sir Rolf assessed each other's strengths. Both recognized that despite Justin's wish to meet under more peaceable circumstances—"I would rather break bread with you than cross spears"—the two would have to fight: Justin because he was challenged, Sir Rolf because tournaments were the way he made his living.

As the tournament began with a melee, Justin and Rolf were placed on the same team to fight a fierce mock battle during which many knights were wounded so severely that they were unable to attend the ensuing castle festivities. On the first of three subsequent days of jousting, Justin nervously anticipated being called to joust with Rolf. His dreaded turn finally came when Sir Rolf interrupted the sequence of jousters by challenging Justin to a duel. Justin's youth and slight build enabled him to tolerate the intense heat of the day better than his older opponent, who grew tired and suffered from blurred vision. Thus, when Justin's lance struck Rolf's shield, the knight-errant fell from his horse, leaving Justin the victor. While being assisted to his feet by his squires, Rolf looked at Justin and repeated the younger knight's earlier words—"It would have been better to break bread than to cross spears." After the tournament, Justin admitted to his father that he had been frightened and that Rolf was the better knight. Baron Orlando expressed pride in his son's bravery and courage in spite of his fear.

Lasker's brightly colored illustrations employ firm, angular, geometric lines to portray the power and fortitude of castle fortresses, muscular horses, and heavy armor and courage of the knights. Terminology is explained simply in both the text and in an appended glossary. Young children interested in knights and armor will enjoy the vivid descriptions of a medieval tournament, while more thoughtful readers will seek comparisons with contemporary forms of physically dangerous sporting events.

Lasky, Kathryn. *Puppeteer.* Photog. by Christopher G. Knight. New York: Macmillan, 1985, unp. (Intermediate)

Children are invited behind the scenes to visit a puppeteer as he prepares for a performance. Paul Davis is introduced as he is getting ready to produce *Aladdin and His Wonderful Lamp,* including constructing the puppets, designing the set, and deciding on the voices he will use, the special lighting, and much more. To achieve the right effect, Davis begins by searching for ideas and then researching for accuracy in story, clothing, set design, and character. Davis essentially runs a one-man show, since he alone must make the necessary decisions leading up to the performance.

Davis demonstrates the hand puppet and the small movements that make it appear alive. To create a one-man show, he prefers to work with two hand puppets, adding his voice and special inflections. (A rule in puppetry is that only two puppets can be on stage at any one time; however, voices of others can be heard in the background.)

The artist's experience with puppet shows began in his garage when he was a child. He acquired all the necessary materials—props, staging, lighting—and produced a puppet show himself, learning from these experiences how to improve his performance. Gifted children will be inspired by these early beginnings, realizing that the basic requirements are imagination, creativity, and a desire to perform.

In Davis's upstairs workroom we encounter a creative clutter consisting of an assortment of puppets, some needing repair, others ready to perform. Many other related items are scattered about the room—boxes of parts, sewing supplies, fabric, pieces of cardboard scenery, materials for producing certain sound effects, costumes, and much more. All these materials have been used previously or will be adapted for the story of *Aladdin and His Wonderful Lamp.*

In addition to the basic ingredient—the plot—Davis must concentrate on the sound, appearance, and the nine characters involved in the play. Wanting to bring the story to life and instill in the audience what it must have been like to live during that time, he spends many hours sketching and drawing Aladdin, studying colors and architecture, writing the script for the play, and deciding how to produce the voices.

From his drawings, Davis shapes and models the clay for the puppets' heads, carefully constructing the planes and hollows that allow light to enliven the characters' faces. The features must be exaggerated to project across the stage. It takes Davis a month to make the heads plus the duplicates for the changes Aladdin undergoes from being a poor boy to a prince. From the clay heads, Davis makes the molds. The step-by-step process is so carefully explained that readers could duplicate it and make their own puppet heads. A tremendous amount of time and patience is required to create the heads exactly right, however. Although the painting process of applying makeup to the puppet heads is shown in black-and-white pictures, one can imagine the colors from the description.

Continuing his preparations for the show, Davis builds the bodies of the puppets and cuts out camels and elephants to parade across the stage. In some instances, he seeks expert advice to create the fancy costumes and colors for the royal figures. He details every stitch and seam, every trinket and tassel used for the costume, until he gets it just right.

For the rehearsals, a director is called in for assistance, as Davis stays behind the stage and cannot see the performance. Finally, everything is ready and the play is magically presented to an audience of adults and children. Davis has produced a memorable one-man show that enchants all who came to see it. Both puppeteer and reader are rewarded for the meticulous preparations.

Lasky has produced a superior account of a craft most everyone enjoys. The reader's respect for the puppeteer and his profession will be enhanced after experiencing this quality book. The photographs are clear and crisp, focusing on detailed close-ups that help convey the fascinating story. Planning, analyzing, and synthesizing are important elements behind the puppet production, and readers are encouraged to exercise evaluative thinking throughout the book. Lasky appears to respect the child's ability to understand and sustain the book to the end. The technical information is communicated in a creative manner that challenges potential young puppeteers to engage in the unique craft of preparing and performing puppet shows.

Lauber, Patricia. *Journey to the Planets.* Photographs. New York: Crown, 1982, 90 pp. (Intermediate)

What would it be like to take a journey to each of the planets? Lauber offers a well-documented adventure with stunning black-and-white photographs that inparts this experience to her readers.

Earth is visualized as the blue planet an alien would see from outer space. The reader, as an alien, is led to speculate about the possibility of intelligent life on earth. Changes in landscape are used to make this important decision. Photographs depicting coastal areas reveal details of patterns that signify intelligent life on this planet. The physical characteristics of earth are described clearly, yet scientifically. Lauber provides much more information than most books about planets for young readers, delving into such aspects as earth's magnetic field, climate, content of the crust, mantle, and core. The continental drift theory and tectonic plates are addressed, as are earthquakes, volcanoes, and mountain building. Illustrations include excellent photographs of Mount St. Helens and the Himalayas.

Astronomical acceptance of theories of star formations will challenge readers to investigate this phenomenon in greater depth, although Lauber's description and explanation are thorough.

Photographs of the moon and its history are intriguing, leaving unanswered questions for readers to ponder. Pictures supplied by the National Aeronautics and Space Administration (NASA) allow a close-up look at rocks and craters with recent information included. Comparisons of the moon's craters and craters on Earth, such as Meteor Crater, stimulate analytical thinking.

Chapters on Mercury, Venus, Mars, Jupiter, Saturn, Uranus, Neptune, and Pluto contain many known facts, but also give rise to thought-provoking questions that will trigger creative and critical thinking. The section on Saturn's two newly discovered rings is a case in point: "How can the ringlets be twisted? What are the 'spokes' and why do they appear and disappear? What keeps them from breaking up? Could they somehow be caused by the lightning? Why does lightning occur? Just what are the rings? How did they form?"

Accompanying photographs, many of which have not otherwise been readily available to children, require sharp observational skills. Perhaps the addition of color would have made the photos even more awesome and effective. The book is a short course in astronomy with details about the similarities and differences among the earth, moon, and planets. Readers may puzzle over the information and be tempted to do some telescopic investigation on their own. Lauber examines many mysteries, but also leaves many others for readers' exploration.

The detailed language in the book is more specific and in depth than the ordinary reader selects. The overall approach to this current topic is refreshing, adventuresome, and challenging.

Lauber, Patricia. *Tales Mummies Tell.* New York: Crowell, 1985, 128 pp. (Advanced)

Using an illustration of a baby woolly mammoth that has been preserved in ice for thousands of years, Lauber clarifies the term "mummy" in this fascinating book on mummies of all kinds, ages, and nationalities by telling us that mummy means "any well-preserved body—animal or human." The baby woolly mammoth was found in 1977 by Soviet gold prospectors and taken to Leningrad where it was refrigerated for later scientific analysis. The author gives a thorough and lucid explanation of carbon-14 dating, used to determine approximately when the animal had died. The dating does not tell why the woolly mammoth died out, but interested readers will be eager to pursue this topic in more depth.

In other chapters Lauber elaborates on the different kinds of mummies, not just the commonly represented Egyptian mummies but also naturally formed mummies, such as the woolly mammoth. The process of decay and the absence of it help explain how something becomes mummified. In addition, formal embalming, a process that preserves bodies until they become mummified by cold air, is described using explicit photographs of embalmed mummies.

Customs of head-hunting and shrunken heads made of enemies, called tsantsa, recognized by Jivaro Indians as a skill and an art are also described in unusual detail. Children, who are sensitive, may not wish to digest all the details of making shrunken heads.

The author also presents several cases of people becoming mummified accidentally, such as John Paul Jones and a Chinese mummy from the Western Han Dynasty. These mummies were so carefully preserved that scientists have been able to determine diseases, cause of death, and many other facts about the dead persons. Additional information was obtained from the Chinese tomb, from articles buried with the woman, and of some of the ceremonies and customs of the time.

A discussion of Egyptian mummies and the beliefs surrounding this custom explains the practice of adding to the grave articles that the person would need in his or her next life. The Egyptians experimented with several methods of mummy making until they found the best means of preserving a person's lifelike characteristics. Mummy making ended when Christianity was adopted.

The final two chapters of the book present fascinating accounts of mummies in ancient Peru and Denmark. Every specimen is described in detail and accompanied by excellent photographs.

Scientific analysis of ancient mummies can supply information about people and their diseases, diet, longevity, and many other factors. The author points out that X rays offer more accurate identification and clarification of objects than autopsies when the ancient bodies are unwrapped and analyzed. To illustrate modern methods used to analyze mummies, Lauber devotes a full chapter to the unwrapping of a mummy at the Manchester Museum. From this explicitly detailed venture emerges the likeness of a teenage girl who lived 3,000 years ago and obviously suffered many hardships.

Lauber emphasizes that scientists still have much to learn about the practice of mummifying people, the different methods used, the reasons for mummification, and the identity of these well-preserved mummies.

Lauber has meticulously researched her subject, and her treatment of this mysterious topic is both powerful and spellbinding. The reader becomes absorbed in what first appear to be morbid accounts but prove to be factual information presented in clear and easily understood style. It is not a book for young children, but will provide intermediate-level and older children with abundant material about mummy exploration. A bibliography for further reading and an index are included. Gifted children who are interested in this topic will be stimulated to explore the subject in greater depth.

Lauber, Patricia. *Volcano: The Eruption and Healing of Mount St. Helens.* New York: Bradbury, 1986, 60 pp. (Intermediate)

At its eruption in 1980 after many years of silence, Mount St. Helens became one of the most devastating natural disasters of our time. Lauber's compelling narrative effectively documents this event with excellent color photographs that also take in the surrounding area.

After being introduced to the geological history behind the formation of volcanoes, details of rock content, and the changes it undergoes, the reader will understand how a volcano reaches the point of eruption. In addition to carefully selected vocabulary and writing style, clearly labeled diagrams and maps facilitate this understanding. Readers learn that alert geologists' careful scrutiny and observation of the majestic Mount St. Helens had increased their awareness of its dangerous potential. The eruption in March 1980 confirmed their scientifically based conclusions.

Lauber's description of the blast gives readers a personal panorama of the events that precipitated the explosion as well as the power of the eruption: "Before the eruption Mount St. Helens was like a giant pressure cooker.... The superheated water flashed to steam. Expanding violently, it shattered rock inside the mountain and exploded out the opening, traveling at speeds of up to 200 miles an hour." Photographs of flattened forests and ash-covered vegetation, as well as the huge lava and mud flows, vividly document the immediate aftermath.

In the latter part of the book Lauber focuses on the survivors of the eruption, animals and vegetation, using both narrative and pictures: "Fireweed appeared through cracks in the ash.... Ants survived underground. So did eggs laid by insects. Many other small animals, such as springtails and mites, lived through the eruption in their homes of rotting logs." To show the continuation of the life cycle, Lauber relates how many larger animals, such as deer and elk, eventually found their way into the area where they were able to find enough vegetation for food and thus stayed on.

Younger children may understand the book, while older readers will particularly enjoy the 80 fascinating photographs and perhaps be stimulated to investigate in greater depth volcanoes and their eruption. This large picture-book-size volume includes a table of contents and an index for easy location of specific information about volcanoes.

Leaf, Margaret. *Eyes of the Dragon.* Illus. by Ed Young. New York: Lothrop, 1987, unp. (Beginning)

Leaf and Young have collaborated to produce a memorable story that captures in brilliant color the ancient art of dragon painting.

The setting is a small village in ancient China where the village magistrate has his people surround the village with a high wall to be safe from intruders, man or beast. The wall becomes a source of pride and admiration for the magistrate. So, when he discovers his grandson and other children drawing on the wall, he scolds them. Later, he agrees that a bit of decoration might enhance the wall, however.

The magistrate subsequently summons all the whole village to a meeting to discuss this idea. The people decide to employ a great dragon painter to paint the Dragon King on the wall. Before the painter begins, he requires that the magistrate promise to accept the painting as completed and to pay him 40 silver coins for the job. Having reached this agreement, the dragon painter begins his work.

When the portrait of the dragon is finished, the village people, who have been watching the artist at work, are breathless at the magnificence of the painting. The Great Dragon stretches all around the wall with its head finally meeting its tail. According to Chinese tradition, the dragon has 81 scales; its feet are the paws of a tiger and the claws those of a hawk.

The magistrate withholds the 40 silver coins as payment until he has carefully inspected the painting. As he and the village elders walk around the wall, they are speechless at the size and beauty of the painting. However, when the artist repeats his request for payment, the magistrate insists that the dragon have eyes before payment can be made. Thus, the magistrate breaks his promise to accept the painting as completed by the dragon painter. The wise elders fear the magistrate's demands, but the magistrate disregards their warnings of dire consequences, and the painter unwillingly adds the dragon's eyes, which he has deliberately left out. Having finished, the painter takes his coins and leaves the village.

Then, before the astonished villagers, the Great Dragon's eyes begin to glow and smoke curls from his huge nostrils. A black cloud suddenly appears, and the dragon begins to move. The shaking of the dragon's great body causes the wall to crack and crumble as the dragon himself rises up into the black cloud.

Leaf drew her inspiration for this story from research on a thirteenth-century dragon handscroll. According to folklore, when its eyes are painted, the dragon will fly away. The story builds dramatically, setting the reader up for something mysterious and thought-provoking. To reinforce these feelings, Young's sweeping illustrations captivate the reader as he portrays the foreboding consequence of a promise broken, using washes of pastels over the double-page spreads in this large-sized picture book. Young artfully conveys the anticipation, admiration, and terror of the villagers while concentrating on the giant dragon as the central focus. Colors range from soft, delicate pastels of pinks, blues, violets, yellows, and greens to vibrant reds and purples used to illustrate the dreadful dragon, and end with dark, muted shadows to designate the despair that covers the village.

The story is appropriate for reading aloud to young children while providing the comfort of a return to reality. Older children will contemplate this illustration of greed and the consequences of dishonesty. The author's notes at the back of the book and her explanation of the meaning of a Chinese seal at the front may inspire older children to research the ancient art of dragon painting.

LeTord, Bijou. *Good Wood Bear*. Illus. by author. New York: Bradbury, 1985, unp. (Beginning)

On his way to meet Bear, Goose finds a bird's nest full of eggs on the ground. He takes it to Bear and they discuss the nest's construction and the material the birds used to built it.

Bear then decides to make a birdhouse for the birds. He sets to work with Goose looking on. First, he selects and measures the wood. He also uses the necessary tools to cut out the pieces, including a heart-shaped window. Other building steps include drilling and shaping wooden pegs, planing the wood, and fitting the various parts together. Finally, Bear puts it all together with nails and paints it. Having placed the house on a pole, Bear and Goose watch the birds cheerfully inspect it. Finally, in keeping with the professional, businesslike tone of this book, Bear gives Goose a drawing and plans of the birdhouse to take with him. The last page shows the careful plans for how to construct a birdhouse.

Illustrated in delicate line drawings against pale pastel colors, each page is a discovery for the young preschooler. At the same time, the vocabulary and theme of the book will attract primary children. The author respectfully assumes readers can follow the step-by-step directions and be able to construct a birdhouse with adult assistance.

Mathematical terms, such as the concepts of length and width, and the use of fractions (on the last page) will challenge the older child. Young gifted readers, in particular, will be challenged to apply skills of analysis and synthesis as the author takes them from beginning to end of this unusual book about birdhouse construction.

Levitt, Paul M., Douglas A. Burger, and Elissa S. Guralnick. *The Weighty Word Book*. Illus. by Janet Stevens. Longmont, Colo.: Bookmakers, 1985, 100 pp. (Intermediate)

The Weighty Word Book presents a polysyllabic word for each letter of the alphabet—thus "weighty." The meaning of each word is described in a humorous, imaginative short story that concludes with a pun to help readers long remember the word itself, which appears in large letters at the end of each segment. According to the authors, the words were chosen for both frequency of use in written language and for their sounds, which suggest puns. For example, a pickup truck with a mind of its own displays bad temper through its fierce and reckless antics on the road—cutting off other drivers and honking rudely. Unable to be repaired or made to behave by the city's best mechanic, Hugh Crackenblock, the truck sits on Hugh's lot until a farmer, desperately needing transportation, borrows it. The truck rages all over the road, causing damage to other vehicles and coming to a halt after landing upside down. When a policeman arrives on the scene, the farmer claims it is not his fault but rather due to the "truck Hugh lent" (truculent).

The youthful illustrations, depicting plump animals dressed as people in humorous situations, are somewhat incongruent with the complex, rather literate words chosen to represent each letter of the alphabet. The book is especially appropriate for gifted children because of the challenging vocabulary. It should delight verbally adept youngsters who enjoy word play, and may send them on a search through the dictionary to find other words that lend themselves to puns.

Livingston, Myra Cohn. *How Pleasant to Know Mr. Lear!* *Edward Lear's Selected Works.* New York: Holiday, 1982, 123 pp. (Intermediate)

An opportunity to "know" Mr. Lear awaits the reader of this remarkable collection of the poet's work. Livingston provides a lengthy introduction to Edward Lear and includes comprehensive notes about the sources of her selections. Eleven chapters of words at play exemplify Lear's almost eccentric life. Thematically arranged, each chapter focuses on the deeper aspects of Lear's eccentric behaviors, revealing his sensitive nature behind the jovial one. Each section is accompanied by a short narrative describing the reason behind the emphasis of the collections. Each chapter's introduction describes some facet of Lear's personality—his concerns and his idiosyncrasies.

Lear's ability to poke fun at himself endears him to the reader and often becomes the subject of his poetry. For example, as a result of his preoccupation with physical features, Lear drew his self-portrait with an unusually long nose (he was obsessed with his nose), and many of his characters also sport huge or extraordinary-looking noses. Other facial features were of special interest to Lear, who wrote limericks to share his exaggerated observations. For example:

There was an Old Man of the South,
Who had an immoderate mouth;
    But in swallowing a dish,
    That was quite full of fish,
He was choked, that Old Man of the South.

There was a Young Lady whose eyes,
Were unique as to color and size;
    When she opened them wide,
    People all turned aside,
And started away in surprise.

But as Livingston reveals, there was a lot more to Lear than his nonsensical, imaginative, and captivating humor. He was not without sadness, despair, rejection, and hardship, as reflected in some of his poems.

Herons and Sweeps,
Turbans and Sheeps,
Set him a weeping
and see how he weeps!

There was an old man whose despair
Induced him to purchase a hare:
Whereon one fine day,
He rode wholly away,
Which partly assuaged his despair.

Written with relish, zest, and gusto, Lear's lilting limericks and other verses portray his beliefs, likes and dislikes, and his good-naturedness meshed with wit and humor. The mood is fun and intended to entertain. Rhyme, rhythm, and unusual juxtapositions of sound stretch the imagination. Lear's use of repetition and rhyme results in effective metaphors. Readers are required to discern analogies and associations from his whimsical works that are seasoned with a sophisticated vocabulary—for example, "assuaged," "dolorous," and "syllabub." Along with the challenge to create imagery and follow Lear's often unexpected and nontraditional lines of thought, gifted readers will savor the saltiness of the keen language and Lear's ridiculous pen-and-ink illustrations.

Livingston's thorough research of Edward Lear's life preserves the background of experiences of a memorable poet and confirms that it truly is "pleasant to know Mr. Lear!"

Livingston, Myra Cohn. *I Like You, If You Like Me: Poems of Friendship.* New York: McElderry, 1987, 144 pp. (Intermediate)

This superb anthology of poems, representing more than 50 distinguished and not so well-known poets—both traditional and contemporary—deals with friendship. Divided into nine sections, the poetry appeals to various emotional/experiential backgrounds of children ranging from feelings of loneliness to the joyfulness of acceptance. For example, at some time in their lives, many children experience the despair of friendlessness, real or imagined. Specifically selected for such readers are the poem "Hope" by Langston Hughes and Livingston's poem "Lonesome."

Hope
Sometimes when I'm lonely,
Don't know why,
Keep thinkin' I won't be lonely
By and by.

Other poems are lighthearted and humorous such as those in the section entitled "Would You Come and Be My Friend": "The Owl's Bedtime Story" by Randall Jarrell and "Miss M.F.H.E.I.I. Jones" by Karla Kuskin. A section on the unique friendship between humans and animals includes the memorable "The Erie Canal" by an unknown author and William Jay Smith's "Coati-Mundi." Best friends and the special feelings they evoke are found in Eve Merriam's "Secret Talk" and "What Johnny Told Me" by John Ciardi. X. J. Kennedy's "Agnes Snaggletooth" lends some absurdity and fun to the collection, while "Friendship," translated from the Aztec by John Bierhorst, appeals to our aesthetic nature. Edward Lear's "The Duck and the Kangaroo" and "The Friendly Cinnamon Bun" by Russell Hoban can be found in a section emphasizing the value of having especially good friends. David McCord's "At the Garden Gate" and "Friendship" by Shel Silverstein may already be familiar to many children. The book ends with a somewhat serious selection of poems, "Missing You," which includes a poem by Charlotte Zolotov of that same title, W. S. Merwin's "Separation," and "Letter to a Friend" by Lillian Moore.

The unifying theme of this collection of poetry is friendship in its various aspects. Appropriate for all children, the verse is particularly meaningful for gifted children many of whom sometimes experience solitude and feelings of separation from their peers. By selecting the talents of a diverse group of poets, the author provides some of the best poetry available to children on this extremely human topic. The language, with its unexpected rhyming patterns, speaks directly to the reader without condescension or sentimentality, thereby broadening the child's experiences related to personal relationships. The simple expressions of the desire to have a friend and to be one and the devastation of losing a friend are sensitively presented in this work.

This splendid volume includes a table of contents, an index of titles, index of first lines, and an index of authors and translators.

Lobel, Arnold. *Ming Lo Moves the Mountain.* Illus. by author. New York: Greenwillow, 1982, unp. (Beginning)

Living in the shadow of a huge mountain, Ming Lo and his wife are constantly troubled by such misfortunes as loose rocks falling on their roof and heavy rains from clouds on top of the mountain. In response to his wife's request that they move the mountain so they can spend the rest of their lives in peace, Ming Lo seeks the advice of the wise man in the village. Several of the wise man's suggestions are not successful, including pushing a thick tree against the side of the mountain to move it and frightening the mountain by banging pots and pans. Finally, after considerable thought, the clever wise man proposes taking the house apart stick by stick, packing up all their possessions, and stepping to the dance of the moving mountain by taking one step forward and two backward. Eventually, the couple rebuild their house under the open sky, convinced that they have moved the mountain.

Lobel's green, gray, and red-orange watercolors, reminiscent of Chinese paintings, characterize the simple text. Beginning readers will enjoy the wise man's absurd advice and Ming Lo's foolish behavior. Perceptive readers will take pleasure in interpreting the dance of the mountain.

Mabey, Richard. *Oak & Company.* Illus. by Clare Roberts. New York: Greenwillow, 1983, unp. (Intermediate)

The "company" in *Oak & Company* refers to the wildlife on and in an oak tree. Mabey presents a case for recognizing the sturdy forest oak as one of the oldest and greatest trees, used by both humans and animals. The life cycle of an oak is told as a narrative from its beginning as an acorn, through its various growth stages and injuries inflicted by nature and humans, to its death after 283 years of serving as a home to various wildlife. Even after its death, the oak's cycle begins again as its stump serves as a host to toadstools and insects. Mabey describes the tree-animal relationship as:

> A whole community of creatures traveling, working, eating, sleeping, singing, and bringing up young, on every part from the topmost spring buds to the dead gash blasted out by a lightning flash.

The oak's story is told through the seasonal changes that mark major growth stages and events and illustrate its remarkable endurance in spite of the destructive efforts of both animals and humans. Of the thousands of acorns produced by the parent tree, only a few survive to establish roots suitable for growth. Subtle destruction of an oak begins early. When a sapling is only a few feet tall, it begins to be invaded by creatures that suck sap from its leaves. As it grows, the oak is subject to further devastation when its branches are wide enough to be reached by deer and cattle. Humans enter the cycle when farm workers inadvertently trim the top of the five-year-old oak to only four feet above the ground.

Weather conditions also affect the tree. For example, strong winds snapping off branches produce a wound that dries the wood, which is further eroded by a woodpecker that drills a hole for a nest. Later, this hole becomes large enough for an owl to roost and bring up her young.

At age 120, the oak has housed more plants and animals than the total of its years. More tree-animal interaction occur underground where an almost identical number of creatures live among the oak's roots—wood mice, rabbits, foxes. Many live in a partnership relationship. For example, worms enrich the soil, and even the company's waste products are used—dead insects, green acorns, young leaves, and bird droppings become part of the humus or are eaten by deer and squirrels.

Damaged by lightning, and with rotting wood and holes and gashes, the

283-year-old oak finally falls to the ground as its branches and roots are weakened by freezing snow. Its offspring provides a home to the company of woodpeckers, butterflies, mosses, and beetles, thereby starting a new cycle.

Alternating pages of text enhanced by a panel of colorful drawings and full-page illustrations give readers a feeling of being surrounded by forest life. The watercolor illustrations are filled with important, minute details. Individual leaflets of ferns and mosses are detailed as if the reader were looking through a hand lens. At first glance, a caterpillar seems suspended in midair against a white background, but a closer look reveals the fine silk thread on which the larva is suspended. The illustrations unite with the text to form an integral whole.

Mabey describes the events in the oak's life in a fascinating yet factual manner. Readers are eager to turn each succeeding page to find out what happens next. The tone of the book conveys a sense of respect for the intricacies and balance of nature, with the implicit understanding that a change in one aspect of the environment affects other forms of life. Highly able readers can use skills of observation and analysis to respond beyond the literal level and gain an appreciation and understanding of the interrelationships of a tree's life cycle.

Macaulay, David. *BAAA*. Boston: Houghton Mifflin, 1985, 62 pp.
(Advanced)

The story begins with an announcement that all the people of the world have disappeared from earth, leaving a flock of sheep as the only living creatures. After depleting the food supplies in their pasture, the sheep find an abandoned town where they begin eating familiar food—grass and flowers. Not yet satisfied, they wander indoors and sample food left in a refrigerator. Weary from their travels, the sheep eat, drink, and sleep indoors for several days. After exhausting the food supplies in 17 houses, the sheep stumble upon a supermarket and, annoyed by the unpleasant piped-in music in the store, they carry their favorite foods back to the houses. While frolicking in a family room, a lamb accidentally turns on a television, and the flock gathers around the set for several days. Becoming bored, some sheep go outside to play in the fresh air until that, too, becomes tedious. With the discovery of a VCR, the sheep play movies until they learn to speak and read. The more the animals learn about people, the more they want to emulate them, and soon the sheep begin wearing clothing. From that point on, the sheep follow in the historical footsteps of their human counterparts, establishing schools, pursuing careers, producing offspring, and enjoying prosperity.

As in any society, leaders arise, and the population growth makes life more complicated as evidenced by long lines at supermarkets and gas stations. Eventually, food supplies dwindle, and although warned of shortages on the omnipresent television commercials, the sheep ignore the cautions and, for the first time in their new community, some of them go to bed hungry. Leaders impose rationing, which only exacerbates the food shortage and reveals the difference between the haves and the have-nots. After angry sheep turn to crime and rioting, TV programs offer more comedies, and the leaders present statistics to prove that there is no more hunger. Finally an inexpensive and nutritious food product, Baaa, is made available to all, but it is so popular that soon its supplies decrease, bringing the return of rioting and unrest. Although the population declines steadily, the demand for Baaa increases, and the remaining sheep appear contented. More and more sheep disappear, leaving ghost towns behind. One day only two sheep remain. After eating lunch together, they disappear, one after the other, without the reader knowing what becomes of them. Some time in the future, an ocean fish swims toward land. It cautiously surveys the area and considers crawling onto the land but decides to return to the ocean.

Without labeling the sheep's government as democratic or totalitarian, the author identifies the problems of any society—overcrowded cities, hunger, crime, and governmental attempts to manipulate its people via the media. The black-and-white pen drawings depict life from a sheep's point of view in a picture-book format. Despite the serious tone of the book, the author injects humor. When they started wearing clothes, the sheep discovered that many are made of wool "(so that's where it went!)."

Macaulay's allegorical tale offers a springboard for discussing contemporary issues. Macaulay depicts sheep with blank, vacant stares symbolic of a society consuming itself and helpless to prevent it.

Macaulay, David. *Unbuilding*. Illus. by author. Boston: Houghton Mifflin, 1980, 80 pp. (Advanced)

Many stories have been written about the Empire State Building, but Macaulay's approach to this famous landmark is unique and unrivaled. In this unusual and inspiring work of fiction, Macaulay builds the story of unbuilding the Empire State Building.

After an overview of the history and construction of this phenomenal skyscraper, the author proceeds with a detailed description of its demolition. The year is 1989 and a new headquarters must be established for the Greater Riyadh Institute of Petroleum (GRIP). Unable to agree on an architectural plan, Prince Ali, the manager of GRIP, eagerly proposes to buy the Empire State Building, dismantle it, and transport and resurrect it in the Arabian desert. This preposterous suggestion meets with contempt from New Yorkers. But after appeasing them with promises to replace it with a park and oil for taxis and buses, Ali overcomes their resistance. Dismantling begins. In the process it becomes necessary to demolish some parts that will later be replaced in the reconstruction, such as the concrete floors.

Descriptions of workers and their specific jobs, machinery and equipment, and the purpose of each are explicit and many are illustrated. The indispensability of interdependence among everybody involved is stressed. For example, safety precautions are taken, inspections made, and permits obtained before any work can begin.

> To reduce the risk of falling debris even further and to make it possible to work from the outside of the building, a scaffolding of prefabricated sections was erected around the entire structure.

Then, piece by piece, floor by floor, the building comes down, with each stage carefully explained and illustrated. It is the year 1992 before all structural components and materials are finally aboard ship, ready for transport to the Middle East. Then a tragedy occurs in the Atlantic. A storm causes the ship to collide with an iceberg and lose its cargo. Luckily, the crew is rescued. The news of the misfortune is received with varied feelings across the world, but New Yorkers rebound at the opening of Empire State Park with a celebration. Then Prince Ali begins thinking of his next venture—dismantling the Chrysler Building!

An aesthetic study in architecture, *Unbuilding* offers readers a thoroughly researched and detailed account of an enormous and intriguing undertaking. Demanding the exercise of skills in observation, analysis, and synthesis, the work exposes readers to an element of excitement throughout the book. As participants in this destructive yet creative endeavor, readers will employ their problem-solving skills in how to dismantle the building, what to retain, what to destroy, how to dispose of the rubble, and the timing of all the necessary phases.

Macaulay is a master of meticulous, intricate, black-and-white drawings that stimulate readers' appreciation for the architectural profession. An investigation in visual thinking, *Unbuilding* is an ingenious tool for imaginative minds. The language is rich and vigorous, utilizing a vocabulary unique to the profession.

McDermott, Gerald. (Retold). *Daughter of Earth: A Roman Myth.* Illus. by author. New York: Delacorte, 1984, unp. (Intermediate)

This mythological adventure explains the beginning of the seasons in a picture-book format using superb, sweeping illustrations of dynamic colors and design.

Ceres, goddess of agriculture, and her lovely daughter, Proserpina, stay busy during the year going from field to field across the earth. They attend to the sowing of seeds and watch the grains and fruits grow, while being greatly loved by the people of the earth.

Proserpina has specific charge of all flowers. One day, when left alone by her mother, she decides to make a surprise bouquet for her. In her delight at this idea, Proserpina runs about a meadow gathering blossoms and spots a narcissus of stunning beauty. She struggles to free it from the earth, and when it is finally released, a great rumbling and crashing of the earth bring forth Pluto, King of the Underworld, in a huge chariot pulled by dark fierce horses.

Pluto immediately decides to claim Proserpina as his bride. She cries out in vain as he swiftly carries her away, informing her that she cannot escape the deep, dark underworld. Proserpina is led to Pluto's palace where she is guarded by Cerberus, the three-headed hound that hovers over the palace door.

Meanwhile, Ceres has heard her daughter's cries and hurries to rescue her, but to no avail. After days of searching, the beauty of the fields begins to fade and die and everything turns brown. In her distress, Ceres finally implores Jupiter, King of the Sky, to help her, but he can do nothing, for he rules the skies while Pluto is in charge of the Underworld. One god doesn't interfere with another's kingdom.

Finally, the god of the sun tells Ceres where her daughter may be found. Angry that the gods have not interfered with Pluto's plan, Ceres threatens famine and drought as revenge. In the meantime, in his deep caverns, Pluto tries to persuade Proserpina to eat of the fruit of the dead to make her his forever, but in her sadness, she wants nothing.

As Ceres threatened, the earth finally dries up, and in their desperation the people call out to the gods for help. Jupiter sends Mercury to warn Pluto to release Proserpina. Knowing that Jupiter is King of the Gods, Pluto is afraid and pleads with Proserpina to stay. He joyfully discovers that she has eaten a pomegranate, and that her fate is sealed.

In retaliation, Ceres freezes the earth in blankets of ice and snow. Mercury is again sent on a mission to rescue Proserpina, and explain to her captor that she may join him for a third of the year. Pluto reluctantly agrees to let her go. So, as the myth goes, Proserpina returns to Pluto in the Underground during winter and emerges in spring to live on earth.

McDermott's mural-like illustrations depict the gaiety and happiness of Proserpina, in contrast to the tragedy and anger of Ceres, as she wraps her cloak about her and searches in despair for her daughter. The overall effect is a magnificently three-dimensional design with stark and dramatic contrasts between brightness and darkness.

This book is appropriate for introducing gifted children to myths by calling into play their imagination and ability to perceive good winning over evil.

MacDonald, Suse. *Alphabatics.* Illus. by author. New York: Bradbury, 1986, unp. (Beginning)

Seemingly engaged in acrobatics—hence the title *Alphabatics*—each alphabet letter jumps and turns as it is creatively altered in size or position to become part of an accompanying illustrative example. For instance, with the addition of a few feathers and an eye for a beak, the letter r looks like a rooster; a capital F turned on its side becomes a fish with long fins. Each letter presentation occupies a double-page spread with the capital and low-ercase letters printed in bold color on white background on the upper-left portion of the page. At the bottom of the page either an upper- or a lower-case version of the featured letter is shown undergoing a sequence of spatial alterations. After flip-flops, turns, reversals, or enlargements, the letter lands at its special position as an object or part of the scene depicted on the facing page. Each transformation consists of three or four stages, and letters are shown within boxes. For example, lowercase n loses its straight line and is gradually turned over to become a bird's nest in a tree. Lowercase m is widened to become a thick, brown mustache. In three sequences the letter o is transformed into the eyes of an owl. First one white o is shown; then two o's with the centers filled in by a gold color; in the last boxed sequence, feathers are added. The complete owl figure sitting in a tree appears on the facing page.

Although this alphabet book resorts to a few too-familiar, overused words such as "xylophone" and "zebra," most other words are more original and have fresh appeal, such as "quail" and "dragon." Language is limited to one-word examples. The bright, bold colors against a background of plenty of white space keep the pages uncluttered and visually interesting. *Alphabatics* should stimulate the imagination and creativity of preschool and other beginning readers and inspire some youngsters with an inclination toward figural creativity to draw some of their own "alphabatics."

McGovern, Ann. *Nicholas Bentley Stoningpot III.* Illus. by Tomie dePaola. New York: Holiday, 1982, unp. (Beginning)

Nicholas joins his family on a cruise but is largely ignored by his parents who are busy with their adult friends. Nicholas feels lonely, goes to bed early, and longs for some excitement. One night his wish for excitement is fulfilled as a severe storm causes the boat to sink. The adults sail away safely in a lifeboat, but Nicholas is left clinging to a piece of the destroyed ship. After floating for several days, Nicholas lands on an island paradise that he subsequently claims as his own because the inhabitants—parrots, goats, and a monkey—welcome him. He quickly adapts to his new life-style, using his survival skills to construct a house and furnishings and reveling in his free-dom from parental control.

His parents, once they discover their son is missing, offer a million-dollar reward, and soon helicopters and boats search for him. Not wanting to be recognized by would-be rescuers, Nicholas disguises himself in clothing that has drifted ashore from other shipwrecks. Alternately dressed as an old lady, a clown, a pirate, and a wild beast, Nicholas avoids detection. Gradually, Nicholas learns to cope better and better, for example, by reading books he finds in trunks washed ashore from previous ship disasters. He contemplates leaving the island but decides to wait until he is ready.

McGovern contrasts two different life-styles in the transformation of Nicholas—the neatly groomed, well-dressed but lonely, dependent young-ster and the wild-haired, casually attired boy who is master of his own world. Although this imaginative story will appeal to many children, it is particularly attractive to gifted youngsters who long for the freedom and opportunity to explore their own interests and develop self-reliance.

McMillan, Bruce, and Brett McMillan. *Puniddles.* Photog. by Bruce McMillan. Boston: Houghton Mifflin, 1982, 32 pp. (Beginning)

In this innovative book of photographs, a father and his 13-year-old son introduce a new game called *Puniddles.* The two authors define Puniddles as "a pair of photographs that suggest a literal or obvious solution in a funny way, . . . A game using the pair of photographs to deduce the punny solution."

The preschool set will delight in applying the visual clues in an attempt to discover the one- or two-word solutions to the puzzles. The book consists of 28 pairs of black-and-white photograph puzzles. Some are simple puns, some are catchy. Some of the more elementary examples include a picture of a bear and a picture of a person's feet below it (bare feet); a picture of a burning fireplace with a photo of crackers below (firecrackers). More in-triguing examples include a seascape and saw (seesaw); a collie dog and a flower (cauliflower); and an ear of corn and a person's knee (corny). Clever combinations require higher-level thinking skills such as analysis and synthe-sis: a boy's chest and nuts that fit on bolts (chestnuts); a pig and a child's bare back (piggyback); and a bee and a seagull (beagle).

All photographs are sharp and clear and of easily recognized objects, freeing the observer to concentrate on the puniddle, rather than trying to identify the picture. Little adult introduction or assistance is needed to enjoy this book as it is textless except for the two-word answers at the bottom of each page (written upside down). On each page the combination of photographs is the same size, thereby creating a sense of balance. Young children will want to "do" this book over and over as well as share it with others. Young gifted children will be encouraged to invent some of their own puniddles.

McNulty, Faith. *The Lady and the Spider.* Illus. by Rob Marstall. New York: Harper & Row, 1986, unp. (Beginning)

This is a poignant story of a little garden spider and a tenderhearted young lady. Although told in the third person, the story can almost be realized from the spider's viewpoint.

In a lettuce garden lives a little spider just trying to exist from day to day by avoiding being consumed by some pernicious predator and hopefully finding food for herself. Her choice for a home is inside a head of lettuce leaves where she feels warm and protected and where she can obtain a drink of water from a drop of dew on the leaves. The spider finds food in the garden each day, maybe a fly or maybe a moth trapped in the dew. She is always wary that she, herself, may end up becoming some hungry bird's lunch.

Just the trauma the spider experiences when the lady's footsteps cause the ground to quake or the brush of her dress, is terrifying, for the garden in which the spider lives belongs to a lovely lady who tends it well. Each day, the lady picks a head of lettuce until one day she unknowingly selects the spider's home and carries it in her basket to the kitchen. There, on the counter, rest the lettuce house and the little spider, unaware of what is to come. When the lettuce is washed under cold running water, the spider struggles for survival by climbing onto a leaf. Here she is discovered by the lady, who immediately prepares to dispose of her, leaf and all. But, on second thought, she decides to set the spider free and takes it back to the garden. She drops the spider into another head of lettuce where the spider begins her little existence all over again.

A strong message of a tenacious determination to survive is conveyed in this simple, stunning story. The young gifted child may identify with the spider and its seemingly insignificant life that, yet, is of utmost importance. The book is an excellent example of perfect harmony between text and illustration. The pale greens and blues of the illustrations appear delicate and fragile surrounding the spindly little creature in its tiny world.

The lettuce is large and looming on the pages, sometimes covering them in color. The gentle lady is in a white summer dress, sometimes with a bit of lace showing as she bends down to loosen the lettuce leaves. Sometimes only her sandaled feet are showing, but all the while, the focus is on the little spider, portrayed as not harmful, but dainty and vulnerable. The wash of cool, crisp color surrounding the tiny spider enhances the effect of the total design. The lady allows the spider to continue her existence, demonstrating the privilege and purpose of each living thing. The story is beautifully illustrated and beautifully told.

Malnig, Anita. *Where the Waves Break: Life at the Edge of the Sea.* Photog. by Jeff Rotman and others. Minneapolis, Minn.: Carolrhoda, 1985, 48 pp. (Intermediate)

This is not just another ordinary book about small sea animals at the ocean's shore. It is unique by showing fascinating animals in their natural habitat.

The book explains high and low tides through diagrams, and describes the animals who live in tide pools, including jellyfish, clams, hermit crabs, sea urchins, sand dollars, starfish and brittle stars, snails, periwinkles, sea squirts, seaweed, and sponges. While most animals are presented rather conventionally, some of them are photographed upside down to give a fuller impression. A giant clam hidden in the sand reveals only its ruffled edge to an observer. The large transparent moon jellyfish floats through the water just beneath the surface. A hermit crab is tucked away in its shell with only its claws visible to seal the door. The nutritional value of seaweed and its other uses are also explained. A scientific classification in the back of the book includes kingdom, phylum, class, order, family, genus, and species of each animal. An index is also available.

Malnig's book offers an excellent treatment of an intriguing subject—life at the edge of the sea. The full-color photographs are of excellent quality, focusing on microscopic details with close-up enlargements. Each photograph is carefully captioned and arranged on the page in a way that makes the book easy to read.

Young gifted children can read and understand this exquisitely presented material on well-known and not so familiar sea animals. Factual information is presented in such a manner that a child will want to find out more about the little creatures.

Markle, Sandra. *Digging Deeper: Investigations into Rocks, Shocks, Quakes, and Other Earthy Matters.* New York: Lothrop, 1987, 120 pp. (Intermediate)

This book explores the formation of rock and subsequent changes. Beginning with a brief overview of the planet earth, the author poses questions to the reader about the age of rock, for example.

At the beginning of the chapter on the forces that shape and build the earth, a photograph shows the aftermath of an earthquake followed on the next page by a detailed description of the Alaskan earthquake of 1964. A scientific explanation and diagrams of the underlying structure of the earth are accompanied by an experiment readers can do to understand better the shock waves and vibrations of the devastating quake in Alaska. Several other interesting experiments are offered to help the reader understand how earthquakes are measured. Another chapter explores tectonic plates, mountain building, and volcanology. Again, various experiments are included to help children relate more closely to the geological changes discussed.

An historical account of the formation of the Grand Canyon and the process of rock weathering is found in the chapter about forces that break down and move rocks. For example, the author explains cave formation and stalactites and stalagmites, and describes an experiment whereby children can grow crystals to witness these occurrences.

Discussions of wind and water erosion, landslides, soil composition, and glaciers are each accompanied by an experiment children can perform using easily obtained materials.

There is also a chapter describing minerals found in the earth, including their location, characteristics, quality, usefulness, and the difficulty of mining them. A description of crystals is accompanied by a diagram of the six basic formations. Procedures for how to identify minerals and an explanation of hardness value and mineral properties provide young children with information usually found in more advanced works.

Photographs of rocks and their interiors afford children an opportunity to understand the composition and formation of various kinds of rocks. The geological calendar, as accepted by geologists, is presented with entries of possible changes and formation of rocks for each era.

The book presents an excellent, readily understandable account of some otherwise complicated geological processes and properties. Actively involving the reader with pertinent questions and follow-up experiments, Markle has explored a great many topics and posed many more questions for children to investigate. Her encouragement of rock collecting may further inspire children who already have an interest in this area. The book contains enough information to increase the reader's understanding without totally satisfying his or her curiosity, thereby leaving room for further independent exploration. The book, well written and using scientific and geological terminology, involves the reader in a participatory role throughout.

Mayer, Mercer. *East of the Sun and West of the Moon.* Illus. by author. New York: Four Winds, 1980, 48 pp. (Intermediate)

Once upon a time, a beautiful maiden lived with her father and mother in a faraway land. Their lives were complete until war broke out. Food was scarce, the father became ill, and the daughter was sent to find food. The beautiful daughter, who had always had her choice of any man in the kingdom, was now no more attractive and appealing than a hardworking peasant. She felt her unattractiveness, and bitterly anticipated a solitary life.

The mother sends her to the house of the South Wind for the clear water needed to prevent the father from dying. With a silver cup, the maiden sets out on her journey. When she arrives at her destination, she discovers that the South Wind has gone and that the spring has turned murky. Hearing her lamenting her misfortune, a frog guarantees the water if the maiden will grant him three wishes. She agrees. The water clears and the frog fills the cup. His first wish is that she will permit him to visit her, which the maiden quickly grants and leaves.

After drinking the water, the farmer's health and fortune are restored. Time passes and the maiden forgets her promise to the frog.

Then, suddenly, one day the frog appears on her doorstep and reminds her of the promise. She allows him to visit her, and after seven days, the frog asks the maiden to grant his second wish. She is appalled to learn that he wants her to become his bride. Disgusted, she runs to her room, but the frog follows, insisting on her promise. The maiden furiously flings the frog against the wall, killing him. A handsome youth appears. He informs her that the death of the frog has freed him, but that he must go far away to wed the troll princess because the maiden broke her promise to the frog. The maiden vows to follow him and become his bride in spite of the youth's warning that the kingdom is east of the sun and west of the moon.

After the youth is carried away by demons, the maiden weeps in helpless sorrow and utters aloud her dilemma. The high moon hears her and directs her to the ice cave where she is to ask for help from the salamander in a chamber of fire. When she arrives at the cave, the salamander tells her that he knows the lovers' hearts, but can only tell her the land is east of the sun and west of the moon, and that it will not be a pleasant place to visit. The salamander refers her to Father Forest, who knows everything. To reach Father Forest, the maiden is to find the tinder box outside the cave and ride the unicorn waiting there. On reaching her destination, she is to keep the box but send the unicorn back to the salamander. When the maiden arrives in the forest, she follows the salamander's orders before lying down to rest. As she sleeps, Father Forest tells her that although he knows the youth's and the maiden's desires, he cannot tell exactly where the kingdom lies, only that it is east of the sun and west of the moon.

Father Forest directs the maiden to the Great Fish of the Sea for help. The Great Fish gives her similar instructions; find a bow and arrow to keep, and ride in a cart pulled by a goat. She finds the Great Fish and is told to seek the North Wind for help, and he offers to let her ride there on his back.

On reaching the North Wind's house, the Great Fish leaves her with a scale from his back. When the maiden learns that the North Wind is out, she waits in the garden to meet him the next day. Finally, the North Wind agrees to take her to the land east of the sun and west of the moon, but cautions her that she will not be welcome there.

Arriving at the troll kingdom, the tired maiden knocks at the castle door pretending to be looking for work. The troll princess eagerly greets her with intentions of turning the maiden into a stone statue, as she has done to many previous visitors. The maiden is ordered to clean everywhere except behind the door with the gold knob.

As she works, the trolls taunt and tease her, ruining her efforts by throwing soot and sand everywhere she cleans. Eventually, she finds the room behind the gold knob and releases the youth imprisoned in a block of ice by igniting it with the tinder box. The youth is weak, but they manage to escape only to encounter the troll princess poised with an ax. The maiden takes the small box and arrow and shoots the troll in the heart, instantly turning her into wood. As the other trolls rush at them, the maiden holds the shiny fish scale up so they can view their ugliness and, in horror, they turn to stone.

The castle immediately returns to a happy place and the people in stone return to life. The youth and the maiden are married and a new castle is built for them where they remain in the land that is east of the sun and west of the moon.

Mayer has created an enchanting version of a classic fairy tale. Although all ends well, the maiden's adventures in her persistence to find her true love are memorable. The illustrations are rich and colorful with sweeping, romantic, and detailed images. In contrast, the wicked trolls are depicted as coarse and vile in their atrocities. Although the text does not describe the maiden's character in depth, the illustrations depict the range of emotions felt by the girl as she seeks her prince.

In fairy-tale style, the language is rhythmic and repetitive, yet holds the reader's interest and anticipation regardless of the somewhat predictable ending. This well-written and beautifully told story will captivate the gifted reader with its rich language from beginning to end. In addition, the illustrations stimulate the reader to contemplate the story contained within them.

Merriam, Eve. *Fresh Paint.* Illus. by David Frampton. New York: Macmillan, 1986, unp. (Intermediate)

This well-known and much-loved author brings her readers another wonderful collection of original poems filled with vivid imagery and lilting rhyme. Using a variety of subjects—from the world around us to the world inside us—each poem nudges children to think, imagine, and wonder.

For example, a poem entitled "Peeling an Orange" conjures up the pungent, delicious aroma of the freshly peeled fruit. An accompanying illustration aptly shows orange segments with the peel spiraling away. "Quaking Aspen" reminds anyone who has ever seen an aspen tree of how all its leaves seem to tremble and rustle at one time. In her poem "Questions for an Angel," Merriam has three questions to ask an angel, while "Quest" echoes the forlornness of a wasted planet when environmental concerns are ignored. In an amusing poem called "Artichoke," a turtle is made from artichoke leaves.

Highly able readers will internalize the meaning of the more serious poems, such as "Summer's End," while delighting in the carefree ones, such as "Butterflies." Only a master poet such as Merriam can write such beautiful, meaningful, and fun-to-read poetry for children. Using figurative language, as in "Sunset," clever analogies, as in "Anticipation," and sensitive phrases, as in "New Moon," the poet always stimulates readers aesthetically. Many of the poems have an enchanting effect on the reader, requiring them simply to sit back and enjoy.

The collection contains poems that appeal to children of all ages, provoking the reader to find their own special meaning. A slim volume of 45 verses, the book is elegantly illustrated with black-and-white woodcuts.

Monroe, Jean Guard, and Roy A. Williamson. *They Dance in the Sky: Native American Star Myths.* Illus. by Edgar Stewart. Boston: Houghton Mifflin, 1987, 130 pp. (Intermediate)

This beautifully written book contains legendary tales of American Indians' interpretation of the constellations. Eight chapters extol the beliefs of Indian tribes, including the Pawnees, Plains Indians, California Indians, and several others. The tales were handed down orally from one generation to the next with each tribe slightly altering them by adding some of their own observations. Emphasizing humankind's relationship to nature, the stories do not attempt to explain that world scientifically. Rather, they are intended to reveal man's harmony with nature that emerges from observing the laws of nature.

Beginning with the Seven Dancing Stars, known as the Pleiades, the first group of legends shows how North American Indians used this small constellation to plan their calendar. Originally, the name "Dancing Stars" was given to this constellation because it looks like two rows of dancers moving across the sky. Onondaga Indians called the constellation the "Bright Shining Old Man"; a California tribe, the Monache, referred to it as "Wild Onion Women." Yet another tribe named it "Baakil and His Five Wives." As illustrated in this collection, each tribe had an entertaining story that explained the name it had given to Pleiades.

Another constellation, the Big Dipper, is sometimes linked to animals, such as a large bear or a coyote. The Navajo and Pueblo Indians, tribes of the Southwest, had their own mythological versions of star tales and used constellations to guide their planting of crops and to determine their harvesting time.

"Where the Dog Ran" is a story of the Cherokee Indians' description of the Milky Way, which they represented as cornmeal sprinkled across the sky and being highly visible during corn harvesting season. According to legend, a dog invades the corn mill, scatters the meal, and then runs away as he is chased by Indian women.

Some of the tales may be compared with Greek myths. For example, "The Little Girl Who Scatters the Stars" bears resemblance to "Pandora's Box."

The carefully researched stories are charmingly illustrated with soft, black-and-white drawings. Simply yet elegantly written, the tales adhere as closely as possible to the original version. Consistent with the oral tradition, therefore, the stories are enhanced if read aloud. This Native American Indian heritage, tastefully depicted in these tales, provides the able reader with a rich background of imaginative interpretation of the constellations.

The book contains a table of contents, glossary of the names of constellations and Indian tribes, a suggested bibliography for further investigation, bibliographical notes for each chapter, and a helpful index.

Munro, Roxie. *The Inside-Outside Book of Washington, D.C.* Illus. by author. New York: Dutton, 1987, unp. (Beginning)

With its clear, sharp, intricate lines, this large, handsome picture book is an aesthetic and architectural delight.

Our visit starts on the front cover jacket inside a helicopter. Hovering over the White House lawn, the helicopter is preparing to land so we can enjoy an outside-inside look at famous landmarks in the nation's capital city.

Illustrated with spacious crisp, clean lines, the massive, gray, monolithic Library of Congress confronts us. The reader immediately has a feeling of being at the bottom of the steps leading up to this huge structure. The next double-page spread takes us inside the building, enabling us to look down at the quiet activity of the library floor. In full view is the delicately designed ceiling dome with sculptured arches and stained-glass windows. The vastness is almost overwhelming.

Next, the regal Corinthian columns of the Supreme Court Building loom high above several brick umbrellas on a rainy day. Inside we see the members of the Supreme Court, robed in black, in session above the floor. Sections of the artwork on the ceiling and surrounding sculpture appear above the heavy maroon velvet draperies. Over the shoulder of a sketching artist we peer down at the justices of the Court.

An unassuming presentation of the exterior of the Bureau of Engraving and Printing appears on the next page accompanied by illustrations of children enjoying refreshments from a street vendor. The double-page spread of the inside of this building is astounding as we watch paper money being printed. Our vantage point allows a closer look at this fascinating process.

The Organization of American States Building's wrought-iron entry gates open to a throng of people who join an assembly of brightly costumed representatives of other countries and cultures. A crystal chandelier hangs above the stately columns.

Continuing her practice of using nontraditional vantage points, Munro introduces the inside of the Space Museum from the cockpit of a DC-7 where instruments and technological apparatus are realistically illustrated. Children will marvel at the impressive assortment of airplanes in this building.

The East Room of the White House is filled with reporters during a news conference. Gold curtains hanging from the windows match the opulence of the ornate chandeliers. We also witness an on-the-spot news broadcast outside the White House and get a behind-the-scenes look of a newscast. The news coverage is also represented by a double-page spread of the *Washington Post* as the paper rolls off the press and later is found rolled up on a doorstep somewhere in the city.

Next, the reader is taken by car to Robert F. Kennedy Memorial Stadium where the astounding spaciousness of the interior of the arena is presented, filled to the brim with colorfully clad spectators watching a football game.

An exquisite drawing of the Capitol dome against a soft blue sky captivates the readers before they are invited into the Senate floor.

The book ends with a view of the Lincoln Memorial as a group of children on a field trip is leaving. We stand before the impressive statue of Lincoln and sense the quiet dignity of this overwhelming, meticulously carved monument.

Munro's book is a you-are-there visual experience, memorable long after its cover is closed. The rich color and the clean, sparkling lines of every illustration evoke the reader's appreciation of the craft and detail that have gone into the magnificent structures presented. Readers will wish to investigate further certain buildings of particular interest. A spectacular introduction to the nation's capital for many children, the book includes an annotated bibliography on each building shown.

Munthe, Nelly. *Meet Matisse.* Illus. by Rory Lee. Boston: Little, Brown, 1983, 45 pp. (Intermediate)

This book introduces the reader to an exploration of the works of the final years of Henri Matisse, a French artist famous for his oil paintings. As Matisse became ill and grew weak, he no longer had the strength needed to work in oils and subsequently began to produce cutouts using scissors and paper. The artist selected a special quality of paper and had his assistants paint large sheets in his preferred colors before he began his unique way of sculpting with scissors. The resulting cutouts were unusual in that Matisse's choice of colors and shapes came from his imagination and self-expression, not from the ordinary shapes of nature. Matisse was influenced by the world around him and the special world inside him. For example, in *The Sheaf,* he used irregularly shaped leaves in various bright colors to illustrate his interpretation of life.

To make Matisse's techniques more practical and "live," readers are given directions and illustrations in double-page spreads on how to create their own compositions using painted paper and scissors. The theory behind color contrasts, complementary colors, and background emphasis is explained along with brief interpretations of the psychological and emotional effects of specific colors. Using direct quotes by Matisse, the author invites the reader to examine two of Matisse's works: *Composition, Violet and Blue* and *Composition, the Velvets.* Each is carefully analyzed and its intended effect explained according to feeling, images used, and colors. These analyses will inspire participants to examine other works of art using the same applications as with other of Matisse's specific artistic processes.

In addition, techniques related to light and color and texture and color are introduced through an art activity illustrated on a double-page spread using bright blue paint. In a further attempt to involve the reader, Munthe suggests the reader observe a shell, draw it from every possible angle, investigate each curve and spiral, and try to concentrate totally on it as Matisse would. To accompany this suggestion, the book includes a color illustration of a snail's shell depicted from various sides.

Matisse's genius is shown through the examples of other of his works. For example, when he was commissioned to create some murals, he drew from his own rich experiences of travels to exotic islands in the South Pacific, producing *Oceania* and *Polynesia*. He focused on corals, birds, jellyfish, and sponges for his stark, white cutout shapes and beiges and blues for background colors. Matisse employed positive and negative shapes to create *The Swimming Pool,* one of his greatest works in the medium of cutouts, completed when he was old and ill in 1952. Matisse's unique work can also be found in the Chapel of the Dominican at Venice for which he created the *Rose Chasuble* and *The Tree of Life.* The beauty of these compositions is enhanced by the light streaming through the stained-glass windows. In these compositions the artist was expressing the light he had inside of him: "One must observe a lot. One has only one life, and one is never finished."

In this book the author "allows" Matisse himself to explain his deep, inner motivations for each work and tries to draw the viewer into his world. His apparent obsession with color was organized and balanced, yet always changing. For him, the choice of color for a composition was always meaningful, never random.

Matisse also emphasized the lifetime of discipline and effort that went into his work regardless of the simplicity of design. To him each creation was important, and each time he began a new project he started anew and renewed.

Munthe's introduction to the twentieth-century master concentrates on Henri Matisse's final years without much attention to his earlier work in oils. Observations are aesthetic, detailed, and thoughtful, emphasizing Matisse's deep emotional involvement in the art medium of cutouts. Matisse's art is expressive, communicating a message with rhythmic arrangements of shapes and colors—to him the placement of objects and the space around them were equally important.

Accompanying black-and-white photographs are skillfully and effectively presented, from Matisse painstakingly drawing on the walls around his bed to create a garden atmosphere to practical instructions and illustrations on how readers can make their own wall friezes. The book's format is crisp and clear with splashes of bright and cheerful color. It's a delightful visual experience that challenges children to create and encourages the more serious student to investigate Matisse's earlier work after this introduction to the creations of his later years.

Murphy, Jim. *Guess Again: More Weird & Wacky Inventions.*
New York: Bradbury, 1986, 92 pp. (Intermediate)

Where there is a need for improvement, someone will find a solution. To back up this assertion, Murphy has described 45 little-known inventions, a few serious, but most of them humorous, by would-be inventors using a quiz format. In this sequel to his earlier title, *Weird and Wacky Inventions* (see Baskin and Harris, *Books for the Gifted Child,* Bowker, 1980, pp. 203–204), Murphy uses the same format: Actual inventions by inventors who were never recognized are presented in pen-and-ink drawings from the original patent drawing and a brief clue describing the object followed by multiple-choice guesses as to the function of a particular invention. Answers are presented in a more complete explanation of how the device worked and are accompanied by a more detailed drawing showing the invention in action. Illustrations are clear, black-and-white sketches from actual patent drawings and magazine illustrations.

In his introduction, Murphy relates the invention of the Kentucky long rifle, an invention essential to the survival of early settlers, as an example of the necessity of invention for man's survival. Inventions from the 1800s and 1900s reflect concerns related to the economy and transportation systems of the times as well as personal safety and recreational needs. Specifically, inventions are grouped under the headings "The Animal Kingdom" (most dealing with concerns of farmers), "What You Wear," "Getting Around," "Fun and Games," "Personal Hygiene," and "Odds and Ends." Many inventions were attempts to meet serious needs, such as a life preserver for horses (inflatable rubber bags strapped on a horse's stomach) to enable cavalries carrying heavy equipment to cross deep water quickly without the aid of boats. Several intriguing, often silly, solutions were devised to help alleviate some of the annoyances and dangers facing farmers and the animals. For example, a metal antibutting device worn by a bull between the horns and nose ring was supposed to prevent bulls from butting anything in sight. Other creations seem more frivolous. For example, in the early 1920s when it was fashionable for women to sport full, cupid-style lips, a device was invented for shaping the upper lip to keep it in the desired shape for hours. Of special interest to children might be the hypodermic needle shaped as a bunny patented by Dr. Robert Smeton in 1967.

The last chapter offers insight into the creative process itself and describes the attitudes of five inventors, not all successful: Benjamin Franklin's efforts to deal with inferior competitors for his stove; John Fitch's largely unsuccessful experiments with steamboats; Catherine Beecher's concept of a central kitchen; Louis Braille's writing system, little recognized until after his death; and mechanical engineer Arthur Rayment's attempts to devise a crab sheller robot as efficient as a human. To remind readers that humorous inventions are not merely a thing of the past, the author describes a motor-driven flag-waving machine designed for the enthusiastic patriot by William E. Bounds in 1984. Finally, a list of government publications related to patents and other books about inventors and inventions is included for readers' reference.

The underlying message of this entertaining and informative book, stated in the afterword, is that as long as there are problems, there will be people willing to spend the time and energy to solve them. Creative intermediate-level readers can analyze the examples in this book and draw the relationship between an identified need and a proposed solution. Even though not all inventions were successful, readers can benefit from studying the process of divergent thinking.

Nolan, Dennis. *The Castle Builder.* Illus. by author. New York: Macmillan, 1987, unp. (Beginning)

Rich in imagination, this is the story of a little boy who builds an elaborate sand castle on the beach. He thinks aloud as he plans to build the largest and best castle ever made. Beside the boy stands a miniature toy figure, and nearby is heard the gentle lapping of waves. The boy works industriously to shape the walls, towers, windows, and battlements as the tiny figure looks on. Finally, the castle is finished and the boy is very proud of his creation.

In his imagination, he now enters the giant castle and climbs the stairs. Surprised, but not frightened, the boy discovers that a huge, fire-breathing dragon inhabits the castle and soon roars up the stairs after him. Fearlessly he commands the dragon to stop and obey, and the dragon complies.

As Sir Christopher, the name the boy has given himself, stands on top of the castle wall, he sees a ship of pirates approaching. He bravely commands them to retreat, but they continue rushing in for the attack. However, when the boy orders the dragon to destroy the pirates, they quickly turn and flee.

When the wind suddenly increases as a storm approaches, the dragon flies away. Left alone in the castle, the boy is unable to command the ocean to obey him. Instead, the water rises as he rushes up the castle stairs. Soon, huge, powerful waves crumble the walls of the sand castle, and just as the boy screams, a hand reaches down to save him. The hand belongs to the boy; the figure he rescues is the toy; and the imaginative adventure is over. The boy places the toy figure in his sand bucket and leaves for home with plans of making an even bigger and better castle the next day.

Large, soft, black-and-white illustrations are composed of tiny dots. On cream paper these lend a dreamy quality to this imaginative story. The boy's fantastic imagination allows young readers to share an experience they won't soon forget. Children will utilize their own imagination to ponder the events of this superb tale. The story is aesthetically appealing and stimulating for youngsters, many of whom may have built their own castles in the sand or in their dreams.

Novak, Matt. *Claude and Sun.* Illus. by author. New York:
Bradbury, 1987, unp. (Beginning)

Focusing on French Impressionism, this exquisite picture book presents a refreshing approach to children's literature.

The main character, Claude, is a little old man with a fluffy white beard who clearly resembles the great painter, Claude Monet. In this charming story, Claude is shown on hands and knees caring for his vegetable garden while a lemony-yellow sun shines on. Against a sun smiling over cottony clouds, he is subsequently dwarfed by giant golden sunflowers reminiscent of those painted by Vincent van Gogh. Next, we see Claude and the sun playing on a pond of lily pads, reminding us that Monet was an avid painter of water lilies. Deep in a forest, Claude is busy gathering blackberries as the sun streams through the trees. He then discovers a secret path to a lovely rain shower that produces an abundance of brightly colored umbrellas, not unlike Auguste Renoir's theme for his famous painting by the same name. Soon the sun peeps out from behind gray clouds before it bursts upon the antics of a group of children who use the umbrellas in a delightful game of hide-and-seek.

Finally, Claude and the sun return home, prepare for bed, and bid the world good-night. Even the sunflowers retire for the night, closing themselves amid the pinks and blues of sundown as beautifully depicted on the last page.

The book is brilliantly illustrated in the pointillist watercolor style of Georges Seurat, thereby enhancing this little story that cleverly interweaves art history into its otherwise simple plot. The ever-present sun brightly illuminates Claude's happy world from sunup to sundown, always hovering close to this little man.

The brief text allows greater concentration on the art theme, which can be developed with younger children with help from an adult and can be realized by older children as they feast on this work independently. The incorporation of the symbols and styles of well-known painters suggests the book could be used for deeper art appreciation.

Nozaki, Akihiro, and Mitsumasa Anno. *Anno's Hat Tricks.* Illus. by Mitsumasa Anno. New York: Philomel, 1985, 44 pp. (Beginning)

Simple in appearance, *Anno's Hat Tricks* is an introduction to the challenge of solving logical thinking problems by elimination. The problems relate to guessing which color hat—red or white—each of the children is wearing. Four figures remain rather static throughout: The hatter, who is reminiscent of Sherlock Holmes, distributes red and white hats from his long hatbox; a boy and girl, the recipients of either a red or a white hat; and "Shadowchild," representing the reader, a gray shadowlike figure who also wears hats provided by the hatter. The first few problems use only three hats, but later problems are more difficult involving five possibilities.

To start, the boy figure is shown wearing a red hat. Shadowchild also wears a hat, but cannot see its color. The reader is led to recognize that, given two hats—one red and one white—if one can see the color of the other child's hat, he or she will know the color of his or her own hat. If Tom's hat is red, mine (the reader's) must be white. In the next problem, the number of hats increases to three (two red and one white) and, through dialogue, the reader is led to understand the reasoning process. Later problems involve combinations of five hats (three red and two white) and include a girl figure.

Both text and illustrations are sparse, but concise. The uncluttered, simple illustrations are an integral part of communicating the process of how to eliminate possibilities.

In a note to adult readers, Nozaki and Anno explain the importance of if-then reasoning, warn against making erroneous assumptions, and give examples of hat problems using flowchart diagrams that illustrate the binary logic and display all the possibilities.

To guess the hat colors correctly, readers should have attained the cognitive stage beyond egocentricity that enables them to examine data from another's point of view. Deceptively simple in appearance, the book offers a cognitive challenge to young readers who have the ability to manipulate data mentally as they examine several possibilities. Although some readers can interact successfully with the text and illustrations to solve the problems independently, others need adult assistance.

Oakley, Graham. *Hetty and Harriet.* Illus. by author. New York: Atheneum, 1981, unp. (Beginning)

Harriet was never satisfied. An opportunist at heart, she was constantly seeking the "Pathway to a New Life" and was continually reminding her good friend, Hetty, of her desire to run away. Hetty, on the other hand, could not be bothered, she was content with her complacent and calm existence. So goes the introduction to this story about two hens who lived in a farmyard.

The opportunity to escape occurs right after a storm. Most hens, including Hetty, preferred to reap the rewards of the storm in the form of lots of newly exposed delicious worms. Harriet's mind was on other things, however, and after the feast she announced her decision to leave for "just over there" where things were more wonderful. Easily influenced, Hetty agrees to accompany her friend. They find the perfect place and enjoy a fruitful day, but then Harriet begins her perpetual complaining again and encourages Hetty to come with her to a more perfect place. Along the way the two hens mistakenly claim a hungry fox's den for a nice nesting place and narrowly escape when he returns.

Next, they decide to nest at the top of an abandoned windmill where the eerie night becomes illuminated with many pairs of eyes. Frightened, they leave the windmill, but not before Harriet spots the beckoning bright lights of a city.

Their next roosting place during their wanderings becomes a street lamp pole. In the city the hens find scratching ground in a flower box at the entrance to a shopping mall, but are chased away by exasperated shoppers. By now, the two heroines are starving, but learn that a flock of pigeons is unwilling to share breakfast with them. An episode in a candy store also leaves them wanting.

Finally, a policeman donates the two bewildered hens to an auction. Their new owner takes them to what appears to be a farm. However, while out looking for greener grass the exploring duo comes upon the Techno-Egg factory. Frightened at the prospect, they escape through a hole in the fence, but are immediately snatched up and placed in separate cages, joining many other female fowls. Soon the other "girls" inform them of their obligation to produce a daily quota of eggs. They refuse to lay eggs and eventually the egg collector arranges other plans for Hetty and Harriet.

On a rainy night, a small flock of hens is herded to a van headed for the chicken soup factory. Anticipating this grim destination, Harriet and Hetty make a run for it and the other hens follow suit. They all flee into the night, and thanks to Hetty, all stick together. The next day they are trapped by a fox between the bushes and a nearby stream. At last, they flap their way onto a floating branch and are safe from the villain. Very soon, Harriet again sees the most absolutely perfect place, "just over there," as they enter a wonderful barnyard again.

Oakley's humorous story of *Hetty and Harriet* is adventuresome and delightful. The characterization of the two hens is unique, conveying the familiar message that the "grass always seems greener on the other side." Harriet, the willful one, undauntingly searches for the Pathway to a New Life, while Hetty is characterized as a follower who never has the courage to adhere to her inner convictions. Their experiences together are genuine, without elaboration, and all finally ends well.

This is an excellent picture book for young gifted children to read or have read to them. The language is rich and varied without being condescending. A sense of sophistication prevails in this folksy, friendly book, providing intrigue and anticipation of the hens' unexpected experiences. The format is enchanting, with text written in different places on the pages. Quaint, soft colors emphasize the intricately drawn illustrations. Information is presented that may be new for many young children, such as the egg factory, requiring them to assimilate ideas and exercise such thinking skills as application and evaluation as they realize that Harriet is ready to repeat her mistakes.

O'Dell, Scott. *Streams to the River, River to the Sea: A Novel of Sacagawea.* Boston: Houghton Mifflin, 1986, 191 pp.
(Advanced)

O'Dell has carefully chronicled the adventures of the remarkable Sacagawea, the young Shoshone woman who accompanied Lewis and Clark on their journey to the Pacific Ocean. Written from Sacagawea's viewpoint, the author skillfully conveys the journey without minimizing the hardships and dangers experienced by the group along the way.

The story begins when the Minnetarees, an enemy tribe, attack Sacagawea's camp, killing her mother and leaving many others dead as the camp is burned. Sacagawea is kidnapped along with several other women and children and taken to the Minnetaree camp as slaves. The camp is ruled by Chief Black Moccasin, who plans to present Sacagawea to Red Hawk, his spoiled and arrogant son, as his wife.

Soon, Tall Rock, the Indian who captured Sacagawea and killed her mother, steals her away in the night and takes her to the cruel Le Borgne. Sacagawea has heard stories of Le Borgne's violent temper and she fears for her life. Consequently, she steals a horse and leaves, knowing she will be followed and, if found, killed. The young woman travels far away from the enemy camp and sets up her own small campfire, hoping her people will see it and eventually rescue her.

Instead, it is Charbonneau, a French trader, who comes down the river by canoe and offers to take Sacagawea back to her people. Charbonneau is known to the Indian villages as a "white trader" and is welcomed for the many useful and beautiful items he brings in exchange for animal skins. When they reach Black Moccasin's village, Sacagawea is won in a hand game by Charbonneau, who takes her as one of his wives. Terrified of the "white trader," she wants to be free, but she is bound by Indian law to remain his wife.

Soon, Captains Lewis and Clark arrive at the village to trade. Sacagawea has not known people who speak, dress, and behave differently from her. She immediately likes them and the rest of their group and is particularly attracted to Captain Clark. The explorers decide they need Sacagawea to travel with them because she knows the country well. As a result, they hire Charbonneau as a helper, and all depart, including Sacagawea's infant son, who rides in a cradleboard on her back.

The long journey is treacherous, the mountains are steep, the weather is damp and cold, and often the hunters are without food. Still, Sacagawea looks forward to the adventure and the possibility of seeing her own people again since they are to travel near their village. Clark is helpful to her and the baby, whereas her husband selfishly looks out only for himself. Thus, when she becomes very ill, it is Clark who takes care of her. Sacagawea realizes how deeply she feels about Clark and how much she fears and hates Charbonneau.

Finally, the party reaches the Pacific Ocean and turns back inland, the men having completed their mission of tracking a waterway to the sea for traders to use. Sacagawea is given the opportunity to remain with her people when they visit them, but she refuses, wanting only to be near Captain Clark. Eventually, she accepts the fact that her marriage to a white man would only create problems for him. She leaves the man she never wanted and the only one she really loved.

O'Dell's fictionalized account of the historical journey is suspenseful and penetrating. While Sacagawea's feelings for Clark are a strong feature of the story, the vividly portrayed experiences of the entire group are absorbingly realistic. Older children will marvel at the endurance of the hunters and their leaders' determination to continue to the sea regardless of the dangers encountered—it never occurred to them to turn back, for they had an important mission to accomplish.

Olney, Ross, and Patricia Olney. *How Long? To Go, To Grow, To Know.* Illus. by R. W. Alley. New York: Morrow, 1984, unp. (Beginning)

Curious youngsters with a penchant for facts should find that this book stimulates their desire to learn more about the fascinating world in which we live. Filled with facts about how long (how much time) it takes for various life forms to grow and how long (tall) certain objects grow, the book is illustrated with colorful cartoonlike drawings. Some of the illustrations include balloons with comments that add humor or underscore the comparisons being depicted.

In a simple manner—without directly explaining the different meanings of spatial or temporal changes—the Olneys present the concept of change by exploring the relationships among the growth periods of humans, animals, and plants. For example, we are told that the blue whale is the fastest growing animal, but the deep-sea clam is the slowest growing, taking "about 100 years for it to reach a size of less than ½ inch long." Other facts relating to "how long" include how long something will last (stone faces at Mount Rushmore, a television set) and the speed of light and sound. Facts related to size are humorously depicted in both text and accompanying illustrations. One double-spread shows the following sequence of relationships: a germ, a flea with millions of germs, a dog with thousands of fleas and millions of germs, and a blue whale covered with dogs from head to tail, representing hundreds of dogs with thousands of fleas having millions of germs.

Many gifted youngsters enjoy gathering facts and often possess a store-house of interesting knowledge. This book offers more facts to ponder. Whereas less capable readers might not understand the different meanings of "how long," young gifted readers should be able to comprehend the concepts underlying the facts without more explicit explanations.

O'Shea, Pat. *The Hounds of Morrigan.* New York: Holiday, 1985, 469 pp. (Advanced)

Fantasy at its finest awaits the persevering reader in this far-reaching, highly absorbing story. The adventure begins in Ireland when Pidge, a schoolboy, happens upon an old book with a picture of an evil serpent, Olc-Glas. Accidentally, Pidge releases the snake and receives instructions to imprison it again in iron. Therefore, accompanied by his younger sister, Bridget, Pidge begins the long, eventful journey that finally destroys this dreadful creature. The two children encounter what seem to be insurmountable dangers and evils along the way, but remain assured that they will always be protected by Dagda, Lord of Great Knowledge.

When Morrigan, the triple witch-goddess of evil, battle, and sorrow, discovers that Pidge has imprisoned the serpent, she reveals her obsession to obtain the power of Olc-Glas. Thus, Morrigan and two other wicked women take up residence near the children's home and begin to cast their evil spells.

Pidge and Bridget are to retrieve a blood-stained pebble that will determine the future of the world, but first they must experience many hardships. The action-filled tale moves swiftly from one bizarre event to another without yielding the slightest clue to what will happen next. The children sense forthcoming danger—at times frightfully so—but always continue toward their goal. Although the reader remains confident that the two protagonists will not meet fatality along the way, such assurance does not lessen the thrill of the dangers and the obstacles in the two children's path.

Morrigan's horrible hounds, who are capable of assuming human forms and habits, follow Pidge and Bridget, knowing they can only track, not hunt, and that they must not chase the children unless they see them run—only then are the children fair game.

Beginning with the Great Eel, Pidge and Bridget meet numerous unusual and strange creatures, many of whom are helpful to them and play an important part in their mission. Examples include a talking frog who sends them into peals of laughter; Serena, a talking donkey who gives them valuable advice; and great flocks of white birds who shield them from the hounds. At one point, the children are rescued by a spider who leads them to his wonderful family deep in the ground under a tree. Here they meet all his tiny spider children, who delight their young visitors and thereby almost create a story within. Another animal, Coo-roo, a beautiful fox, uses his skills and trickery to cover their scent as he guides them over dangerous mountains and through steep valleys.

When the children finally locate the fateful pebble and retrieve it from a dead giant's hand, they are witness to an evil battle of great magnitude involving Morrigan and her two witch counterparts and other warring figures summoned by both good and evil forces.

Eventually, Pidge and Bridget are returned to the safety and comfort of their hometown. What seemed like endless days of travel actually was only about an hour or so in time.

O'Shea's beautiful command of language will capture readers' attention and tempt them to continue the very long tale to its conclusion. Never does the story lag, never does it bore; rather, it mystifies and magnetically compels rapt attention throughout. Amidst all the horror and ugliness of evil characters and events, a thread of humor and enchantment is expertly interwoven to soften any anticipation of hopelessness or doom. At times, even the slithery, sly hounds are depicted in a dignified manner.

Pidge is portrayed as a rather calm, thoughtful boy, intent on accomplishing his mission. He tries to remain stoic and undaunted even when he is terrified. His strength is partly for the benefit of Bridget, his cheerful, lighthearted sister. Bridget, on the other hand, is a straightforward, rather outspoken little girl who seems wise for her years. True to her character, she approaches the wicked and cruel characters with a "just try me" attitude that elicits a smile from Pidge even in the direst situations. Despair almost overcomes the children near the end, but just when they believe they can no longer continue, a rainbow of hope appears.

O'Shea's imaginative description of the brilliance and beauty of the countryside is breathtaking. For example, "The sky was streaked with long, ruby gashes frilled with apricot clouds" and "Lightning like whips of fire appeared in the sky, lashing and cracking and belting the clouds which scattered like sheep from dogs." The book abounds with analogous writing.

Children who seek out fantasies will marvel at the author's ability to create verbally fascinating images that leave behind a powerful and memorable story.

Peyton, K. M. *"Who, Sir? Me, Sir?"* New York: Oxford University Press, 1983, 172 pp. (Advanced)

One day, after a few too many pints at a local pub, form master Sam Sylvester, disgusted with his students' lack of ambition, arranges an athletic competition between his physically unfit students from a lower-class school and a team of four athletic boys from an affluent school. Realizing he can only achieve through their successes, Sylvester sets out to prove that his school, Hawkwood, merely lacks the facilities and that, if properly trained, his boys can perform as well as the Greycoats. With one year to train, the Hawkwood team at first consists of the following motley crew: Hoomey, a small, thin boy whose nickname is suggested by the title (He always responds with surprise to comments directed his way with "Who? Me, Sir?"); Jazz, a Sikh boy who, in keeping with his family's Indian culture, wears a turban and is set apart because of the darker color of his skin; and two other reluctant students, Bean and Gary. Nutty, a determined, goal-oriented 13-year-old girl is the only true athlete—already an accomplished show horse rider. However, she is not allowed to participate because she is a girl, so she serves as captain/coach.

To begin preparing for the tetrathlon events—swimming, running, riding, and shooting—the parents' association purchases horses otherwise destined for the slaughterhouse, and Nutty arranges for Gary's brother, Nails, an excellent swimmer, to teach the boys to swim. Nails and Gary have unhappy family lives—their mother has deserted her family, and the father is abusive.

When the parents do not want to fund expensive riding lessons and Sylvester refuses to participate, Nutty organizes an unofficial team composed of those who really want to continue—herself, Nails, Jazz, and Hoomey. Biddy Bedwelty, a young accomplished rider accepts the challenge of teaching the beginners to ride, agreeing to forgo her usual fee if the team wins. Self-motivated, the Hawkwood students continue their training in earnest, while the Greycoats, believing they are facing no serious competition, relax.

Nutty's sister, Gloria, who is dating Seb and some of the other Greycoat team members, tells Nutty that Seb's swimming pool is available for practice on Friday nights, so the youngsters, tired of the crowd at the public pool, make use of the private one. Returning home earlier than expected and discovering the Hawkwood team practicing at his pool, Seb's father decides the competition is stimulating for his son's team. Consequently, he not only invites the Hawkwood group to continue using his pool, he also loans them pistols for target practice.

When Nails resisted the routine attempts of a social worker accompanied by the police to question him about his home life, he was taken to the police station on the night before the tetrathlon and nearly missed the event. From the police station, Nails telephones Biddy, pretending she is his mother, who quickly gets him released and drives him to the tetrathlon. Meanwhile, the Greycoats cheated by substituting a skilled swimmer for a team member who did not excel at swimming. Gloria reports to Nutty another Greycoat plan—to distract Jazz's horse. Since the Greycoats had cheated twice, Nutty had few qualms about disguising herself as Jazz and riding again because she knew she could control the horse better. The officials agree that because of the cheating, the schools would have to compete again. In spite of this decision, the story concludes with each member of the Hawkwood team feeling a sense of great accomplishment. Nails is offered a job at Biddy's stables; Hoomey realizes he has ambition; and Jazz is asked to join the prestigious swim club.

This challenging story, which should appeal to gifted readers, revolves around an unpredictable plot, filled with action, humor, and spirited characters, and culminates in a satisfying conclusion with each character attaining a positive self-image. Sentence structure and vocabulary, including British expressions, combine to make challenging reading for highly able upper-intermediate-grade readers. All the characters are memorable as they mature physically and emotionally due to their training. Particularly endearing is Nails, whose juvenile delinquent behavior and angry attitude gradually soften as he recognizes his concern for his horse and her colt.

In the course of the story each character achieves some measure of success, develops insight, and recognizes the value of ambition and hard work. Young people who ascribe success or failure to extrinsic sources such as luck or task difficulty rather than intrinsic values such as ability and effort would do well to read this book.

Phillips, Louis. *263 Brain Busters: Just How Smart Are You, Anyway?* Illus. by James Stevenson. New York: Viking Kestrel, 1985, 87 pp. (Advanced)

This thought-provoking little book contains six chapters full of tricky teasers. Each chapter provides a different kind of problem, making it easy for children to locate quickly their preferred puzzler. A chapter on verbal posers presents plays on words gifted students will find particularly challenging. The last chapter has the answers, which are in chronological order. The mathematical problems may contain a few old favorites, however, most of them are new and different. Bright trivia buffs will be pleased with an unusual assortment of tantalizing tricksters that may be too complicated for the average student. Logic is dealt with in an entertaining manner that encourages children to arrive at clever calculation and stimulates higher-level deductive reasoning.

The book is a combination of riddles, jokes, and puzzles that will stimulate the thinking of the gifted child, while providing information. Black-and-white illustrations add interest and decoration only. All in all, it's a handy little volume of memorable mindbenders that could become a favorite.

Phillips, Louis. *The Upside Down Riddle Book.* Illus. by Beau Garder. New York: Lothrop, 1982, unp. (Beginning)

Fourteen stimulating and challenging riddles are accompanied by brightly colored illustrations that, turned upside down, reveal the solution to the riddle. Written in verse, some of the riddles are familiar and easily identifiable; others are more obscure. Easy riddles include one about an elephant that carries his trunk wherever he goes.

In this instance, the reader can see the bright red shape of an elephant against a vivid green and blue background even before turning the book upside down for the answer. However, in another example, the solution is not as readily discernible. An eagle is described in the riddle, but whenever the book is turned upside down, the reader sees a white jet plane against a bright pink and blue background.

Each riddle is written in white letters in the upper-left corner of a soft gray page; the illustrations occupy the adjacent page. Colors are crisp, clear, and cheerful. Riddles and pictures are carefully selected for a young audience and are especially appealing to the gifted child who must supply the solutions to the riddles from visual clues.

Phillips, Mildred. *The Sign in Mendel's Window.* Illus. by Margot Zemach. New York: Macmillan, 1985, unp. (Beginning)

In the small Russian town of Kosnov where all the inhabitants know one another, the butcher and his wife, Mendel and Molly, decide to earn needed funds by renting out half of their shop. They are delighted when a well-dressed newcomer named Tinker offers to rent the space, for nothing more than a place to sit and think. Separated only by a bedsheet hung from ceiling to floor, the butcher shop is occupied by Mr. Tinker on one side and Molly and Mendel's business on the other. As he counts his weekly earnings aloud, everybody in this small town of tightly clustered buildings hears Mendel's voice. At the end of the week, Mr. Tinker borrows Mendel's horse for a weekend trip to the city. Returning the following Monday accompanied by two policemen, Mr. Tinker points to Mendel's money box, proclaims the amount contained in it, and accuses Mendel of stealing the money from him. Knowing that Mendel's weekly earnings are no secret, Simka, Mendel's friend and an elder citizen, urges the police to question other citizens about the amount of Mendel's weekly earnings. But it is Molly's quick wit that saves her husband from jail. She asked Tinker a series of questions, leading him to admit that if a butcher had handled the coins, there would be fat on them. She places the disputed coins in a pot of boiling water and a layer of fat floats on the surface. She points to this as evidence that the coins had been handled by a butcher, not a thinker. In this ingenious manner, Tinker is soon identified as the thief.

This story is appropriate for young thinkers, since it introduces them to deductive thinking by providing an opportunity to predict how the tale ends. Phillips uses foreshadowing early in the story when Simka expresses caution about the gentleman tenant who claims he wants nothing more than a place to sit and think. The story is told with subtle humor and illustrated by watercolors filled with penned details.

Phipson, Joan. *The Watcher in the Garden.* New York:
Atheneum, 1982, 203 pp. (Advanced)

Kitty, a 15-year-old girl, lives a miserable existence. Feeling unloved, although her family is close-knit and caring, Kitty continually compares herself to her older sister, Diana, who, in Kitty's opinion, is prettier, smarter, and more popular. Kitty's unpredictable, explosive temper and unkind words keep her family in constant turmoil and anxiety. She escapes the family circle as often as possible, taking refuge in a huge garden owned by an old man named Mr. Lovett, whom Kitty eventually meets. He knows that Kitty has been making regular visits to his garden, and respects her need for solitude, contemplation, or whatever else brings her there.

Kitty learns that Mr. Lovett is blind but possesses a keen sense of hearing and intuition. The old man is able to communicate with her as no other and consequently draws her to him. Thus, Kitty visits Mr. Lovett and his dog as often as possible, to share her concerns.

One day, Kitty becomes aware that someone else comes to the garden almost as often as she. In fact, she senses the other person's presence long before she sees him, always feeling fearful and anxious when the other person is around. When Kitty learns that the mysterious visitor is Terry, a town hoodlum, her fears increase. Terry is nursing a grudge against Mr. Lovett for not selling his father land to build a gas station. As a result, he secretly plans to destroy the old man and merely uses his visits to the garden in preparation for this act. Eventually, one of Terry's hoodlum friends takes a job as a gardener for Mr. Lovett, thereby helping along Terry's plan for Mr. Lovett's harm. At the same time, the garden, both enchanted and haunted, begins to play tricks with Terry by creating in him feelings of powerlessness.

When Kitty warns Mr. Lovett about Terry, he assures her that he feels protected by his garden. Yet, obsessed with the threat Terry poses, Kitty begins to spy on him as a precaution.

Meanwhile, Kitty's family relationship is tempered somewhat by her association with Mr. Lovett. Her family knows nothing about him, but Kitty feels that Mr. Lovett understands her and gives her a sense of worth.

Terry becomes irritated with Kitty always lurking around and hopes to scare her away from the garden. Among other things he tries to run her over with his motorcycle but, instead, is seriously injured himself.

Gradually, Terry and Kitty begin to read each other's thoughts. Informed by his friend, the gardener, of Mr. Lovett's habits and of the construction of a new lookout place for the old man, Terry plans to make Mr. Lovett fall down this point, making it appear to be an accident. However, Terry barely escapes death himself, and believes the garden is threatening his life. Finally, just as Terry approaches Mr. Lovett to push him to his death, the garden is shaken by an earthquake. Concentrating with all her mind on replacing

Terry's evil thoughts with good ones, Kitty causes the boy to save Mr. Lovett without really understanding why. In the end Kitty and Terry come to share a special relationship.

Phipson's story is powerful, magnetic, and at times, disturbing. Kitty, around whom the entire story revolves, is presented as an authentic, anxious, young girl. Unsure of how to deal with her own turbulent personality, her relationship with Mr. Lovett instills in Kitty a confidence that gives her unexpected strength.

Readers are presented with abrupt changes of scenes from Kitty's home life to her sojourns in Mr. Lovett's garden. Continually evaluating her behavior and reactions to incidents, readers respond with analysis and criticism of a character whose faults and strengths are realistically portrayed. Some readers may identify with her solitary preferences, her hours of introspection in the garden, and her self-isolation from her family. This strong, stirring story is stunningly written and contains many surprising incidents that keep readers off balance until the end.

Pinkwater, Daniel. *The Frankenbagel Monster.* New York: Dutton, 1986, unp. (Intermediate)

Daniel Pinkwater has whipped up another zany tale. In this one, kindly but ambitious Harold Frankenbagel, proprietor of the Glimville neighborhood bagel shop, turns into a mad scientist at night as he seeks out distant bagel shops in his quest for highly unusual bagel combinations, including ice cream, celery, and prune and even bagels that can sing and fly and those that have computer capacities to answer questions.

Not finding these odd concoctions available, late at night in his bagelshop, Frankenbagel experiments with creating strange bagels. The most unusual of these—the Glimville Bagelunculus—is a huge, robotlike bagel subject to Frankenbagel's commands. This bagel monster assumes a power of its own after encountering a bag of bright blue garlic and roams the streets at night, frightening Glimville's citizens.

Concerned that the giant bagel might cause harm, Frankenbagel admits responsibility for the bagel monster and seeks the counsel of Professor Sir Arnold Von Sweeney, an expert on food-gone-mad events, such as the Night-Stalking Celery of New Jersey. Shortly before the professor devises a plan for dealing with the robotlike bagel, the Bagelunculus attempts to break into a warehouse filled with nutritious lox, which, if eaten, would increase its powers, possibly causing it to become grouchy and destructive.

Clinging to the universal truth that "bagels always go stale just before you're ready to eat them," the professor talks aloud with Frankenbagel about their plan to cover Bagelunculus with cream cheese and jelly. This clever plan works—Bagelunculus's movements become slower and slower as the monster goes "stale." Although Harold Frankenbagel has learned his lesson—not to make a bagel more powerful than himself—readers are left wondering whether the giant bagel is indeed really "stiff, stale, and harmless."

Brightly colored computer-generated illustrations embellish this ludicrous story, which is spiced with puns. The humor should be appreciated by primary and most intermediate-grade readers.

Pomerantz, Charlotte. *If I Had a Paka: Poems in Eleven Languages.* Illus. by Nancy Tafuri. New York: Greenwillow, 1982, unp. (Beginning)

Original and creative, the 12 poems in this collection, mostly in English, also contain words from other languages: Swahili, Serbo-Croatian, Native American, Samoan, Dutch, Vietnamese, Japanese, Indonesian, Spanish, and Yiddish.

Each word and phrase in the foreign language is easily identified in context and through repetition; for example, in Serbo-Croatian, "Yes, It's Raining" or "Pada Kisa." Also, "paka," from the title, means "cat" in Swahili. The poem is written in a chanting style with a lion, rooster, donkey, sheep, and a friend portrayed in each verse.

Similarly, rhythm and repetition help clarify meaning in a poem in the English language called "You Take the Blueberry." This poem delightfully continues for two pages and concludes with a surprise ending. Simple in style, yet challenging in vocabulary, the poems will sharpen the young gifted child's awareness of words in other languages.

Pomerantz's book is distinguished by its pattern, a line of foreign language followed by a line of English interpretation, rather than a complete verse of each language. This feature sustains the reader's interest and enjoyment.

Tafuri's clean, simple drawings in clear, crisp, vivid colors perfectly complement the poems. The intriguing illustration of a cat, "paka," and a mouse on the cover of this charming collection entices the reader to immediate investigation of its contents.

Porter, David Lord. *Help! Let Me Out.* Illus. by David Macaulay. Boston: Houghton Mifflin, 1982, unp. (Beginning)

This is an unusual story of a little boy, Hugo, who reads an ad about how to throw your voice. Intrigued, Hugo mails in his quarter for the how-to book about ventriloquism. Immediately, he can throw his voice and does so, right into a trunk in his room. But when he tries to retrieve his voice, it is gone. He looks everywhere in his house, but to no avail. Hugo ends up going to bed not feeling well, as his concerned and confused mother tries to console him with tea and honey. When he begins to cry, his mother inquires.

Meanwhile, Hugo's voice is ecstatic over its freedom and bounces around the countryside, trying out the mountains, fields, and the seashore. It even goes to the moon. The voice continues its adventures by going on a date, to the zoo, school, and the circus. It surprises people wherever it goes by unexpectedly using words quite inappropriate for the occasion at hand. Finally, the voice becomes bored and lonely and longs for Hugo.

But back at the house, Hugo's parents seek expert advice as to the whereabouts of Hugo's voice. They consult a doctor, a lawyer, and a detective, none of whom can discover the reason for the lost voice—or the cure. So they decide a trip to France just might do the trick.

Hugo's voice eventually enters a trunk in a railroad station and unknowingly becomes baggage on an oceanliner. In the darkness of the trunk, it calls for help, but is unheard. Finally, a redcap hears some disturbance and unlocks the trunk from which the sound seems to be coming. This frees the voice, which races back home to Hugo. Too late, however, for unhappy Hugo and his parents are in a hotel far away in France.

In their absence, Hugo's voice searches the house and discovers the detective in the basement looking for a clue to the lost voice. Intent upon his investigation, he answers the voice without even looking up, explaining that Hugo is in France. The voice sends a telegram to Hugo, requesting that he eat the message. Hugo obeys, proclaiming a loud "*yum*" as he happily regains his voice.

Macaulay's cartoonlike watercolor illustrations depict a typical boy's room and a rather studious-looking boy with large glasses. All characters in the story look as though they came from the comic section of the newspaper, including the balloons used for the voice's spoken words.

This very different picture book is highly entertaining, and, although unable to speak for most of the book, Hugo remains a strong main character. Appealing to children with a keen sense of humor, the story is both appealing and absurd. The book design begins and ends with a view of an open trunk suggesting an impending mystery.

Reading Is Fundamental. *Once Upon a Time... : Celebrating the Magic of Children's Books in Honor of the Twentieth Anniversary of Reading Is Fundamental.* New York: Putnam, 1986, 64 pp. (Intermediate)

Readers are immediately invited inside the book by the tempting cover that depicts a fairy-tale-like forest scene with pictures of illustrations from the book hanging on trees. Assembled to celebrate the twentieth anniversary of Reading is Fundamental, *Once Upon a Time...* is a collection of childhood memories, stories, and anecdotes about the early reading experiences of well-known contemporary children's authors and illustrators. Each of the featured 26 authors and illustrators has contributed two or three pages—written or drawn in his or her individual style.

As Jim Trelease writes in the introduction to this unique collection, of all the wonderful information books can give readers, none is more important than finding out more about ourselves. "How is my *own* story going to turn out? What's my plot?" Characters we meet in books help us learn about ourselves and the world around us, thereby extending and enriching our sense of self.

The first entry is Jack Prelutsky's grinning, gruesome dragon protruding from a book and his poem describing the exciting creatures—trolls, dragons, pirates, and others he has met while reading. The next double-page spread is a pastel-colored futuristic rendering of two children reading together by Leo and Diane Dillon, followed by two pages of text by Katherine Paterson, who reveals her "secret life"—imaginary friends—as a child reader. The book continues with Tomie dePaola's handwritten, uppercase anecdote telling how he drew all over his white bedsheets as a child, crawling under and using a flashlight—until his mother came one day to change the sheets. The accompanying illustration shows a boy, arms extended from the top sheet sketching people and animals on the bottom sheet. Other delightful childhood memories include contributions from Judy Blume, Jean Fritz, Trina Schart Hyman, Jamake Highwater, Shel Silverstein, Steven Kellogg, and many other well-known authors and illustrators.

This varied book will have wide appeal to both children and adults—parents as well as educators. Many adults, but few children, will relate to authors' memories of the Dick and Jane readers. Both children and adults can appreciate the exotic characters and humor of Dr. Seuss and the comfortable, family interactions of the Berenstain bears. The book can be read on different levels—for pure enjoyment, to become acquainted with an author or illustrator, and to evaluate the role of books in one's own life. Serious, insightful young readers can use this unique "book about books" as a means of analyzing and comparing the styles of different authors and illustrators.

Richardson, I. M. *The Adventures of Hercules.* Illus. by Robert Baxter. Mahwah, N.J.: Troll, 1983, 32 pp. (Intermediate)

Recounting the birth of Hercules and his mission to overcome 12 tasks, this adaptation is easily accessible to middle graders while retaining the eloquence and history of the longer original version.

Hercules' extraordinary strength was first observed soon after his birth by his mother, who witnessed him strangling two poisonous snakes sent to kill him by Hera, a jealous goddess. Clearly stronger than ordinary men, Hercules emerges as a hero to his people. Consequently, he is sent to the mountains to kill a huge lion with his bare hands. Later, he demonstrates his great strength by defeating entire armies. Later, when he is married and has children, the jealous Hera causes him to destroy his family, thereby bringing him immense suffering, pain, and grief. When he finally visits the Oracle at

Delphi to seek release from this sin, he is told to go to Mycenae to serve the king for 12 years.

Realizing that the strongest man in the world has come to serve him, the king becomes ecstatic and devises a plan with Hera for Hercules to face 12 deadly tasks known as the "labors of Hercules." The first consists of killing the fierce lion of Nemea, which Hercules strangles with his hands. The second task is to defeat Hydra, the huge, many-headed monster of the swamp. His next task involves capturing the golden-haired stag and a wild boar. Again, Hercules performs his duty without any problem. To accomplish the fifth labor—cleaning the stables of great masses of cattle—Hercules changes the course of two rivers to supply the necessary water. Additional challenges require him to kill man-eating birds and a wild bull, tame man-eating horses, and retrieve a golden belt from Amazon women. Hercules heroically survives these and several other seemingly insurmountable tasks. Finally, the 12 labors are performed, and Hercules confirms the prediction of the Oracle of Delphi by becoming the world's hero.

Individual victories consume him temporarily, but once he achieves his goal, he moves on to new battles. Children may wonder what finally happened to this immortal man. Comparison of the athletic and intellectual qualities of this hero may propel youngsters to analyze the emotional aspects of his compulsively violent personality. Does Hercules suffer remorse for his deeds? Why is this powerful man always forgiven for his acts?

The language in this single-myth presentation is rich and varied. Although delicate color and soft line dominate the illustrations, violence and destruction are visible in Hercules' triumphant behavior. The text appears underneath beautiful watercolor illustrations depicting Hercules' magnificent physique against the dangerous and cruel obstacles he must overcome. Action coupled with rhythm in both illustration and text enlivens the format and enthralls youngsters who may be new to mythology. This vivid and powerful tale will stimulate many readers to investigate more complete mythological works.

Rodowsky, Colby. *The Gathering Room.* New York: Farrar, 1981, 186 pp. (Intermediate)

Unable to accept the assassination of his friend, a gubernatorial candidate, Ned leaves his legal work and city life behind and takes his wife, Serena, and their young son, Mudge, to live in the gatehouse as caretakers of the old Edgemount Cemetery. Living within the confines of the cemetery, the family is isolated, without even a telephone. Mudge receives his schooling from Ned in the gathering room—the large area where eighteenth- and nineteenth-century mourners assembled for funerals.

Without the company of schoolmates and neighbor children, Mudge makes friends with an assortment of persons resting in the cemetery. For example, he plays with the little girl Dorro, converses with the serious judge, enjoys the poetry recitations of the Butterfly Lady, and visits the Captain who was accidentally shot before the War of 1812 by another cemetery inhabitant—Jenkins—one of the captain's own men.

One day Ned's older sister, Ernestus, who raised him as a child, learns of the family's whereabouts and comes to visit to renew her relationship with her brother and his family. Aunt Ernestus reminisces about Ned's childhood, and her presence is a reminder of the world outside Edgemount. Mudge resents the intrusion of his aunt and her dog, Thanatos, feeling crowded. Consequently, he rejects his aunt's friendly overtures and accuses her of invading his life. Before leaving to care for the ailing mother of a friend, Aunt Ernestus tells Mudge that he may call upon her if ever needed.

After her departure, Aunt Ernestus's impact continues to be felt. For example, Ned and Serena begin to show more interest in the area outside Edgemount as they plan a trip to the library and a special treat for Mudge—eating at McDonald's. Mudge, however, refuses to accompany them, preferring to stay home. Gradually, Mudge becomes accustomed to accommodating others in his life. For example, he makes a real live friend, Marcus, who comes to fly kites in the cemetery and later invites Mudge to join his family on a picnic. As Mudge allows Marcus into his life, the graveyard friends lose some of their former attraction.

Ned and Serena continue to lessen their isolation, as when they have a telephone installed. Also, the historic preservationists who had been working for years to establish Edgemount as a historic site finally achieve their goal, and the family must move. Sensitive to the conflict within himself and his father, Mudge summons Aunt Ernestus, who comes to stay with Mudge while his parents plan to relocate. Aunt Ernestus helps Mudge realize the vulnerability that accompanies caring for others by revealing the hurt she felt when Ned abruptly took his family away. At the conclusion of the story, Mudge has accepted the family's leaving and is ready for a new beginning.

Life is composed of endings and new beginnings, the underlying theme of the story. The well-developed characters grow as individuals, gaining insight into themselves and others. Ned prepares to find a job; Serena looks forward to locating a house; and Mudge accepts the friendship of people outside his immediate family. At the same time, Aunt Ernestus comes to understand why her brother felt peace of mind at Edgemount.

Mudge's ambivalence about admitting others into the closed circle of his life is clearly conveyed, yet not overstated. Although the theme is of a serious nature, the story is not gloomy and captures the reader's interest. Children who feel secure in their environments but sometimes become fearful of change can empathize with Mudge. Gifted youngsters, who, because of circumstances or their own special abilities, have felt different from others, can relate to Mudge's isolation and his special relationship with imaginary friends.

Sancha, Sheila. *The Luttrell Village: Country Life in the Middle Ages.* Illus. by author. New York: Crowell, 1983, 64 pp. (Intermediate)

Rural living in the Middle Ages is depicted in this rich, descriptive story where every detail is clearly labeled. Luttrell Village, named after Sir Geoffrey Luttrell, was reconstructed from a psalter, or prayer book, now on display in the British Museum. The grayish black-and-white illustrations are intricately and laboriously drawn to exemplify the bustling activities of the people of the time.

Each citizen had a specific responsibility—farming, sewing, building homes, gardening—making the community self-sufficient, yet interdependent. Life seems simple compared to ours, but one ascertains that many hardships were endured. For example, traveling involved long wearisome journeys along bumpy roads. Furthermore, the privileges of the rich and the plight of the poor contrasted sharply. For example, the poor rarely had meat to eat, their diet consisting mostly of vegetables, whereas the more affluent feasted on meats and spices.

Inspired by the psalter, Sancha has created a unique and unusual book full of wonderful information of busy country life in the Middle Ages. Diagrams and reconstruction of the village were developed after carefully studying maps and archaeological reports. Double-page spreads of numerous little buildings connected by narrow, winding roads create a cohesive community.

New vocabulary is introduced in heavy black type and a descriptive glossary appears at the end of the book. The book is of large picture-book size, but its fascinating contents will appeal to the older child. The gifted child, in particular, may be stimulated to seek additional information about this topic.

The illustrations and text are compatible and complementary. Sancha has managed to portray the people at work in a most captivating manner.

Sandak, Cass R. *Tunnels.* Photographs. New York: Watts, 1984, 32 pp. (Intermediate)

Tunnels hold fascination and mystery for most people, and a better treatment of the subject could hardly be found than that in Sandak's unusual book. A history of tunnels from ancient times to present day includes photographs and diagrams of complicated underground systems as far back as ancient Egypt. Many original elements of design are presented and elaborated upon in this book.

This carefully crafted work begins with an overview of underground passageways before delving into descriptions of tunnels and their uses. A section on tunnels in nature explains underground passageways built by many animals and how they are used. Rock and earth tunneling is also explained, along with the special equipment needed for this difficult engineering endeavor.

The building of the first underwater tunnels and modern-day attempts to improve them may help clarify for children where the water goes while the tunnel is being built. Finally, alpine tunnels and modern tunnels in the United States are explained and illustrated. Sandak points out that plans to build tunnels using nuclear energy and lasers have already begun, and that the possibility of connecting continents via undersea tunnels has been discussed.

Sandak peaks the reader's interest in tunnels from the very first paragraph by alluding to the thrill and adventure surrounding the advent of a new tunnel. The remainder of the book informs, analyzes, compares, and distinguishes the many kinds of tunnels constructed. The format of the book requires children to analyze the tunnels and synthesize the information. Usually, parts of a tunnel are described with a clear diagram, and the related vocabulary is set in heavy type. Excellent photographs, many in color, lend additional emphasis to the text.

The different kinds and shapes of tunnels presented help make this book a cut above other tunnel books for children. Even adults may be enlightened with the procedures used to plan and build a tunnel. Photographs show tunnels from the inside out and from the outside in, allowing the reader a closer look at the intricate construction required.

Captions accompany each illustration. An extensive glossary plus a table of contents and index make this book a challenge for young minds.

The author's exploration of tunnels leaves much unresolved in the building of tunnels, stimulating gifted children to evaluate the information to get more understanding of the topic.

Sargent, Sarah. *Watermusic.* New York: Clarion, 1986, 120 pp. (Advanced)

Sensing a strangeness in the world and always feeling there is something beyond that is unknown to us, 13-year-old Laura is a prime candidate for Mrs. Uhrlander's unusual request—that she put her flute playing to use by playing a special white flute to help arouse a bat that has been sleeping for a thousand years.

Mrs. Uhrlander, Laura's anthropologist neighbor, who lives in an old Victorian house, requests Laura's help in unpacking artifacts from South America after first sharing with her accounts of different cultures she and her husband have studied. Mrs. Uhrlander asks her young friend not to reveal anything about their work together, emphasizing that Laura will be exposed to mysteries and secrets. Mystified and excited, Laura unconsciously makes comparisons between Mrs. Uhrlander's old, musty house and her own sparkling, clean home, and somehow anticipates that her new experiences will be unusual.

Laura soon learns her part in Mrs. Uhrlander's bizarre plans. She is to play a special white flute, but only after a large crate is opened to reveal a huge white bat, known as a seraph, that has been sleeping for a thousand years. The music from the flute is the richest and deepest sound imaginable, and it slowly arouses the bat. At the same time Laura notices an odd gurgling and gushing sound in the water pipes that Mrs. Uhrlander dismisses as air bubbles.

One day Mrs. Uhrlander leaves Laura to play the flute while she remains upstairs with the bat. The music creates beautiful images of birds, butterflies and flowers. At another level, Laura envisions mathematical-like formations and complex structures. She learns the effect her playing has on the bat and Mrs. Uhrlander when she finds them both in a trancelike dance, with Mrs. Uhrlander beginning to resemble the bat in appearance with a silvery-pale whiteness. Laura is hurt and confused when informed that Mrs. Uhrlander's work is near completion and that she will be leaving on a trip, but she forces herself to accept that Mrs. Uhrlander has apparently arrived at the same level as the bat and, consequently, no longer needs her.

One day the water pipes and drains in Laura's house begin to bubble and cough; her mother becomes concerned and her father calls the plumber. Laura remembers Mrs. Uhrlander explaining the flute music might attract an ogre and she is terrified. She has to accompany the plumber in his investigation of the Uhrlander's plumbing while they are away. When they search the dark, wet basement, Laura spots two glittering eyes behind a pile of rubble, but for reasons she cannot explain, she does not alert the plumber, and they both leave the basement. Later, during a storm, Laura sees a beastly creature at the window, but her mother reassures her nothing is there. When she checks outside the window the next morning, her fears are confirmed, for something has left telltale signs behind. Laura summons enough courage to seek out the ogre from the Uhrlander's basement, and sees for herself that it is an ugly but harmless creature.

Meanwhile, Mrs. Uhrlander has been found supposedly dead at the top of a snow-covered mountain in South America, apparently from a plane crash. Her husband brings her body home, but during funeral preparations, she is found to be alive. Knowing of Laura's involvement in past incidents with his wife, Mr. Uhrlander requests her assistance in reviving his wife by playing the flute. When the music fails to arouse the sleeping woman, Laura summons the ogre, who turns out to be a mermaidlike woman who expresses love and warmth and brings her cold body back to life. Only Laura witnesses this phenomenon. Laura, regretfully, must send away this creature to whom she has grown attached by ceremoniously setting up the ritual for its departure and throwing away the flute.

Watermusic quickly captures the reader's attention and holds it throughout the book, moving back and forth between Laura's orderly and attractive home and the Uhrlander's old, dark, dilapidated house and causing her continually to make comparisons without necessarily making judgments. She also finds herself comparing the rather unrealistic Mrs. Uhrlander with her own mother, who is depicted as a compulsive housekeeper who continually cleans and polishes. While obtaining comfort from her home and its meticulous order, Laura is constantly drawn to the spooky and foreboding mansion and the frightening mysteries it holds.

Sargent's unearthly tale spins a web of wonder in protagonist Laura, who is fascinated with the details of a dark, remote culture hidden in the South American jungle. Far removed from the usual good-against-evil pattern in much fantasy literature, comparisons between the seraphs representing intellect and the ogre symbolizing love, regardless of its hideous origin, will appeal to intellectual minds and challenge higher-level thought processes.

Scarry, Huck. *Balloon Trip: A Sketchbook.* Illus. by author. Englewood Cliffs, N.J.: Prentice-Hall, 1982, 71 pp. (Intermediate)

This full-blown portrayal of the lively experience of ballooning includes technological and romantic aspects. As a spectator during an international balloon meet in Switzerland, Scarry originally became intoxicated with the excitement surrounding this sport and, years later, welcomed the opportunity to take a trip in a balloon. His on-the-scene description invites readers to climb aboard for an account of a fantastic flight that includes the events leading up to the flight, the preparations for launching, the trip itself, and a most unusual landing in an evergreen forest.

Full-page drawings of balloons and parts, all carefully labeled and described, fill the pages. Step-by-step preparations are illustrated and carefully detailed, including the kind of gas and equipment required to fly a balloon. Other technical information includes the physical characteristics of hydrogen and its properties, and discussion of such factors as wind, temperature, clouds, and sunlight, which influence a balloon's ability to rise and stay aloft. A full explanation of the function of the "guide rope" further clarifies how to maneuver the aircraft's rise and descent.

Also included is the story of hot-air ballooning, how it originated, the trial flight, and an account of the continued development that has made ballooning a popular sport. Directions for how to make a hot-air balloon are clear enough for an older child to try.

The author's heady description of events high above the earth appeals to one's aesthetic nature. For example, "Alone, like pioneers, we left our friends on the bottom of the great atmospheric ocean." *Balloon Trip* is an unusual presentation of a topic that holds interest for many children. The format of the book is light and airy, and the theme is uplifting, to say the least. The gifted child will particularly be intrigued by the intricate details and designs of these balloons.

Schwartz, Alvin, comp. *The Cat's Elbow and Other Secret Languages.* Illus. by Margot Zemach. New York: Farrar, 1982, 96 pp. (Intermediate)

The "Cat's Elbow" is one of 13 different secret languages—codes for speaking—designed to challenge young readers who enjoy language play. Starting with the familiar and easy pig Latin and progressing to more complex languages, Schwartz explains each code with a brief history, step-by-step directions for speaking, and a riddle, rhyme, famous saying, or short story for readers to decode. The secret languages in Schwartz's collection originate from such diverse places as the United States, Russia, Jamaica, East Africa, Germany, and China.

Secret languages are devised by altering standard languages through certain operations, such as rearranging the position of a syllable, transposing letters, adding a syllable or letter, repeating a syllable, or substituting new letters or words. Code words were used hundreds of years ago by thieves to communicate and mask their plans. The code is based on replacing whole words to hide the meaning of certain words.

Plenty of white space interspersed with Zemach's comical ink drawings of animals and people exaggerating the text invites the reader to discard typical language conventions and explore the endless possibilities of secret languages. In addition to the solutions to practice problems presented, Schwartz includes notes containing more details about secret languages, sources, and a bibliography to stimulate further reading.

Both the variety and challenge of decoding secret languages will appeal to intellectually capable readers who have high verbal skills. Mental manipulation of letters and word parts places demands on higher-level cognitive skills. Intermediate readers who are interested in language will be intrigued with the possibilities of inventing their own secret languages.

Schwartz, David M. *How Much Is a Million?* Illus. by Steven Kellogg. New York: Lothrop, 1985, unp. (Beginning)

Fantasy and realism are juxtaposed in a lively, airy style to elucidate the often baffling concept of large numbers. A kindly, wizardlike character, Marvelosissimo the Mathematical Magician, leads four jovial children and their pets—a dog, two cats, and a unicorn—in demonstrations of the meaning of million, billion, and trillion. Explanations of these abstract entities are conducted through several dimensions. The concept of a million, for example, is introduced through height (children standing on top of each other's shoulders), length of time ("If you wanted to count from one to one million . . . it would take you about 23 days"), and volume (a huge bowl holding one million goldfish would be "large enough to hold a whale").

To illustrate a billion, the human tower is used again. This time the row of children reaches past the moon. The bowl needed to hold a billion goldfish is depicted in a double-page spread as big as a stadium. To add further interest, spectators are shown watching men in rowboats, colliding as if engaged in a sport. Continuing the visual comparison, the human tower reaches nearly to Saturn's rings to show a trillion.

Kellogg's pastel watercolors and line drawings carry the meaning of the text, which is printed in large, bold, uppercase letters—one or two lines per illustration. Illustrations are inventive, lively, and brimming with detailed figures and amusing scenes. For example, one drawing shows the four children, old and gray-haired and sitting in chairs next to Marvelosissimo's gravestone marker, counting from one to a billion. Unique is the set of seven pages filled with tiny white stars in straight rows on a blue background used to concretize 100,000 stars. From the hot-air balloon in which the main characters travel throughout the book, Marvelosissimo tells the children that by taking the trip ten times they will travel past a million stars. The book concludes with a thorough explanation of the calculations on which the examples are based. For instance, the number of stars printed on each page is given with an explanation of how many pages it would take to illustrate a million and a billion stars.

Large numbers are difficult for children and many adults to understand. Beginning readers and older, more experienced individuals who learn best from a visual presentation will enjoy the humorous examples that can clarify their conceptions of large numbers. Gifted youngsters who are intrigued by numerical facts will stretch their imaginations as they read this book.

Senn, Steve. *In the Castle of the Bear.* New York: Atheneum, 1985, 135 pp. (Advanced)

Having lost his mother, who has died, as well as his dog, who was killed in an accident, Jason faces a new agony: His father is remarrying. Unlike his two sisters, who are accepting of Lauren, his soon-to-be stepmother, and eagerly look forward to having a mother again, Jason hates the whole idea, including Lauren. Thus, this 12-year-old boy internalizes his grief and sorrow, unable to express it except in the poetry he writes. His poems are sensitive, secret, serving as a means of escaping from a world he feels no longer understands or cares for him. He imagines he is a famous poet, such as Poe, without an audience who really appreciates him since he carefully protects his poems from anyone seeing them.

Soon the family moves to Lauren's 100-year-old house in another town. Named the "castle" by Jason, this dark, dreary, and foreboding building with its secret passageways and rooms appears to Jason to be haunted. In his new neighborhood Jason soon meets Cleve, who attends the school he will be going to. He finds that they both are trying secretly to learn about the unknown spirit world. Hence, both are intrigued with the old books of magic found in Cleve's Aunt Tilda's old house. Tilda, a writer, becomes a magnet for Jason because he feels they share a love of written expression. When Tilda commits suicide in despair of never writing anything worthwhile, Jason is further saddened. Somehow he senses that, like his mother, Tilda has found a peace that only can be found in death.

Meanwhile, Lauren continues to appear in Jason's imagination as someone to fear, despise, and resent. He has a dream in which "Bear," a spirit, has come to possess him, to forever cast darkness and gloom on his life. Jason transfers the Bear to Lauren, believing she is a witch, Bear being her "familiar" who roams the castle. Feeling that Lauren is always watching and spying on him, he tries to gain power over her by learning her secrets. Obsessed with this desire, Jason secretly spies on Lauren as she paints and leaves hateful poems about her work pinned to her easel to torment her.

When he finds a large footprint in the tower of the castle, Jason believes it belongs to Bear. He senses the strangeness of another presence within the walls, hovering over his every move. His imagination continues to tell him that Lauren is Bear, the thing that caused Tilda to die and that will eventually take his life.

During his explorations of the castle, Jason discovers an old dumbwaiter where he can hide and watch Lauren paint. His poems continue to send her the message that her painting is common, without feeling or creativity. He also begins to write her poems about Bear. Eventually, after much struggle and distress, Lauren decides to paint Bear. Indeed, when this painting becomes her first to sell, Lauren concludes the success is due to the influence of Jason's poetry. She tries unsuccessfully to develop a relationship with the boy, but is abruptly rejected and regarded with suspicion, especially when she tries to explain to him how much alike they are. Finally, in a fit of pent-up anger and hurt, Jason lashes out at his stepmother before she finally reaches him and helps him understand that "Bear" is really himself. When he finally lets it go, he also lets his mother "go" and he is able to warmly accept Lauren as his new mother.

The story is complicated and tragic, but with an intricate complexity of writing and content that will appeal to gifted children. The absorbing account of a child who has lost a parent and a pal and of the depression and loneliness that follow is both moving and contemplative. Senn leaves readers with the knowledge that there is hope at the end of a long, dark journey through much hurt and disappointment.

Service, Pamela F. *Winter of Magic's Return.* New York: Atheneum, 1985, 192 pp. (Intermediate)

Set in Wales 500 years after a nuclear devastation and during a period of nuclear winter, the story begins at Llandoylan, a former monastery, now a boarding school for children of wealthy survivors. Society has become barbaric with warring independent duchies and shires complicated by roving bands of mutated animals and humans. Except for Sunday outings, students stay within school grounds. Lessons include lectures about scientific accomplishments of the past, ancient written English, and geography.

Welly, Heather, and Earl—misfits according to peer standards—begin their association on a Sunday venture outside the school grounds. By imitating an animal's howl, Earl distracts a pack of dogs that threatens Welly and Heather who had fallen into ancient ruins while searching for lost jewels described in an old historical novel.

Soon Earl's alleged Aunt Maureen and Uncle Garth arrive at Llandoylan to convince the headmaster that Earl is their nephew. Suspecting their evil nature, Earl bids good-bye to Heather and Welly and runs away. Heather and Welly subsequently slip out of the school grounds to help Earl survive by giving him scraps of food. While the three children spend the night in the ruins of an old mine shack, Earl senses the presence of evil. Confronted again by Maureen, who tries to persuade him to come with her and Garth, Earl struggles against the woman's grasp and falls backward into a mine shaft. Thinking him dead, the couple leaves, planning to return to conduct "laying rites" during the dark of the moon. A blow to his head causes Earl to regain his memory of his former life as Merlin in the days of King Arthur.

Merlin and King Arthur had been working to unite Britain. The evil sorceress, Morgan, had trapped Merlin in the mountain that was destroyed during the nuclear devastation, releasing Merlin. While in the mountain Merlin used his power over time to reverse the aging process, leaving him a youngster with no memory after the explosion that tore open the mountain. Merlin believes that he still has power, but because magic comes in cycles and changes over time, he has lost contact with the ways of magic.

Returning to Llandoylan for food, Heather and Welly encounter the mean boy, Nigel, whom they manage to bind and gag after he threatens to turn them in to the headmaster. Deciding they have gone so far already, the two friends join Earl whose mission is to find Arthur—left in the once parallel world of Avalon to heal until needed again.

Having an intuitive feeling about the place where Avalon and earth cross paths, Earl leads the children southwest. Along their journey, they meet a troll who threatens them because they cross his bridge, several unsavory humans, dangerous mutant beasts, and the evil Morgan and Garth. Trying to destroy Heather and Welly, Morgan creates the illusion of an overwhelming tower of waves mixed with the reality of fish, ocean plants, and a sinking Eldritch ship. Warned by Earl to continue breathing, Heather and Welly survive the evil illusion. Afterward, Earl unearths swords with built-in protections left by the Eldritch people when the ship sank years ago, as well as several gemstones later to be used as payment for food and lodging.

Finding refuge from harsh weather, the three stay at the Penrose family farm where they are encouraged to remain after Welly is nursed back to health from a high fever. The trio leaves after an evil-looking beast nearly injures the Penrose boy. Concerned for their welfare and claiming he does not need them, Earl dismisses Heather and Welly, who are heading back toward the farm when they suddenly encounter Morgan.

This time Morgan tries to entice Heather with visions of beauty and Welly with dreams of leading a battle. Clinging to the Cracker Jack ring given to her earlier by Earl, Heather chooses not to join Morgan. Touching the plastic chess knight in his pocket, Welly makes a similar decision.

Alone, facing the cold, snowy elements, Earl declares his wish to become one with them or die. He succeeds in temporarily leaving his earthly body, mixing with the flying snow and regaining his understanding of his magic powers.

Soon Morgan tries again to destroy the children. An army of screaming, ugly, mutant men and beasts launch an attack. Outnumbered, Earl uses his regained powers to produce deadly flames, purple mist, and a humanoid, mud figure that breaks into pieces and multiplies as he hurls it into the enemy crowd. Morgan counters with a glowing serpent that hurls firebolts. Unable to perform magic, Heather and Welly wield their swords, which seem to move automatically in their hands, and Welly saves Earl from an attack by a wolf who turns into Garth as he lies dying.

As the threesome comes closer to their journey's end, Morgan directs a tidal wave at the part-real, part-magic boat Earl has constructed to take them across a stretch of sea to the entrance to Avalon. Seeing Morgan destroy what he thought was the entrance, Earl recognizes the actual entrance and leads his two friends through the passageway. In contrast to their stark, cruel world, Avalon offers pleasant, sunny sights and sounds, including varieties of delicious food and abundant animal and plant life the children had only read about. Finding Arthur asleep, Earl wakes him and convinces the young leader he is needed to help the remaining survivors of earth find a better life. The group returns to Wales to set forth on their quest.

Strong characters, an unusual setting, and a plot that involves legend and magic with the stark features of a future world devastated by nuclear war combine in a fast-moving story that appeals to the imagination. The self-sufficient, courageous young characters who persevere in their inventive efforts to overcome evil and find a better world are likely to appeal to gifted readers. The writing is direct and descriptive. The author maintains a balance between the severe environmental conditions of the nuclear winter, ugly mutant creatures, and the evil sorceress and the children's concern for one another and their positive outlook. The sequel, *Tomorrow's Magic,* continues the quest of the young characters as they begin to mature.

Shannon, George. *Stories to Solve: Folktales from around the World.* Illus. by Peter Sis. New York: Greenwillow, 1985. 56 pp. (Intermediate)

Stories to Solve is a collection of 14 folktales, written as riddles or puzzles, and each concluding with a question that asks readers to come up with a solution to a difficult or seemingly impossible situation. Solutions are given on the page following each folktale riddle.

Some tales have a familiar theme—the farmer who must take a goat, wolf, and cabbage across a river or the wise king who decides which of two women is the mother of a child. Other stories, most only a page in length, may be new to most young readers. A few tales deal with wrongdoing that is uncovered. For instance, there is a thief who stole a gold ring, a thief who stole a boy's coins, and a boatman who killed a merchant to obtain his goods. Clever readers will discover how thieves and other characters give themselves away by their actions or words. One tale, "Heaven and Hell," demonstrates the value of cooperation. Armed with three-foot-long chopsticks, the people in Hell starve while those in Heaven feed each other.

The stories are illustrated with soft, black-and-white stippled drawings of rounded human figures and thatched-roof cottages that add an appropriate touch of old-world charm to this enjoyable collection of folktales without giving clues to the solutions. The stories are written in a straightforward, easy-to-read manner. The challenge is in the reasoning skills needed to solve the riddles. Most gifted children relish the intellectual challenge of unraveling clues to solve ambiguities. Solving the riddles and puzzles in these stories requires analyzing relationships and reasoning in addition to both divergent (identifying a range of possibilities to arrive at an answer) and convergent thinking.

Sherman, Ivan. *Walking Talking Words.* Illus. by author. New York: Harcourt, 1980, unp. (Beginning)

Illustrations partially camouflage the letters of word concepts that accompany the limericks in this unusual book. For example, the word "eat" is portrayed as a huge mouth formed by the letter E. The A is shown inside the mouth and appears to be eating the T with rows of teeth nestled between the letters. In another example, the word "eye," taken from a limerick on the adjacent page, is illustrated as the lowercase letter e between an upside down y. Each e is an open and a closed eye.

Another concept, "open," is elaborately introduced with each letter of the word as an open door: One opens horizontally and one opens vertically, thereby creating a structure that requires close observational skills to discern the word. In another instance, a limerick about a forlorn little girl is accompanied by a drawing of the girl sitting on a "chair" made from the h and holding the a. The other letters of the word are positioned as stools or items of furniture.

"Jump" and "walk" are illustrated in the act of doing just what they imply. In "jump," the j and p turn the rope while a little girl, u and m, jump. In "walk," the w and a ride on a horizontal l with the k underneath—all being pulled by a dog. In a poem about an oyster, the word "inside" is depicted with the letters packed inside a crate. A limerick about the "squeeze" received from a great aunt is illustrated with huge representations of the letters of the word being squeezed in the middle and the "aunt's" legs and arms being visible around them.

Visually appealing and whimsically illustrated in soft blues and yellows, each page of this book is a delightful puzzle for the able reader. Very young children may need assistance to decipher word concepts since many letters appear in unusual positions, some of them reversed. Each double-page spread contains an illustration of the word and a poem that includes that word in italics.

Simon, Seymour. *Earth: Our Planet in Space.* Photog. by author. New York: Four Winds, 1984, unp. (Beginning)

Simon presents a splendid introduction to the planet Earth. Stark, black-and-white photographs, some topographical, and diagrams combine to project a clear view of the earth from outer space. This large, picture-book-size volume is an excellent addition to nonfiction collections on space.

The book begins with a view of Earth from space to introduce readers to their home. The dark and light shadows of the planet are then explained to be seas, land clouds, and Antarctica. The comparison between Earth and the sun is beautifully accomplished with few words and striking photographs. To introduce the other planets, Simon combines eight photographs in one, naming the planets that are shown and those that are not. To demonstrate the earth's shape, he uses the moon and the earth's shadow, photographed in stages, as the moon travels across the earth.

Night and day are carefully explained as the earth spins on its axis, without using difficult vocabulary. The orbital path and position from the sun are shown in a simple diagram. The changing seasons are illustrated with distinct diagrams.

Atmosphere, the magnetic field, and geological land formations, such as mountains, oceans, and valleys, are clearly viewed from space. The effects of erosion from water, ice, and snow are easily distinguished, and the photographs of Phoenix and New York City show how people have also changed the land. The book concludes with a rocket ready to be launched into space, holding the possibility that we will learn more about the earth's history by space exploration.

This book contains basic information presented in text that is not overwhelming but complements the unusual photographs. Set in type that is large enough for young children who can read, the book would be interesting and thought-provoking for youngsters who are expanding their knowledge of our world and beyond. The use of actual photographs acknowledges the young child's ability to comprehend the topic.

Simon, Seymour. *Hidden Worlds: Pictures of the Invisible.* New York: Morrow, 1983, 48 pp. (Intermediate)

The paradox suggested in the subtitle, *Pictures of the Invisible,* is resolved as the reader delves into this fascinating introduction to those "hidden worlds" that are either too distant, too small, or too fast moving to be seen with the naked eye. Large photographs, both black and white and color, convey the extraordinary shapes, configurations, and textures of microscopic plants and animals, parts deep inside the human body, moments of action seemingly caught in time, atmospheric and environmental features of earth, and objects in space.

A variety of technological methods underlies these extraordinary photographic revelations. For example, use of microscopes at various magnifications allows interesting photographic close-ups of familiar objects such as a snowflake and a bar of soap. Sharp photographs of a male mosquito seen through a scanning electron microscope highlight the mosquito's feathery antennas. A look at a mouse's tongue reveals its rough surface, which resembles jagged curves. Readers with allergies may be especially interested to see the unusual configurations of pollen grains magnified about 160×. Even atoms can be seen, appearing as tiny dots of light.

Similarly, technological advancements such as fiber optics and the X ray make it possible to look deep inside the human body. Illustrations of this hidden world include photographs of a stomach ulcer, a skull showing blood vessels, a six-month-old human fetus (sonogram), red blood cells, and the surface of a tooth.

High-speed photography enables dramatic action to be captured on film such as a drop of milk splashing like a crown ringed with pearls and the sequence of a diver's motions. Perhaps more familiar because of their use for weather map photos on television, satellite photographs expose views of earth's land and water features and sometimes also reveal the effects of pollution and unwise use of resources. Photos taken from Skylab beyond earth's atmosphere and other results of using interferometry show distant galaxies as well as our own sun.

The text briefly and concisely describes a given technology and comments on the accompanying photographs. Vocabulary is within reach of most high-ability intermediate readers. *Hidden Worlds* serves as a motivating introduction to current and future photographic technology and the realms of science available for future study. Going beyond a mere factual account, photographs and text combine to illustrate the beauty and aesthetic form of nature. This work serves to stimulate and extend the often insatiable curiosity of many intellectually able youngsters who may respond beyond an initial reaction of fascination to analyze and question further. Concluding by posing questions such as "What happened to the dinosaurs?," Simon suggests that we have only begun to examine the mysteries of our vast universe. "Who knows what strange and wonderful hidden worlds remain to be explored?"

Sperling, Susan Kelz. *Murfles and Wink-a-Peeps: Funny Old Words for Kids.* New York: Crown, 1985, unp. (Intermediate)

Filled with old-fashioned words—so old that they are no longer in use—this book is both fun and informative for middle graders and older readers. As Sperling explains in the introduction, the words were used 200 years ago by our great-great-grandparents. The words are all of old English origin and do not appear in today's dictionaries. They resemble slang words, but unlike today's slang, they sound funny and sometimes simply ridiculous. For example, the title words, "murfles and wink-a-peeps" means "freckles" and "eyes." Sperling also points out how pronunciations and spellings of words may change over the years. "Muckender," meaning "handkerchief," originally was "mokedore," then changed to "mucketter" before becoming "muckender."

Sperling has selected 60 obsolete words and combined them with contemporary English ones to create seven rounds. A "round" is made up of five of the words, introduced one at a time, whereupon the first word is repeated at the end of the round to form a circle of words. For example, "Glop means to eat greedily, so you glop your belltimber, which means food which keeps you strong, but lubber-wort, which is junk food, doesn't. Eating too much lubber-wort makes you sloomy, which means sleepy, and this, in turn, makes you pingle, or eat very little at meals, but what you pingle over will make a greedy person glop." In this manner, all words are defined and their meaning is further illustrated in a subsequent example. The book also includes rhymes using the unusual words, with the English translation appearing on the same page.

Children fond of word plays and games will have fun with these hilarious linguistic oddities that go on and on. Names for people, using a combination of "old" words and English ones, such as "true boonfellow," meaning "good friend," or "favorite bellibone," meaning "lovely girl," will also delight.

Various cartoonlike black-and-blue illustrations add further humor to this small book. All new, that is, "old," words are written in blue. The book will be particularly popular with gifted children who enjoy complex language games and unusual word derivations and is bound to stimulate them to explore other words no longer in use. It's an exciting approach to etymology.

Srivastava, Jane Jonas. *Spaces, Shapes, and Sizes.* Illus. by Loretta Lustig. New York: Crowell, 1980, 46 pp. (Beginning)

Using lusty, charming little animals, such as bears, rabbits, pigs, dogs, and lions, with alert expressions, the author has written a book for young children about the concept of volume.

To illustrate space, for example, children can actively participate in the suggested exercises, such as curling their bodies into a ball, uncurling again, and standing up straight to demonstrate that they still occupy the same amount of space. In relation to shape, a potato is examined whole, then cut into different pieces to demonstrate that, when cut, only the potato's shape is changed, not its volume. In addition to such experiments, Srivastava poses questions to the reader about other items to help create a better understanding of shape and space; for example, yarn for a sweater, clay, and sand—things with which young children can easily identify.

In another experiment, the cube shape is introduced with instructions and a pattern for how to make one. Children are directed to use four cubes, or blocks, to build different shapes, then three cubes to recognize that the volume of the cubes does not change, only the shape of each construction. Readers are then invited to join the animals in making their own construction using the cubes, or blocks, to further confirm the point that the volume remains unchanged. To illustrate volume, readers are directed to fill a box with sand, pour it out into other shapes, and then examine the volume of the sand.

> Find a small box. Fill the box with sand. Put a large piece of paper on a table and pour the sand from the box onto the paper. First the sand was in a box shape. Now it is in a cone shape. Has the volume of the sand changed?

The natural progression from cube to box is well executed as children are directed to fill a box with sand, pour it out, and fill another one of different size, while trying to guess how much it takes to fill it. Readers are also encouraged to use other articles, such as crayons and marbles, and are again asked to guess how many of each are required to fill the box. Then they are told to dump them out and count them. This is a challenging exercise in "guesstimation."

Srivastava reminds readers that the volume of the box is unchanged regardless of the type or number of objects put into it. She suggests they use their skills of observation to locate boxes in other places, such as school or in a store, and to notice how they are packed with many different things of various shapes and sizes.

When the concepts of small and large are introduced, the story animals gleefully play inside and outside a huge box to demonstrate how the contents of some boxes rattle when they are only partly full. As part of this section, children are presented with a problem they have to solve by using different small objects and finding a suitable box to put them in. In this example, the author uses health food squares.

A higher-level observation is introduced by means of cereal boxes of the same shape, but with different sizes and volumes. The illustration shows a pig eating from cereal boxes of different sizes, leading the reader to notice how boxes with different shapes may have the same volume. Because this notion is more difficult to ascertain, children are first asked to collect specific small empty boxes. Next comes the fun part when they are invited to make a huge bowl of popcorn and fill each box, dump out the popcorn, and count the individual pieces. Children quickly realize that a different number of pieces of popcorn is required to fill each box, thereby deliciously acquiring the concept of volume. Very young children can conceptualize this geometrical concept in this rewarding manner when assisted in the experiment by an adult.

To clarify the volume of solid objects, the author uses water and crayons. After filling a jar half full of water, children mark the water level and add an object (a potato) to the jar. Children are asked to keep adding water until the potato is covered and then mark the new level to show the volume of both water and potato. Other objects are measured using the same method but different-colored crayons to mark each object. Finally, volumes are compared.

This innovative approach to communicating conservation of space relies on problem-solving skills in an extraordinary manner. Children's spatial awareness does not have to be fully developed before they can attempt the exciting experiments and certainly can be strengthened from the examples. Skills of analysis and comparisons are sharpened by investigating this otherwise abstract geometrical concept. Readers are challenged to demonstrate their mathematical ability in a most entertaining fashion.

The animal characters in the book are winsome but not trite, and their enthusiastic facial expressions invite eager readers to participate in the experiments. Anticipating the outcome of each investigation is exciting for the child while providing tactile opportunities to explore.

Throughout the book Srivastava poses questions for the reader. For example, readers are asked to compare the capacity or space in different sizes of empty cereal boxes. The format depicting the rabbit joyfully tumbling around in an empty box, the pig gobbling down the contents of cereal boxes, along with the ever-present curious, thoughtful expressions of the animals, presents an enticing lesson in volume. The language is fluent and accurate, and use of common mathematical terms credits readers' intelligence to understand the concepts discussed.

Steig, William. *CDC?* Illus by author. New York: Farrar, 1984, unp. (Advanced)

With *CDC?*, William Steig has written another language play book, similar to, yet more subtle than his much earlier *CDB!* (see Baskin and Harris, *Books for the Gifted Child*, Bowker, 1980, p. 234) and with a wider range of content. Black-and-white cartoonlike line drawings provide humorous clues to the interpretation of coded captions composed of letters and symbols in hyphenated strings. Each letter or symbol name suggests meaning.

Although *CDC?* is a children's picture book, much of the humor and vocabulary requirements are beyond the knowledge and experience of many youngsters, such as references to the Roman Forum and to psychoanalysis. Because each page contains a separate cartoon and corresponding caption, readers can select and respond to those messages that fit their experiential level. Decoding letters and symbols requires cognitive flexibility of language usage, as well as divergent and convergent thinking. Many verbally talented youngsters will probably go on to create their own coded messages after encoding *CDC?*

Tchudi, Susan, and Stephen Tchudi. *The Young Writer's Handbook.* New York: Scribner, 1984, 156 pp. (Advanced)

Aspiring young writers will find a wealth of information and motivating ideas in this book especially designed for them. Suggesting that the book be used as a guide to writing, not just a "how-to" book, the Tchudis recommend that the first two chapters be read in order. From then on readers can select chapters of particular interest to them: keeping a journal, deciding on topics to write about, letter writing, writing fiction, plays, and poems, note taking and report writing in school, feature story and article writing, editing, and finally, publishing one's work.

The first chapter examines reasons for writing by giving a brief history of the development of writing. To explore the topic "why write" responses from well-known authors, such as Judith Guest and Mary Stoltz, are presented. First, the well-known authors suggest that readers review their reaction and responses to language in everyday life, the kind of material they prefer for pleasure reading, the kind of writing they would like to engage in, and then list some writing goals they would like to accomplish. True to their belief that one learns to write by writing, these authors recommend that readers ease into writing by not expecting too much of themselves and maintain a positive attitude to learn.

In chapter 2 the Tchudis encourage readers to find their personal approach to writing by putting their ideas on paper quickly, set aside a specific time and place to write, and find the most comfortable tools with which to write. Keeping a journal is described as a private method of recording one's thoughts and impressions without fear of criticism. It becomes a resource of writing ideas and serves as a vehicle for exploring experiences and analyzing individual growth in writing.

In another chapter letter writing is characterized as a personal, efficient, and inexpensive means of communication. The discussion includes advice on how to write friendly letters as well as practical letters such as business letters. Examples of correct form and style are provided.

After reading chapter 6, children will be eager to begin writing fiction and poetry. Without oversimplification, some important points to writing are presented; for example, the importance of plot or story idea in both fiction and nonfiction. For specific school writing tasks, excellent suggestions are given on such activities as active note taking, summarizing, evaluating and critiquing (as in a book report), and report writing, including a bibliography.

Valuable information on editing is provided in chapter 9. For example, the authors recommend that written work be revised according to content, structure, and style. To illustrate, the book contains one of the author's own pages that has been edited. Here the symbols and notations editors employ are demonstrated, accompanied by a discussion of the time and patience required for good revision.

The book is well organized and includes answers to many questions young writers may have about how to get started writing. The style is easy to read, personal, and appealing to middle-grade and older children. Helpful notes and advice from famous authors promote a professionalism attitude toward the child who has the desire to become a writer. For the many gifted children who are interested in writing, this book will become a treasured companion.

Terban, Marvin. *Too Hot to Hoot: Funny Palindrome Riddles.* Illus. by Giulio Maestro. New York: Clarion, 1985, 64 pp. (Intermediate)

Palindromes, or "pals," refer to words or phrases that are spelled the same way backward or forward or numerals that are arranged to read the same forward or backward. Clues, stated as riddles, are presented for several types of word palindromes, often accompanied by a cartoon illustration arranged numerically. One brief chapter explains numeric palindromes, while the last chapter consists of three stories about palindromic sentences featuring palindromes allegedly spoken about or by Teddy Roosevelt, Napoleon, and Adam in the Garden of Eden.

The easiest word palindromes to visualize and the simplest riddles ("What's a three-letter word for mother?") are the single-word palindromes (mom, pup, sis) beginning with three letters and progressing to four- (toot) and five-letter (level) palindromes. On a more difficult level, palindromes may consist of more than one word (nurses run), read by saying each letter separately forward or backward.

Flip-flop phrases exemplify another type of palindrome, constructed by putting together two flip-flop words to answer a riddle. "What spoiled the artist's painting?" "Bad dab." Palindromes can even be extended into palindromic sentences, to be read backward word by word, ignoring punctuation and spacing. An example of a palindromic sentence is found in the title, *Too Hot to Hoot.*

The chapter on palindromic numbers presents examples of calendar dates written in numbers. For instance, the palindromic equivalent of January 4, 1941 is 1-4-41. The reader is challenged to find the palindromic dates in the twenty-first century through a process of adding and reversing numbers. Sometimes it takes many steps to arrive at the palindromic sum, an extreme example being the palindrome of 196, which requires 4,147 steps of reversing, adding, reversing, adding, reversing, and adding.

The author suggests using pencil and paper to record answers in four of the six chapters. However, no writing is required to decode the palindromic sentences, which are merely read backward word by word. A calculator would be useful to compute the palindromic numbers. An answer page for the word palindromes is provided at the end of each chapter. A bright magenta box at the upper right corner makes the answer pages easily accessible to eager palindromic enthusiasts. Humorous cartoon illustrations, done in black, white, and gray tones accented with magenta, abound on every page, providing clues to the riddles.

Palindromes provide readers an opportunity to visualize patterns in language and spelling while encouraging intellectual play. Although the vivid illustrations sometimes give away the answers, intermediate readers should find solving the riddles both fun and stimulating. Many youngsters will want to create their own palindrome riddles.

Testa, Fulvio. *If You Look around You.* Illus. by author. New York: Dutton, 1983, unp. (Beginning)

Geometric shapes—point, line, triangle, circle, square, cylinder, cone, cube, and sphere—are defined by example in this unusual, captivating picture book. By drawing attention to simple shapes, Testa conveys orderliness and the simple beauty of our world. Some shapes result from temporary physical arrangements of objects that interact. For example, a dog straining at his leash held by a child represents a "line," and a paintbrush, pencil, and ruler form a triangle. Other shapes are more permanent, such as the cylindrical shape of a toy drum or a ball indicating a sphere. Because Testa's examples are so disconnected, the reader's curiosity leads him or her to eagerly proceed to see what follows on the next page.

One sentence per page provides a simple description of the narrowly framed drawing on the next page. The simple and direct language leads the reader to examine the accompanying drawing. "A cone is what is left after you eat your ice cream." Perspective and detail are important in the drawings, which sometimes focus on the reader as observer or represent the point of view of the children included in most scenes. Colors are bright with a predominance of earth tones—oranges, browns, blues, and greens.

If You Look around You stimulates thought beyond the apparent focus. Many drawings convey an aura of mystery enhanced by Testa's use of color. For example, a high fence with an opened gate makes the reader speculate what lies beyond. In a scene illustrating a dice cube, only a child's hand and feet extend beyond a flowing pink curtain, and a black cat is shown running from behind the same curtain to chase a mouse. Many young readers will want to look at the illustrations again and again because each observation reveals new detail and wonderment about the world around us.

Testa, Fulvio. *If You Take a Pencil.* Illus. by author. New York: Dial, 1982, unp. (Beginning)

This unusual counting book invites children to "take a pencil" and begin an imaginative journey. Testa treats his readers to a treasure hunt as he illustrates two wide-eyed children drawing two cats. The children are first depicted in a room with shelves of books, a globe, and pictures hinting of other lands, such as a ship at sea. The next page shows the newly drawn cats at play with a third cat added. The three cats curiously watch four birds in a cage before five human fingers release the birds and let them fly away. We follow the birds into a garden of 6 orange trees where children are lazily enjoying the fruit. From there, Testa takes the reader from a fountain filled with fish to a ship of sailors on a deep blue ocean surrounding some islands. On the treasure island, the children find 12 empty treasure chests, one of which holds a pencil. The journey is now complete.

Testa's skillful simplicity of form and design makes this counting book distinctive by the added dimension of discovery. From a child's perspective, Testa successfully conveys the concept of numbers by building on them. The book's simple, semirealistic pictures stimulate further storytelling. Each framed, fully detailed painted page incorporates crisp lines, jewel-like colors of russets, greens, blues, and red (for example, the blue tails of the red fish suggest the deep blue of the ocean). One line of text per page surrounded by ample white space is juxtaposed with the dramatic illustrations. On the endpapers of this attractive book are rows and rows of brightly colored pencils.

While introducing the basic concept of counting, the book is intellectually appealing to the young child in search of an adventure beyond mere
numbers.

Thomson, Peggy. *Auks, Rocks and the Odd Dinosaur: Inside
Stories from the Smithsonian's Museum of Natural History.*
Photographs. New York: Crowell, 1985, 120 pp. (Advanced)

This remarkable book about a world-famous museum gives an overview of
the unusual collections and artifacts a visitor might see there. Thomson has
selected 20 different items—some easily recognizable, others lesser known.
This wide selection offers just enough information about each item to tempt
the curious, yet leaves a quest for further in-depth investigation among older
and more interested readers.

Thomson informs us that three types of visitors come to the Smithsonian:
the Commuters, who race through the great halls hurrying on to something
else; the Cruisers, who drift in and out of the rooms; and the Very Much
Interested People, who know exactly what they want to see and spend well-
planned time with the exhibits.

We learn of the museum's early organization and its acquisition of materials for exhibits and of the meticulous order, classification, and arrangement
of objects today. This information is inspirational for children who may own
small collections of their own. Many of the great collections were begun by
young children who found favorite fossils, nests, and the like and continued
their hobby throughout their lifetime. Such was the case of Spencer Fuller-
ton Baird, who began the museum's acquisition of specimens by bringing in
his own varied and abundant collection. He later became instrumental in
training others to locate, observe, preserve, and bring or send things to the
museum. He encouraged and inspired others to love collecting and generously shared his knowledge.

The exhibits are appealing and exciting for visitors who do not realize the
behind-the-scenes intricate work being conducted by the scientists, such as
decoding, photographing, classifying, repairing, and reconstructing.

The book allows the reader a closer look at specific exhibits and relates
the unusual stories behind them. One such exhibit is that of the Great Auk,
an extinct seabird used for food, fuel, and bait by Eskimos, Indians, explorers, and fishermen. The museum's collection of bones can be credited to
staffperson Frederic Lucas, who carefully researched the birds, obtained
evidence of their existence, and then reconstructed the displayed skeleton
from the fragmented pieces.

Another item, the Kachina doll, was obtained for the museum by Frank
Cushing, who was sent to the Southwest to learn more about the Indians'
life-style, and chose to remain and live with the Indians for five years.

During this time he practiced their customs, habits, and carefully recorded everything.

The chapter on meteorites acquired by the Smithsonian provides insight into the substance itself. Amusing examples of mistaken "meteorites," claimed to have fallen all over the country, point out the difficulty in identifying this rare rock.

To youngsters accustomed to movie and television documentaries about wild animals in their natural habitat, Teddy Roosevelt's safari to Africa to obtain animals for the museum may not be unique. However, the huge giraffe he brought back, now 75 years old, is still striking and rich in color.

Another early contributor, Edward Nelson, went to Alaska to study the Eskimos and collect significant specimens. Here he developed a deep respect for the native people and, subsequently, learned unusual customs and ingenious methods of protection and survival in the harsh country. His findings have also been chosen for display and discussion here.

The book's chapter on the pterosaur flying reptile is one of the most fascinating. Emphasizing the skill and patience paleontologists need to preserve, research, and reconstruct the huge creature, the author explains that scientists have used a great amount of guesswork to reconstruct the reptile. Working with what was presently available to them, they hope to discover a complete skeleton some day and make necessary corrections.

The famous Hope diamond, another museum highlight, has a bizarre history, its rarity not realized for a long time. It is assumed, but not proven, that the Hope diamond is the French Blue, stolen from the French crown jewels. The adventures surrounding the diamond are extraordinary and entertaining, to say the least. True identity remains a mystery, although much examination and experimentation have been conducted with the great diamond. Readers will want to see the diamond for themselves after reading this chapter.

Another chapter describes an unusual worm known as a rift worm, and the difficult process required to preserve it so visitors can enjoy it. The Komodo Dragon and a little-known creature called *Sidneyia inexpectans* are also explored in some detail, enticing children to engage in further investigation.

The story behind a certain suit of armor obtained from the South Seas delves into the relationship between seamen and scientists and provides information that will evoke readers' appreciation.

Because of children's fascination with prehistoric creatures, Arnold Lewis's construction of the skeleton of antrodemus—a massive, meat-eating dinosaur—will prove particularly exciting. Readers are spectators to this two-year project from beginning to end, learning to sympathize with Lewis's tedious task of attaching the body parts to ensure that they will stand correctly, for example. Another unique item will fascinate children familiar with the little house mouse in Beatrix Potter's stories. The museum owns an extensive collection of these small rodents, each identified according to its origin.

The gorgonean coral, another esoteric display, is located in a tank so visitors can observe the feeding process. The impressive, giant blue whale skull hanging in the museum offers yet another glimpse of the behind-the-scenes efforts that underlie effective displays. Thomson relays the interesting story of the decisions involved in its acquisition and the enormous undertaking of transporting a whale. The captioned picture of the hoister hanging the skull from the ceiling suggests that he may have learned how to tie knots from his Boy Scout training.

Children may squeal with fright or delight at the giant tarantula named "Terror." This creature is an unusual visitor attraction during its daily feedings. Henry, the feeder, explains the habits and characteristics of the tarantula to cautious onlookers, as he feeds it a cricket.

Indian navel-cord boys, used as charms for protection and to ensure longevity, are also described. Another item, the bull mummy, is so old and fragile that museum experts touch it as little as necessary. X rays of the mummy reveal that this is not a true animal, but bits of trash—only the head and horns are authentic.

Another unusual exhibit are the "stumpers"—rocks that visitors can actually touch and examine. They are found in the Discovery Room of the museum where they are designated with a big question mark to induce visitors to explore and investigate further on their own.

Children will particularly enjoy the remaining chapter of this highly informative book in which Max, a large German shepherd guard dog, is introduced. Friendly to children, Max patrols the museum with his handler, keeping watch over the exhibits and valuable collections.

The book contains clear, black-and-white pictures of objects and people at work behind the scenes that may appear in few books, if any. In separate boxed areas, additional and unusual information is provided. A table of contents and index are also included.

In this outstanding work, Thomson acquaints readers with the inside workings of the Smithsonian through carefully selected stories that appeal to children. Gifted children, especially, will be intrigued with the research involved in preparing the exhibits and will appreciate the techniques, patience, and perfectionism exercised by the scientists. To be appreciated properly, the topics require synthesization and evaluation. Without being overwhelming, the book is cognitively challenging, giving readers a synopsis of information, capturing their attention, acting as a stimulus, and enticing them to seek more knowledge.

Trinca, Rod, and Kerry Argent. *One Woolly Wombat.* Illus. by Kerry Argent. New York: Kane/Miller, 1985, unp. (Beginning)

By selecting Australian animals as their main characters, Trinca and Argent have created a clever counting book focusing on representation of numbers 1 through 14.

A cover picture of a wombat sunbathing in a beach chair characterizes the unusual animals depicted in this large, picture-book-size book as amusing and entertaining. Colorful wombats, koalas, magpies, kangaroos, platypuses, possums, emus, echidnas, goannas, kookaburras, dingoes, cockatoos, mice, and seals frolic across the glossy pages, engaged in myriad comical activities.

For example, "*Nine* hungry goannas wondering what to cook" shows these playful creatures decked out in chef's hats and aprons, musing over cookbooks, with *nine* brightly colored forks standing in a row on the adjacent page. "*Ten* giggly kookaburras writing riddle books" depicts these native Australian birds with fountain pens in beaks, trying to write in a book. *Ten* colorful fountain pens are shown on the facing page. As in these examples, the child has the opportunity throughout the book to count the same number twice, first the animals, then the accompanying objects that cleverly enhance the animals' activity. On the last page the complete text is repeated as a review of the number of objects presented.

Young gifted children will examine the pages over and over and relish the winsome characters as well as the cleverness of the language in this superb counting book.

Van Allsburg, Chris. *Ben's Dream*. Illus. by author. Boston: Houghton Mifflin, 1982, 32 pp. (Intermediate)

Seeing dark clouds threatening rain, two friends, Ben and Margaret, decide to change their after-school plan to play baseball. Instead, each goes home to study for a geography test on landmarks of the world. Settled in his father's comfortable chair with his textbook, Ben is soon lulled to sleep by the sounds of the rain. He dreams he is floating on a sea past some of the world's most famous landmarks—the Statue of Liberty, the Leaning Tower of Pisa, the Great Wall of China, and the statues of Mount Rushmore. As he passes the head of the Sphinx, Ben waves to a tiny figure in the window of a distant house also floating along.

After the storm, Margaret appears at the window of Ben's house to awaken him and tell him of a similar dream in which she saw Ben waving at her. Margaret expresses her surprise that Ben is aware of her dream when he, in turn, tells her that he saw her. The children appear to have shared the same dream.

Young readers with a broad background base will be able to identify most of the landmarks depicted. However, the half-submerged structures are difficult to identify because most are shown from unusual vantage points—the Eiffel Tower is viewed from a section of supports, the Great Wall of China merges with the sea and presents an incongruity, and the figure of the

Sphinx is incomplete. A wide background of knowledge, typically character-istic of intellectually gifted children, is needed to interpret the drawings. Van Allsburg uses black-and-white line drawings and unusual perspective to produce a visually intriguing work suitable for gifted children.

Van Allsburg, Chris. *The Mysteries of Harris Burdick.* Illus. by author. Boston: Houghton Mifflin, 1984, unp. (Intermediate)

In the introduction, Van Allsburg explains that 14 enigmatic pencil draw-ings, titled and captioned, make up a surrealistic fantasy to be explored. Claiming to have written 14 stories, each illustrated with many drawings, Harris Burdick, years ago, left 14 drawings and their titles and captions with a friend in the children's book publishing business, promising to return the next day with the corresponding stories. Burdick did not return, however, and was never seen again. To help solve the mystery, Van Allsburg suggests that children write the stories.

The 14 drawings are not related except that they share an intriguing, startling quality. For each the title and caption are printed alone on the page preceding the drawing, the brief captions conveying an aura of mystery. For example, "His heart was pounding. He was sure he had seen the doorknob turn." The corresponding picture, "Uninvited Guests," reveals a man's legs descending basement stairs. A rounded wooden door, distorted in size to appear smaller than usual, is depicted on the opposite wall. Van Allsburg's ingenious use of light and shadow and soft background figures creates a misty atmosphere that lends an eerie quality of foreboding, tension, and curiosity about what will transpire next. In "Just Dessert" the author/artist skillfully establishes a mood of impending danger, showing a woman holding a long knife resting on the edge of a brightly glowing pumpkin juxtaposed with a familiar rolling pin and mixing bowl on a kitchen table.

Other drawings are whimsical, such as "The Harp," suggestive of a fairy tale; "Another Place, Another Time" is reminiscent of a childish adventure. In yet other drawings, Van Allsburg's human figures convey a depth of emotion such as the boy gazing from afar at a harp and the girl saying good-bye to two small caterpillars held gently in her hand in "Oscar and Alphonse."

Intermediate-grade readers who have not recently explored a picture book have an opportunity to extend their visual literacy skills by reading this work. Because the text consists only of titles and captions, readers need to interpret meaning. Thoughtful readers will be cognitively challenged to resolve the incongruities depicted. The juxtaposition of reality and fantasy in Van Allsburg's drawings arouses readers' curiosity and presents opportuni-ties for extending imaginative thought. The unique drawings and the under-lying theme of this book will stir the imaginations of many perceptive young readers to add their own words to write stories and thereby bring closure to the unfinished messages conveyed in the mysterious drawings.

Ventura, Piero. *Great Painters.* New York: Putnam, 1984, 160 pp. (Advanced)

Combining reproductions of famous paintings with his own colorful, detailed sketches of people, towns, and historic events, Ventura has produced an unusual work. Itself a work of art, *Great Painters* traces the history of art through representative artists from each period from the thirteenth century to Cubism. Specific topics include Italian, Flemish, German, French, and Spanish painters, Florence and the influence of the Medici, Vatican frescoes, the impact of Gutenberg's printing press, eighteenth-century English painters, influences of major wars on painting, the nineteenth-century Romantic movement, Impressionism, and Cubism.

Individual painters and their works are viewed as reflections of society and as contributors to each period. In a brief accounting of each artist's life, Ventura outlines the artist's major contributions and usually includes an anecdote about the artist's temperament or personal life. Occasionally, a fictionalized account of certain events is added. Readers who seek additional facts will find biographical sketches and descriptions of styles and periods in the appended material. Also included in the back of the book is a list of illustrations, dimensions of each work, dates and present location, and an index of names.

Contributing to the uniqueness of this work, originally published in Italy, are Ventura's illustrations—stimulating colors ranging from bright, sharp figures to soft, muted landscapes—juxtaposed with famous paintings. The layout is a visually appealing blend of color and text with ample white space on each glossy page. Artists' paintings often assume a dominant place on the page with Ventura's figures appearing smaller—whether in the distance or in the foreground. At other times small paintings are placed on easels with the artist either still at work or having just completed a painting while Ventura's drawings surround the scene. For example, the double-page spread of Rubens hosting a reception in his home features a painting that reflects the costumes of the day. Ventura's colorfully costumed figures seem to move from Rubens' painting and across the page. Other drawings depict artists at work, perched high on scaffolding or in their studios; often messy pots of paint and supplies are strewn about. This portrayal of down-to-earth realism makes famous paintings less isolated as works of art and demonstrates their relationship to the life and customs of the times.

Great Painters succeeds in giving young readers a behind-the-scenes glimpse of the lives of famous painters and asks them to understand famous works in terms of the underlying cultural and political milieu. Highly able readers can take a stimulating visual journey into the life and times of painters described in the accompanying informational, concise text. Careful readers will observe subtle, often humorous, details that contribute a light tone to the serious nature of painting.

Von Tscharner, Renata, and Ronald Lee Fleming. *New Providence: A Changing Cityscape.* Illus. by Denis Orloff. Orlando, Fla.: Harcourt, 1987, unp. (Intermediate)

Double-page spreads show the physical changes of a city named New Providence during the period from 1910 to the present.

In 1910, we see a trolley car on cobblestone streets, horse-drawn carts, an old hotel with green and white striped awnings, and lush green trees in the town square where a statue is about to be unveiled in a park that is surrounded by a wrought-iron fence. The huge courthouse with columns, a dry goods store, women strolling by in long dresses, and men in suits and hats add to the vivid details. The few cars on the streets are Model-T Fords. Other minutiae include renovation of a tower on one of the Victorian buildings as evidenced by the wooden framework around it. A little red brick schoolhouse is seen in the distance, and the remaining one single-family home in the town is dwarfed on either side by taller buildings. The overall impression of this early twentieth-century town is colorful and homey. Then the page is turned to reveal a description of the changes that have gradually taken place over a 70- to 80-year period.

The 1935 setting shows the cars of the times, a new shiny shoe store that has replaced the old grocery and market, the hotel losing its awnings, and the tower with a new coat of paint. The original buildings are beginning to show signs of wear and their colors are grayish, although the fall season is depicted in full color. There are fewer trees in the square, and a fountain has replaced the theater in the park. Behind a new post office, the old train station can be seen. Other signs of the times include a billboard advertising a soft drink, a Charlie Chaplin movie at the Strand Theatre, a new apartment building, shorter women's fashions, paved streets, and a traffic light. The last single house has become a laundry, the large department store loses its awnings, and the unemployed are lined up outside the post office for free bread.

The 1955 setting is enhanced by a winter holiday scene showing a sparse landscape with a Goodyear blimp hovering over it, the train station ablaze with a fire, and the school sporting a new addition. Another billboard has sprouted atop the department store, modern cars are parked at meters, the shoestore has given way to a supermarket, and a drugstore and pharmacy have been added. Other signs of change are a liquor store, a modern gas station at the end of Main, and more traffic. Buses have replaced streetcars, few trees remain, and pipelines are being laid. A Disney movie at the Strand, a decorated tree in the park, neon lights and asphalt on the courthouse square, bigger cars, a motel, a new insurance building, a fallout shelter sign and air raid sirens—all are signs of change and signal the arrival of the nuclear age.

By 1970, there is less traffic and fewer people living in the city. The busy town square is enlarged and paved to form a mall to keep out cars, and only two trees remain in the square. The supermarket is gone and a play area is in its place; a boutique and music store replace the liquor store. More houses march along the landscape, the train tower is undergoing repair, and a jet is flying low. Close inspection reveals a protest group outside the courthouse, a holdup in the park, and graffiti. The post office has been replaced by a parking lot. The mill has a for-rent sign, and a Beatles movie is playing at the Strand. The older homes are being replaced by suburban ones, all alike; and the school grows along with more power lines and industry.

The 1980s scene shows trees planted in barrels in the town and park. A freeway divides the landscape, a crane is on top of a building, a new hamburger place is next to an arcade, and a styling salon replaces the boutique where the top floor has burned. Signs of deterioration compete with efforts to renovate. The original statue in the square has been destroyed, litter is obvious, vandals have broken streetlights, there are more people in the town area, and the theater has been changed to a cultural center. The scene is a hodgepodge of quaint old and shiny new features that somehow do not mesh.

However, 1987 reveals a hazy landscape with many trees and houses in a return to fall. In town, a computer store replaces the pharmacy; the trees downtown have grown larger around the grassy square that is busy with performances. People are relaxing at outdoor restaurants, and there are flower gardens. New building fronts are more compatible. Fewer cars, busy shoppers, and a fresher, cleaner atmosphere indicate a similarity to the city's appearance in 1910. The heritage has been maintained with the convenience of city life, keeping the original style.

Truly a study in architectural change, the book is unique and informative, with a nostalgic tone. This visual overview of the period from 1910 to 1987, emphasizes subtle signs and symbols of economic, technological, and social significance and change. Illustrations are in full color and carefully detailed. This book is an outstanding example of change over time skillfully portrayed with illustrations that subtly demonstrate transformation and innovation that gifted children will be able to comprehend. Specifically, an element of abstraction requires the reader to "read" the pictures and then return to the beginning to reread them to pick up new observations each time. This rather challenging activity will be eagerly accepted by most gifted children.

Walsh, Jill Paton. *Gaffer Samson's Luck.* Illus. by Brock Cole. New York: Farrar, 1984, 118 pp. (Intermediate)

Excited, but apprehensive about a move his father has been forced to take, James looks for a tree-lined landscape as they travel by car, since the move is to a marshy flatland many miles from Yorkshire; however, James's expectations remain unmet.

Eventually, they arrive at their new dwelling, much smaller than the home they left behind, for it was used, at one time, as a malting place for barley. Exhausted from the trip and unhappy about having to leave his close friends, James falls asleep and later awakens in a cheerfully lit attic room with a wonderful skylight. His initial attitude soon softens and James decides the new place may hold some promise, after all.

He soon meets an old neighbor, Gaffer Samson, who becomes his first and dearest friend, and later, on a shopping trip, James meets Angey, who also becomes a good friend.

School brings James new problems because he is far ahead of his class in math. Angey is in the class, along with a gang of children known as "the villagers." This group obtained their label from living in a certain section of the community and are not well received by children living in other areas, such as the "estate." James is unfortunate to have moved into the village area. Taunting and ridicule by the gang on the playground intensifies his feeling of being an outcast so he happily anticipates his visits with Mr. Samson, who seems to be his only real friend. The old man fills a void in James's life. James is drawn to Gaffer's loyalty and trust in him and finds he enjoys their discussions of the history of the community.

James is hesitant to become too closely involved with Angey for fear she will become a leech, and also, she is not well accepted by her schoolmates. When called on to assist her with math, he realizes that she is not lacking in intelligence.

When Gaffer Samson has a bike accident, James's world expands as the old man gives him his bike. James also realizes that Mr. Samson is seriously ill and may not live much longer, but will be allowed to return to his little house.

The bike is a windfall! James explores every inch of the community before learning that Mr. Samson wants him to retrieve an old good luck piece given to him long ago by a gypsy. Mr. Samson has hidden it behind a brick in the fireplace in his original home in the marsh. However, the house is no longer there, only remnants of a hearth remain somewhere on the grassy, overgrown plain. Assisted by Angey, James begins an extensive search only to discover that Mr. Samson's directions are confusing. But he is determined to find the treasured token for his friend. After several days of unrelenting rain, the plot where the house originally stood surfaces and James locates the lucky piece.

Meanwhile, Terry, the leader of the village gang, has dared James to cross a dangerous section of a raging river by holding onto chains that mark the weir. James is terrified but astonishes Terry by suggesting that he go first. Terry loses his footing and is seriously injured after being rescued by Scarf, a loyal member of the gang. James finally arrives at his decision to cross the river himself in order not to lose face with the gang. Asking Angey to provide the audience for his feat, James accomplishes the treacherous task and wins the group's approval.

Finally, James places the lucky piece in Gaffer Samson's hand only to have the old man return it to him before he dies. James knows who should really have the lucky piece now, and he sneaks into the hospital to give it to Terry. This act cements the boys' friendship.

Walsh's thought-provoking novel will stir deep feelings as readers identify with James' strong-willed character. Set apart from his new community, his struggle for acceptance is admirable, but his determination to remain true to himself is a distinguishing trait.

In this well-developed plot, Walsh has created memorable characters that become involved in vigorous action and adventure. On another level, Walsh reveals a tale of steadfast friendship, commitment, loyalty, and perseverance. Readers are challenged to discern the various and complicated emotions and sensations presented and recognize the growth and maturity evident in James, his acquaintances, and his family.

The language contains British spellings and vocabulary that eloquently enhances the story without being distracting to American readers. There are several pen-and-ink sketches that provide additional interpretations of events and sensations in addition to being mere illustrations.

Waterfield, Giles. *Faces.* Reproduction. New York: Atheneum, 1982, 47 pp. (Intermediate)

A focus on all facets of faces, including masks, portraits, and sculptures, makes this art appreciation book appealing and informative. Comparisons and contrasts of facial features and expressions from ancient, medieval, modern, and contemporary times are examined and explained. The works of many well-known artists are included in this volume along with those of less familiar ones. For example, Vincent van Gogh is compared with Theodore Gericault. Primitive masks are also included. Some represent gods, particular events, or festivals, such as a mask used by the Iroquois Indians to represent harvest festivals.

Waterfield emphasizes one of the main themes of his book, that is, the personality of the person in a portrait is revealed upon close examination. For example, the portrait of George Washington has a look of authority about it. Waterfield makes readers aware of how and what to look for in faces. For example, when royalty sat for portraits, they were painted with great dignity even if they were children. Similarly, the serious, unsmiling face depicts a person who is important or destined to be special.

The full-color and black-and-white reproductions are of good quality, retaining a great deal of detail. Waterfield explains the colors and contrasts, and what the artist probably intended them to mean. For example, he asks readers to study the eyes, mouth, and expression for the message in them.

The book's format is arranged by juxtaposing two works of similar media on a double-page spread accompanied by a brief synopsis of each and an analysis of similarities and differences. The book includes notes about each artist and a brief index. Headings are thought-provoking and tantalizing.

Children interested in portraits will enjoy the many different faces represented; some will be motivated to seek additional information about portrait painting. Faces is an unusual topic in a series of books on art, but one that is particularly appropriate for gifted children for its aesthetic approach to the study of faces in portraits.

Weiss, Harvey. *How to Be an Inventor.* Illus. by author. New York: Crowell, 1980, 96 pp. (Intermediate)

Practical tips for would-be inventors abound in this lighthearted look at the process of invention. Weiss provides plenty of examples—illustrations and photographs of actual inventions, simple sketches, and copies of patent drawings, each described in captions and text. Defining "invention," Weiss says: "An invention is something new or original—something made up, something that never existed until the inventor thought it up." Yet, later, Weiss reminds readers that most inventions are improvements on existing devices.

Distinguishing among several types of inventors, Weiss directs his commentary mostly toward the inventor-inventor (a person who invents for the joy of the process). Other types include the scientist-inventor (expert), the practical-inventor (one who sets out to solve a specific problem), and the builder-inventor (one who is more interested in the process of assembling objects rather than in the end result).

In the chapter entitled "How to Go about It," Weiss presents a clear example of brainstorming solutions to the problem of putting out the garbage. Pointing out that most inventions result from a need for change or improvement in an existing device, the author briefly emphasizes the importance of being an astute observer.

Believing that models and drawings are central to the process of invention, Weiss elaborates on this aspect of inventing and suggests methods and materials in clear text accompanied by labeled diagrams.

Because most inventions by amateurs are mechanical, Weiss includes several pages of useful suggestions for needed materials and how these can best be utilized. These descriptions take the format of line drawings. For example, the entry for sheet metal scraps is accompanied by brief paragraphs explaining their use, such as the hand crank to move other objects.

For youngsters who need ideas, the several pages of suggestions should prove helpful, such as "a new kind of kite" and "bicycle improvements." In this connection, Weiss cautions young readers not to attempt to invent new chemical combinations and to avoid biology, aeronautics, and electronics unless they have previous training in these fields. He also warns against using 110 volts of electricity, instead suggesting batteries for running small motors on less than 12 volts.

A chapter on patents explains their purpose and the general process of obtaining a patent. The concluding chapter features famous inventors, such as Leonardo da Vinci, Benjamin Franklin, Robert Fulton, George Stephenson, Eli Whitney, and Rube Goldberg. Their most well-known creations are highlighted in a few paragraphs of text accompanied by captioned photographs and drawings. At a personal level, Weiss shares the problem-solving process he used in the development of his own favorite, useless invention, a steam-driven "Beckoning Machine," a hand and finger that beckons slowly. He provides a discussion of his thinking through each step of its creation.

As an introduction to the process of invention, *How to Be an Inventor* gives readers practical advice in a clearly written text enhanced by illustrative photographs, sketches, and diagrams. The idea of utilizing discarded "junk" is not a new one, but Weiss has advised readers how to attach parts and how to get objects to move, providing ideas for young minds to select and choose, experimenting with different combinations.

Weitzman, David. *Windmills, Bridges, & Old Machines: Discovering Our Industrial Past.* New York: Scribner, 1982, 128 pp. (Intermediate)

Author of *My Backyard History Book,* Weitzman makes our past come alive as he describes the workings of windmills, waterwheels and sawmills, canals, aquaducts, steam engines, locomotives, street railways, bridges, viaducts, and trestles. The text describes the origin of each structure or apparatus, its purpose, operation, and place in the community.

In addition to clear black-and-white photographs of many abandoned artifacts of the past, detailed, well-labeled diagrams and section drawings furnish a view of the interiors of antiquated machinery and constructions such as locomotives and blast furnaces. For example, the operation of canal locks is clearly illustrated in step-by-step sectional drawings. The chapter on bridges includes a "Bridgefinder's Alphabet" from A to Z, depicting bridges named after their designers or particular features, including "X is for an unknown bridge you might discover."

Throughout, readers are encouraged to make discoveries and see relationships between inventions of the past. For example, to demonstrate the importance of trusses and triangles in bridge design, Weitzman gives directions for how to make cardboard models to test variations for strength. Again, photos and sketches supplement the textual directions.

Because each piece of machinery cannot receive an exhaustive treatment, lesser known periodicals are recommended as "rainy day" reading in a brief section on how to conduct a library search. A list of specific topics (hoisting machinery, quarries and quarrying, and so on) is provided to practice using the subject catalog available in libraries.

More than a compendium of facts, *Windmills, Bridges, & Old Machines* is a comprehensive coverage of major machinery and constructions of the past that can still be seen today by young readers willing to look around—along a bicycle path or just around the corner. The focus actively involves readers and encourages modern-day discoveries. The book should appeal to youngsters who like to analyze machinery, and may encourage an interest in the history of technical constructions.

Willard, Nancy. *A Visit to William Blake's Inn: Poems for Innocent and Experienced Travelers.* Illus. by Alice Provensen and Martin Provensen. New York: Harcourt, 1981, 45 pp. (Intermediate)

Setting the tone for this book of fanciful verse, Willard tells the reader that she received Blake's *Songs of Innocence and Experience* as a child while recuperating from the measles in her bedroom decorated by glued-on stars on the ceiling. Using humor and unusual relationships between words, Willard describes nonsensical events and odd human and animal characters who occasionally express serious thoughts for the reader's reflections. A young boy who stays at William Blake's inn encounters odd guests, including a tiger, a wise cow, three sunflowers who come to take root in the carpet, and the man in the marmalade hat. Blake's is no ordinary inn, but staffed by angels, dragons, a rabbit, and a bear. "Blake's Celestial Limousine," an open, flying carriage with the wings and head of an eagle and spinning rotors, transports visitors to the inn.

A rabbit serving as bellhop shows the young arriving visitor to his room, which is furnished with a shaggy bear who couples as both a bed and an alarm clock. During his first night at the inn, the guest and the residing animals are awakened by "The Sun and Moon Circus"—noises made by the sun dancing and the new moon singing in the sky. As in many fantasies, there is a timeless quality that lends a feeling of unreality; guests seem to be there for an extended stay. Spring arrives, bringing the man in the marmalade hat scurrying through the inn, awakening the hibernating animals so cleaning can begin.

While at the inn, the King of Cats (tiger) writes a postcard to his wife, entreating her to take care of herself and to keep her whiskers "crisp and clean" and telling her he has come so far he might not be home again. Lastly, the tiger asks Blake for a bedtime story. Blake complies with a story about a tailor who, knowing only how to use the tools of his trade, constructs a flimsy house from fabric and animals' skin, which is soon blown apart by the wind.

The Provensens' unique illustrations, which distort perspective, add to the aura of fantasy and are juxtaposed with the humorous/serious text. The language is rich and expressive and abounds with metaphor: "The sun is opening up his act and crouching for a leap." The idiomatic expression—it's on the house—is depicted by a finely appointed breakfast table perched atop a roof. The young reader's imagination is stretched by both text and illustrations. For example, a sky-dwelling cow is shown breakfasting on a soft, white cloud that had served as the cow's resting place the night before.

A clever play on words is woven into the imaginative verse: "The Wise Cow Makes *Way, Room,* and *Believe.*" As the animals make *way* for William Blake, captain of their boat, "The Wise Cow," being familiar with only grass, says he must make "Way of grass and hay, a nest where he (Blake) can nap like fieldmice in a cap." *Believe* is made in the form of an unusual means of transportation—a combination of a sailboat with wheels, fins, feet, and a hot-air balloon—symbolizing the many ways we can be transported by our flights of fantasy.

Although much of the verse is light and nonsensical there are also serious, philosophical lines to ponder. The Marmalade Man advises:

> Fox and hound, go paw in paw.
> Cat and rat, be best of friends.
> Lamb and tiger, walk together,
> Dancing starts where fighting ends.

The verse can be read and interpreted on different levels, offering a challenge to highly able readers, who will seek meaning on levels other than the literal. The metaphorical language enhances the beauty of ideas expressed. Children who enjoy reading between the lines and experimenting with unusual combinations of language and thought should respond to the fanciful poetry and ethereal illustrations in this beautiful book.

Williams, Terry Tempest, and Ted Magor. *The Secret Language of Snow.* Illus. by Jennifer Dewey. San Francisco: Sierra Club/ Pantheon, 1984, 130 pp. (Intermediate)

Snow has been referred to by many names, as illustrated in this well-designed book that uniquely juxtaposes scientific information and poetic language. The Russian naturalist A. N. Formozov was one of the first to recognize the value of Arctic peoples' (Inuits) snow language. Others who live in snowy climates, including the Russians, use specific words to describe snow conditions. Williams and Magor have selected ten Kobuk Eskimo words as representative of a snow language. One word is featured per chapter.

Preceding the descriptions of individual words is an introduction to the Inuit (IN-oo-it) way of life and language, including a pronunciation key (e.g., "i as in 'stick,' " "u:oo as in 'tool' "). Living in northeastern Alaska in a taiga forest with many open spaces, the Kobuk Eskimos have been influenced by the Alaskan pipeline and other technological advances but have managed to maintain many traditions such as storytelling. Many of these stories tell of the relationships between animals and humans—animals had the ability to become human and often provided needed assistance. For example, the blind boy Tipton had his sight restored thanks to a loon. Later, Tipton turns his grandmother and sister into whales because they tricked him into believing his arrow had missed the bear whose meat they so desperately needed to survive the winter.

Snow in its various forms is also a frequent topic of Eskimo stories, beginning with *annui* (falling snow). Seven structural types of snow crystals—stellar crystals, plate crystals, spatial dendrites, irregular crystals, needles, columns, and capped columns—are described in the text and drawings. *Graupel* (soft hail), hail, and sleet are also differentiated. Unknown to most readers, the effect of snow—its personality—depends on how much water, ice, and air it contains. For example, *api* (snow on the ground) changes as it undergoes temperature fluctuations, melting and freezing and developing enlarged snow crystals. The snow aging processes of temperature gradient metamorphism, equitemperature, and firnification are described. Physical adaptations, migration, and hibernation of large and small animals, such as musk-oxen, caribou, and ground squirrels, are examined in relationship to snow cover. Thus, *pukak* (loose, soft layers that can cause avalanches) enables small animals to claw through to search for food. (A diagram shows *pukak* and compares different layers of "snow geology.") Another form of snow cover, *quali* ("snow that collects horizontally on trees"), offers refuge from predators in addition to causing tree limbs to break, thereby opening up the forest for new plant growth. *Kanik* (rime) appears in a variety of shapes and forms, most familiar as the work of Jack Frost on windows. *Upsik,* the Kobuk word for firmly packed snow, easily supports the weight of humans and animals. Other types of snow include *siqoq,* swirling or drifting snow; *kimoagruk,* a snow drift that can provide a protective shelter for animals and people; *qamaniq,* the "bowl-shaped hollow around the base of a tree"; and *siqoqtoaq,* a glassy, thick, icy-crusted snow.

Through an examination of the Inuit words for snow, readers recognize the role of language in our perception and understanding of the environment. More importantly, Williams and Magor explain the value of snow language in assisting ecologists who study the interaction between plants and animals.

While the language used to explain the concepts presented in this work is simple and direct, the use of folklore, factual information, and poetic descriptions requires a thoughtful, flexible reader. Each chapter begins with a verse that sets the tone for the ensuing description and concludes with a suggestion on how to involve readers in an observational activity (such as examining snow crystals under a hand lens or constructing a simple instrument to measure snowfall).

The book deals with constructs, asking the reader to synthesize, recall previous observations of snow formations, and relate one form of snow to another. In addition, readers have an opportunity to respond at an appreciation level by sharing the authors' love of nature expressed in the chapter introductory verses and other descriptions of beauty often enhanced by pen-and-ink drawings.

Wiseman, David. *Blodwen and the Guardians.* Boston: Houghton Mifflin, 1983, 164 pp. (Intermediate)

In a land of never-never live the wee people, known as the Guardians. Well named they are, as they act as chief custodians and protectors of an ancient tomb and burial ground, Mow Grove.

The Lewis family, including Blodwen, a daughter age ten, and Illtyd, a six-year-old boy, have just moved from the busy city to their cottage in the countryside, little aware of what mysterious experiences lie ahead. Just behind their home in Mow Grove roam their tiny unseen neighbors, the Guardians, who have lived in the tree-lined area for centuries, undaunted in their dedication to guard the sacred mound. Over the years, humans, curious to investigate the Mow, have always turned back when they encountered an eeriness along the path. The Guardians have contributed to this strange feeling by their whisperings and warnings not to enter the sacred ground. To keep aware of stories and happenings about the "outside," the highly organized Guardians hold regular meetings of their Council led by their informer about such affairs, Peridot, who is the only one who can understand human language and ways. It is Peridot who brings the news that Blodwen and her family have moved into the Mow cottage. Smitten by the girl at first sight, Peridot is constantly teased by the Guardians.

Blodwen and Tiddy, as the young boy is called, one day decide to explore the grove of trees at the end of the path, but, as were others in the past, are cautioned back by strange movements and rustlings that sound like voices warning them to stay out. Later, the Lewis family learns from the villagers that Mow Grove is an old chief's tomb. Walter, the town's oldest citizen, intrigues Blodwen and later becomes her confidant regarding the mysterious Mow.

Meanwhile, at their next meeting, the Guardians express concern that Blodwen has ventured so far into the Mow; they are nervous, unsure, and afraid that this stranger intends to intrude. Some of the more outspoken members suggest that they begin proceedings to force the Lewis family out, but Peridot reminds them that their purpose is to defend, not to attack. Consequently, they decide merely to remain watchful of Blodwen while continuing to protect their Trust. Peridot stays close to Blodwen, whispering to her words she cannot hear, but she senses his message and acts accordingly. Consumed with curiosity about the Mow Grove, she glances longingly at the wicket gate leading to it, but something she can't explain always stops her. Tiddy, on the other hand, is insistent about not wanting to explore the Grove, as he is terrified of its dark presence. Finally, Old Walter continues to warn Blodwen of the little people in the Grove without ever fully explaining the mystery.

One day, during one of their walks, the children encounter workmen who have come to build a highway through their wonderful countryside, including the Mow. Blodwen becomes upset and disturbed at this menacing news, as does her mother, who had hoped to leave behind the bustle and noise of the city.

For their part, the Guardians regard the construction workers as a "human army" equipped with huge "beasts" that devour great mouthfuls of earth. Tiddy's pet name for these earthmovers is Bulldosaurus Rex, and like any little boy, he is awed by their monstrous size and power. The Lewis family discusses the future of their cottage surroundings, realizing that the beauty of the country is also attracting other people. As before, it is Old Walter who reassures Blodwen, telling her that the workers will never build on the Mow.

Disdainfully, the children observe the changes brought about in the shrubbery and terrain by the construction crew. Tiddy is impressed with the vast machines, whereas Blodwen is uneasy and worried about the future of the Mow. When she ventures through the wicket gate again, she hears the whispered warnings, this time more alarming than ever.

While the villagers are organizing opposition to the destruction of their peace and solitude, Old Walter steadfastly adheres to his original advice. He stands before the townspeople commanding ultimate respect for his age and wisdom. In addition, he confronts the construction foreman, Mr. Grubitout, and warns him of the little people who will stop the work, one way or another. This threat only confuses and frustrates the contractor.

As always, it is Peridot who brings the latest information to the Council members, referring to the earthmovers as dinosaurs. When Peridot relays the story of Bulldosaurus Rex, as Tiddy has named them, the other Guardians believe him. The Guardians now draw up a plan to interfere with the highway progress. As a result, various minor, and some not-so-minor, events mysteriously occur to complicate the functioning of the machines or annoy the workers. Suspecting the villagers, Mr. Grubitout makes all kinds of threats and becomes even more determined to complete the job.

Meanwhile, Peridot is swept up in a gust of wind and blown into the village inn, where he listens, unobserved, to a conversation among Old Walter, Mr. Lewis, and other villagers. Here he learns that Old Walter knows of the little people and why they guard the Mow. He races back to Gabbro with this important information and to instill in the Guardians a feeling of trust in the townspeople. But they are unreceptive to Peridot's message and distrust him because of his close association with the humans.

The destruction of the countryside is halted when Old Walter plans a party for his ninety-fourth birthday. Blodwen and Tiddy share in the celebration by helping to send out invitations to all the villagers. The party is held in the field where the highway is to be built, and eventually the whole town shows up for the festivity. Even the workmen join in the merrymaking, all except Mr. Grubitout, who finally feels defeated.

In the Guardian camp, Sardonyx, a rebellious member, is striving to destroy the old leadership, as he sows seeds of suspicion about Peridot and casts doubt as to Gabbro's wisdom. Gabbro senses the seriousness of the situation and the Guardians' fear; eventually many of them fly away only to return to the family fold.

A heavy thunderstorm and continuing rains temporarily delay work on the highway. When the rain finally stops, Blodwen and Tiddy decide to explore the Mow Grove. The Guardians keep a careful watch on the two children, hoping for the first time that they will not turn back but find the evidence necessary to protect the ancient tomb. The children finally locate the entrance and Tiddy overcomes all his earlier hesitancy as he ventures forth through the narrow passage. Blodwen expresses fear and urges him to come back; but to no avail. Soon Tiddy emerges with what appears to be an ancient brooch. At long last, the Mow Grove is preserved for its historical significance. The Guardians reunite in peace and Blodwen and Tiddy are well satisfied with the results.

Wiseman's cleverly crafted story imaginatively portrays the little people in an authentic and entertaining manner. For example, each well-characterized member of the Guardians is introduced early in the story, inviting the reader to conjure up mental images of these tiny figures. Gifted children will enjoy the highly organized Council meetings, ceremoniously conducted by Gabbro and often revealing humorous interactions among the Guardians. Peridot's amusing antics are delightful, especially when he is blown into what appears to be an ashtray at the village inn.

The uniqueness of the Mow also challenges the reader to investigate it themselves. Wiseman skillfully builds anticipation about the 3,000-year-old tomb, utilizing an excellent command of the English language. Employment of such terms as "off-load" for unload, "removal people" for movers, "motorway" for highway, are characteristics of British English and add an element of charm to this fantasy. The theme is unifying, the plot compelling, and the conclusion satisfying.

Conservation of natural resources is a strong factor as the villagers strive to save their cherished countryside from the blemish of a modern highway. Many gifted children will identify with this concern for preservation and respect for the natural environment.

Blodwen and the Guardians contains the intrigue and adventure intellectual children seek in a story. They welcome the exciting mystery of the unknown and what it may hold to discover.

Wiseman, David. *Jeremy Visick.* Boston: Houghton Mifflin, 1981, 192 pp. (Intermediate)

Startling events verging on the supernatural dramatize this work of fiction set in modern-day England. Matthew, a 12-year-old boy, is propelled back in time 130 years to an old copper mine accident that took the life of Jeremy Visick, a boy of his age, whose body was never found.

A school assignment requiring Matthew to investigate an old cemetery near his house triggers the boy's interest and he is mysteriously drawn to the tombstone of the Visick family. Unable to explain his obsession with the dead family to his schoolmate, Mary, Matthew sees markings on the stone that are invisible to others. As a result, he begins to seek more information about the family and makes nocturnal visits to the tombstone, sometimes falling asleep there. Although he prefers to keep his illusion about the Visicks, who lived in the very place where his house is, to himself, his strange behavior upsets his sensitive mother and sister and enrages his impulsive father. Nevertheless, Matthew persists in his quest to locate the missing boy. Finally, his middle-of-the-night excursions bring him into contact with Jeremy's ghost. The two converse, Jeremy always reminding Matthew that he cannot come into the mines dressed in his nightclothes. When the voice fades away, Matthew returns home, sometimes not remembering the incident.

Eventually, Matthew is enticed into following the ghost of Jeremy into the dangerous old mine shaft. While his parents become alarmed when he does not return home and consequently start a search for him, Matthew is with his friend, talking to the slumped body at the bottom of the shaft. When he is finally rescued, he shows the search party where Jeremy's body is.

Matthew is not satisfied until the boy's bones are buried in the family grave. He receives a canvas bag with Jeremy's name stitched on it, along with a piece of copper found near the body. This copper rock matches a piece previously given to Matthew by Mary's father, who is knowledgeable about mining.

Wiseman's absorbing tale of Matthew's quest for Jeremy Visick builds continually through a plot of intrigue that interweaves the past and the present. The boy's unwavering commitment to the Visick family portrays him as a strong, central, admirable character that readers will not soon forget. Matthew's identification with the lost boy is sensitively and imaginatively conveyed. Although this engrossing story concludes comfortably, readers will remain uncertain as to whether Matthew's relationship with

Jeremy's ghost was actual or imagined. However, such speculation only enhances the adventure.

The text employs vocabulary unique to mining, such as "adit," "winze," and "sollar." However, since these new words are not extremely technical, this fascinating book is accessible to middle graders and older.

Wyler, Rose. *Science Fun with Peanuts and Popcorn.* Illus. by Pat Stewart. New York: Messner, 1986, 48 pp. (Beginning)

Appropriate for very young "scientists," this book focuses on two favorite snacks of children: peanuts and popcorn.

Beginning with an introduction to a seed, readers are instructed to split open a peanut and examine it under a magnifying glass. At the same time, the text explains what they see. Switching to popcorn, Wyler then suggests that they soak popcorn kernels before examining them more closely.

Readers are invited to try experiments with peanuts and popcorn kernels, which are carefully explained and illustrated. For example, children can see the swelling of peanuts and popcorn when they are covered with water and allowed to soak for a while. Comparisons are made to seeds growing in soil, how they, too, swell and push the soil aside.

At this stage, children are encouraged to plant small gardens indoors using water and paper towels. The accompanying discussion of the elements needed for seeds to grow and what happens if they are deprived of sunlight or water is informative.

In the further progression of this experiment, directions are given for how to transplant starter gardens to soil-filled containers before planting them outside. Additional information about chemicals, such as hormones, and their effect on growth makes this book appropriate for the curious, able reader.

The history and travels of the peanut, including George Washington Carver's work, extend the scientific data bank of youngsters. For example, readers are introduced to the various inedible products made from peanuts and they are shown how to make peanut butter in a food processor with the assistance of a grown-up.

In a math lesson comparing volume of unpopped and popped corn, children are cautioned to secure adult assistance before using a stove. Experiments with the puffy, popped corn involve investigating the size and density of the kernels. Experiments are complemented by answers to questions about the changing characteristics of corn, further informing young readers. Recipes simple enough for children to use, games, and riddles about peanuts and popcorn make this an exceptional science experiment book for youngsters.

Golden-colored illustrations of peanuts and popcorn, explicit diagrams, instructions for experiments set in inserts, and a table of contents make this an attractive and intellectually challenging science book for young talented readers.

Zaslavsky, Claudia. *Tic Tac Toe and Other Three-in-a-Row Games from Ancient Egypt to the Modern Computer.* Illus. by Anthony Kramer. New York: Crowell, 1982, 90 pp. (Intermediate)

How to play tic tac toe in many variations is detailed in this interesting book, including accounts of how three-in-a-row games might have originated in various cultures. Members of ruling classes as well as commoners have played three-in-a-row games, although the names of these games, the materials used, and the rules have changed throughout the ages and from setting to setting. Among its many names, tic tac toe is known as Noughts and Crosses (England), Ecke Mecke Stecke (Austria), and Tripp Trapp Trull (Sweden). Early people probably drew diagrams by scratching marks in the ground or carving in rocks; in colonial days children used their slateboards to play the game, while monarchs used boards with pieces of gold and ivory.

Strategies for winning also vary. For example, in Tapatan, a Philippine version of tic tac toe, the center is the best starting position, but not in Shisima, a western Kenyan octagonal board game, where the center represents a body of water.

Zaslavsky's well-organized book contains a brief afterword, a list of other three-in-a-row games not mentioned in the book, their countries of origin, a map, and a thorough index. Soft, gray wash illustrations add interest to the text, and clear game diagrams enhance the explanation of strategies. Primary or intermediate grade readers who play multidimensional tic tac toe games might be interested in learning more about the history and variations of three-in-a-row games by reading this book. For eager youngsters who enjoy the challenge of strategy games, the book offers a wealth of game variations and many strategy hints for improving their skills. For computer buffs, Zaslavsky provides a step-by-step guide to writing a computer program for playing tic tac toe.

Zelinsky, Paul O. *The Maid and the Mouse and the Odd-Shaped House.* Adapted and illus. by author. New York: Dodd, Mead, 1981, unp. (Beginning)

An old tale from folk literature, this "tell and draw" story was used by a teacher in 1897, who is acknowledged and credited in Zelinsky's book.

The story begins as the wee maid and mouse, boxed in a hexagonal shape, are celebrating their new house. When they build a cozy fire, they realize they need a chimney to release the smoke, and so they build, not one, but two tall chimneys. Satisfied with that endeavor, the maid is observed busily stitching a quilt in a hexagonal pattern, and the mouse is at her feet perusing a newspaper.

Deciding to increase the size of their house, the two make four new rooms by dividing the hexagon equilaterally across and down. Of course, the house needs windows, so they cut two nice round holes for peeking out.

Suddenly, the maid hears a hissing noise outside and hastens to investigate, but not before barring the door behind her to keep the mouse safe. She trips and falls, and trips and falls four times, creating the shape for the cat's legs, and makes it home where she and the mouse decide to clean house just to make sure they don't have unwelcome visitors. When the maid sweeps dust out the door, the whiskers of a cat are formed.

On a following double-page spread the maid is shown sweeping the walk that forms the cat's tail. Again the roar, and then she sees what the reader has already seen—the big cat. She rushes to the house, grabs the mouse, and races down the road, while the cat is busy chasing a bird. The last picture shows the maid and the mouse in a new little house having tea, safe and sound.

Zelinsky's delightful and charming tale requires active participation by allowing the reader a first look at the dilemma the two little ones will encounter. The creative use of limited space introduces various little characters and creatures that engage in much humorous activity in and outside the house. This unusual, large, and spacious picture book about a wee maid and a mouse who live together in a house is written as a story-in-rhyme. Accompanying illustrations are in soft pastels to complement the angular geometric lines that create the house. The wee maid is similar to a pipe-cleaner doll as she frolics and dances about her new house. Each page is nicely framed with trees, flowers, tiny animals, and little people strolling by the house. The happy ending of the story provides comfort and security for very young children. It's a wonderful book to read aloud, but young gifted children will prefer to read it for themselves. The element of discovery and the appeal to skills of observation and identification make this a challenging book for the very young.

Title Index

Level Index

INTERMEDIATE

ADVANCED

Subject Index